The short guide to aging and gerontology

Kate de Medeiros

First edition published in Great Britain in 2017 by

Policy Press
University of Bristol
1-9 Old Park Hill
Bristol BS2 8BB
UK
+44 (0)117 954 5940
pp-info@bristol.ac.uk
www.policypress.co.uk

North America office:
Policy Press
c/o The University of Chicago Press
1427 East 60th Street
Chicago, IL 60637, USA
t: +1 773 702 7700
f: +1 773-702-9756
sales@press.uchicago.edu
www.press.uchicago.edu

© Policy Press 2017

British Library Cataloguing in Publication Data
A catalogue record for this book is available from the British Library.

Library of Congress Cataloging-in-Publication Data
A catalog record for this book has been requested.

ISBN 978-1-4473-2838-4 paperback
ISBN 978-1-4473-2839-1 ePub
ISBN 978-1-4473-2840-7 Mobi
ISBN 978-1-4473-2841-4 ePdf

Cover design by Policy Press
Front cover image kindly supplied by Fotolia
Printed and bound in the United States of America
Policy Press uses environmentally responsible print partners

For my mentors,
Dr. Thomas Cole and Dr. Robert Rubinstein

Contents

List of tables and figure

Tables

Figure

Acknowledgements

There are several people I would like to thank for their help with this book. First and foremost, I would like to thank the anonymous referees who provided input on my initial draft. Your thoughtful comments were extremely helpful and appreciated.

I would also like to thank my two primary mentors, Dr. Thomas Cole and Dr. Robert Rubinstein. Dr. Cole introduced me to the field of gerontology for which I am extremely grateful. Dr. Rubinstein guided me through my doctoral program and the rich world of qualitative research. Thank you both for being a part of my life all these years and for your continued mentorship.

Thanks also goes to my graduate school classmates – Dr. Kelly Niles-Yokum, Dr. Dan Van Dussen, and Mr. David Hamilton. We spent many long nights thinking about what it meant to be a gerontologist. I wouldn't be writing this book if it weren't for you.

My thanks also goes to my colleagues at Miami University. I am fortunate to work with a wonderful group of researchers and scholars who are always willing to discuss and consider gerontology and its evolution. I also want to acknowledge the undergraduate and graduate students who continue to push the field of gerontology forward; the older people with whom I've spoken over the years about their thoughts, experiences and insights; and my family who continue to be a source of inspiration.

Preface

Several years ago, when I was still a graduate student in gerontology, I presented a paper at the Gerontological Society of America conference in a symposium focused on doctoral training in gerontology. The paper's title, 'When I looked around I saw and heard of none like me,' was a quote from Mary Shelly's *Frankenstein* in which the creature recognizes that he and his creator (Victor Frankenstein) are different. Victor had a well-established place in society. The creature was alone, without a defined place or sense of belonging. He bore many similarities to Victor, but was also substantially different. As such, Victor could never really understand the experience of being a new entity set loose in the world.

I found that this metaphor described my feelings at the time. I was learning about gerontology from scholars who were experts in their fields – anthropology, sociology, epidemiology, policy. Yet, they were still embedded within a traditional discipline with corresponding theories, methods, histories, and journals grounded in those perspectives. Even gerontological organizations didn't recognize gerontology as a field of study. Consequently, we – myself and my classmates – were different. We were being exposed to several disciplinary perspectives focused on the study of aging, yet we did not belong to these disciplines. It was difficult to see where we 'fit.' To complicate matters further, most of the gerontology programs hiring new faculty then would not consider candidates with degrees outside of a traditional discipline. It seemed as though our kind of gerontologist was not welcome. Thankfully, times have changed.

The Frankenstein metaphor is meant to suggest that the landscape of gerontology looked and felt very different to those of us who were trying to make sense of the multiple theories, perspectives, approaches and concepts that spanned numerous disciplines than perhaps it did to others who were nested within recognized disciplines. This sense of wanting to see the landscape of gerontology laid out, without disciplinary boundaries, was the motivation behind this *Short Guide*. As gerontology has evolved into its own discipline, now with many others like me as well as people trained in traditional disciplines who focus their research on aging, the time seemed right to try to make sense of it all, if such a thing is possible.

Overview of *The Short Guide*

Since the study of later life or 'old age' covers a vast gamut of experiences, meanings, outcomes and goals, it is important to bring together multiple perspectives to look at aging. Multiple perspectives are what make gerontology both exciting in its possibilities and frustrating in its 'messiness.' I see three overarching aspects of aging that link the topics and perspectives within the chapters, each to varying degrees. These are: structure, experience and care. Structure refers to systems (for example, social, policy-related) and their relationship to aging. Experience describes individuals' reactions to structures and to aging. Care describes both acts of providing care (such as informal caregiving) and of showing concern for or caring about others. These concepts are deeply intertwined. For example, the social location one holds is determined by larger social structures. These structures will affect experience in various ways, such as facilitating or inhibiting access to resources (for example, healthcare, education). These structures also will affect attitudes toward aging individuals (such as concern) and expectations about care (such as are older people expected to care for their grandchildren? Is the government responsible for financing services to provide care for older residents?). Although these concepts are not always explicitly mentioned throughout the text they are present in the background.

In addition, one can't look at the whole of gerontology without being struck by a few observations. First, the fear of death and decline that motivated myths and stories about fountains of youth and quests for eternal life still frame many views of old age. Second, old age continues to be marginalized in society in general and in academic studies. Third, older women have an important (and often negatively portrayed) role in aging. They are the (mostly unpaid) caregivers of others. They are overwhelming more likely to be poorer than their male counterparts. They are likely to live alone. They tend to outlive men albeit with chronic disease, and they are vulnerable to violence and exploitation.

The ultimate purpose of this *Short Guide* is to provide a concise overview of the field of gerontology. Not only are there volumes written on each topic introduced (plus countless topics that have been omitted), but the research literature is constantly being updated. The *Short Guide* should therefore be used as a snapshot of a very expansive landscape. It does not aim to answer questions about why we age per se but, rather, about how the phenomenon of aging has been defined, experienced, studied, regulated, resisted and contested in the past and present. Each chapter is arranged to present historical overviews of the topics addressed, key concepts and findings from several broad perspectives (for example, social sciences, behavioral science, humanities, health sciences, policy studies) and global perspectives and implications.

Areas explored in the *Short Guide* include a historical perspective of gerontology as a field; cultural myths and common assumptions about old age; health and functional abilities in later life; death, grief, loss and loneliness; narrating old age; redefining family and family structures; place and social location; and financing old age. Although these topics appear in different chapters, they are interrelated in many ways. For example, one cannot talk about social location without considering concepts related to access to wealth and other forms of power. Creativity, which is discussed in the final chapter on narrating old age, is also inextricably linked to aspects of the grieving process. Common myths shape ideas about 'normal' aging, and so on. The chapters should therefore not be viewed as addressing discrete subject areas but instead as more of a conversation about a series of issues that can be taken up throughout the book and beyond through further reading and inquiry.

Just as this *Short Guide* uses gerontology to encompass various perspectives on later life beyond the discipline of gerontology itself, it also purposefully avoids the use of the descriptors such as 'theory' or disciplinary names (for example, psychology, sociology). This is not to discount the importance of theory or the need for rich disciplinary perspectives. There are many excellent texts that address various aspects of theory and discipline-specific approaches that will be referenced throughout and listed in the 'Recommended further reading' sections at the end of each chapter. The choice to step away from theory and specific disciplines is an attempt to acknowledge complexities surrounding definitions of theory and recognize that disciplinary boundaries can sometimes create unnecessary barriers to knowledge. Words and phrases such as 'perspectives' (in lieu of disciplines) and 'explanatory stances' (as opposed to theories) will be therefore be used throughout this text.

There are many areas that are beyond the scope of this *Short Guide*. These include the medical and biological literature as well as other health sciences such as nursing, social work, occupational therapy and others. The scope is simply too large to include it all. In addition, since the guide is written from the primary perspective of gerontology, it will not delve into discipline-specific theory or works outside of the context of how these works are applied to later life. Finally, it is not the purpose of this book to give a complete picture of all aspects of gerontology but, rather, to outline some key domains that have been important to the field.

Another limitation is the book's Western focus. Similar to Julia Twigg and Wendy Martin's (2015) explanation in their introduction to the *Handbook of Cultural Gerontology*, the *Short Guide*, too, is from an undeniably Western perspective on aging, heavily influenced by work in the U.S. and the U.K. While there has been a strong attempt to include scholarship and data from other countries and regions in the world, such work is limited to predominantly cross-comparative data rather than rich intellectual underpinnings and influences. For example, population data on countries around the world is now easily available from a variety of reputable sources. Comparing variables such as disease prevalence, life expectancy at birth, fertility rates and others is relatively simple. What is more complicated, however, is an understanding of how (and if) gerontology has developed into the public consciousness in many of these countries, what historical and cultural underpinnings influence current gerontological thought and practice and where gerontology is headed in the future. For many countries, gerontology is a new area of study ushered in by changes in population structures – specifically, the shift from relatively young populations to those relatively 'old' ones.

Overall, my hope is that the *Short Guide* can open new discussions about how we think about and study aging, gerontology's evolution as a field and new directions for research. By looking at the many areas that comprise the field, themes across historical time (such as stages of life) and perspectives will become more apparent.

Reference

Twigg, J., & Martin, W. (Eds.). (2015). *Routledge handbook of cultural gerontology*. London: Routledge.

ONE

Age and aging

Gerontology, simply stated, is the study of old age and later life (however either are defined). Aging is experienced by individuals, organizations, cultures, countries and other units and entities. It occurs within multiple contexts, under multiple conditions and is shaped by factors that are personal, political, cultural, geographic, historical, societal and economic. It is something we may recognize in others (for example, 'My father is old'; 'My neighbor is old) but not necessarily in ourselves ('I don't feel old'; 'I am not old because I can still walk five miles a day') (Jones, 2006). We may be labeled as 'old' because of chronological age (for example, 65 years) or physical features (such as gray hair, use of an assistive device), but not individually identify with such a label. As Jason Powell (2006a) argues, 'The ageing subject is constructed as an object of knowledge and as a seeker of that knowledge (p 5).

In addition to complexities in defining what is meant by old, there is great variability and heterogeneity in 'aging' across individuals, due to myriad factors and experiences occurring over a lifetime such as environmental exposures; genetics; life-style; access to education, healthcare; finances; and so on. Contrary to many ageist assumptions that all people over a certain age (for example, 65 years) are alike, with age comes great diversity. All of these complicating elements beg the question: how can one possibly study something as complex, ill-defined, controversial, yet paradoxically familiar as the time of life called old age?

Fortunately, gerontology brings with it an array of perspectives focused on later life to address many of the ways in which age is and has been defined, experienced and studied. Gerontological inquiry ranges from the humanistic (for example, history, philosophy, literature) to the empirical (for example, psychology, sociology, epidemiology) and is not limited in scope to a single perspective or approach. For example, a topic such as memory and later life can be approached in several ways. A media studies scholar might research how film or print-media portrayals of older individuals as forgetful, incompetent or people to be pitied might reinforce ageist attitudes toward older individuals (Dolan, 2013; Leibing, 2005). From a behavioral science perspective, memory might be addressed in terms of normal decline in memory versus pathological memory loss (such as, dementia) (Salthouse, 2003). From a social science perspective, memory might be viewed in terms of how it has been problematized and stigmatized in the larger society, thereby leading to the creation of subsequent 'solutions' (Katz, 2012). A literary scholar may consider how memory loss is portrayed in novels, poetry or other texts (Goldman, 2012). Gerontology is therefore not about having a particular way of thinking or set of methods, but instead it is unified by its object of interest – those who are considered to be 'aging' or 'old'.

But what is 'old'? The answer to this question has huge implications for people identified as such. It speaks to both the structural and experiential aspects of aging that include privileges and restrictions based on age, role definition, internal and external identity construction and maintenance and other considerations. The next section looks at three ways in which age is conceptualized. This is followed by a brief look at chronological and functional stages of life.

What are 'aging' and 'old age'?

Given that the focus of this book is gerontology, one cannot begin to offer a complete definition of gerontology without first exploring what is meant by aging and old age. As with all of the issues brought up in this *Short Guide*, answers are far from simple or definitive and perhaps ultimately lead to even more questions rather than providing greater clarity. Historian Rivkah Harris (2000), in looking at old age in ancient Mesopotamia, writes that 'the common Akkadian words for "old man" and "old woman" are šību and šībtu, which literally means "grey/white hair"' (p 50). Grey hair is still associated with old age, and is the target of media campaigns aimed at convincing people to cover their grey hair and thereby 'fight' aging.

Corinna Löckenhoff and colleagues (2009) have argued, 'the views of ageing held within a given culture are a form of shared cultural representation. They constitute systems of ideas, values, and customs related to ageing that are treated by members of the society as if they were established reality' (p 942). In this respect, cultural norms and expectations define, to an extent, what aging is. In a similar vein, Rüdiger Kurnow (2015) describes aging 'not as a description but as a judgment' and that it takes two to age: one who lacks the attributes of what is considered young, and one to act on these attributes. In both of these views, age is a cultural construction of a biological phenomenon. It is the way that others react to and make sense of 'the loss of molecular fidelity' (Hayflick, 2007, p 4) that is the hallmark of aging.

Defining old age is certainly complicated. In general, aging is described in three ways: biological, chronological and functional, although there are certainly other ways to think about aging and later life, to include social aging, cultural aging, relational aging and many more. Early gerontologists Ruth Shonle Cavan, Ernest Burgess, Robert Havighurst and Herbert Goldhamer (1949), when commenting on the complexity of defining age, write, 'Not only is an external symbol of entrance into old age lacking, but, as a personal experience, the realization that one is old comes gradually' (p 2). In other words, there is no agreed-upon age at which one becomes 'old'. As will be discussed later in the subsection on chronological age, many societies use age criteria to determine responsibilities, rights and program eligibility. Biologically speaking, there are changes that occur in people over time and at approximate stages in development, but again, there is not an exact age in which one biologically becomes 'old'. Not even subjective evaluation of one's age provides any type of guidance for developing a universal definition of 'old', since people vary greatly in physical change and the cultural contexts in which change is experienced and interpreted. Therefore, in the decades that have followed Cavan and colleagues' observation we are perhaps no closer to offering a complete definition of aging now than they were then. The following sections take a closer look at those three general descriptors: biological, chronological and functional.

Biological age

From a biological perspective, aging is commonly described as the product of time and a series of events – some random, some purposeful – that ultimately end in an organism's death. This conceptualization of age is focused on the organism itself and the relationship between time and change; it is echoed in common phrases such as 'You begin to age the moment you are born' (or maybe even from the point of conception).

It is important to note, however, that in many biological perspectives on aging, aging isn't a life-long process per se. Instead, an organism experiences two stages in his/her/its life: (1) development, which describes changes that prepare an organism for sexual maturity and the ability to reproduce, and (2) aging, which occurs at the point at which an organism reaches sexual maturity (Hayflick, 1988; Hayflick, 2000). According to biologist Leonard Hayflick, aging is 'an increase in molecular disorder. It is a stochastic process that occurs systemically after reproductive maturity in animals that reach a fixed size in adulthood. This escalating loss of molecular fidelity ultimate exceeds repair and turnover capacity and increases vulnerability to pathology or age-associated disease' (Hayflick, 2007, p 4). Such changes after sexual maturity lead to the types of physical and functional change that are key to biological definitions of aging.

Referencing Bill Bytheway (1995), social gerontologist Jason Powell (2006b) suggests 'the notion of "growth" is a central scientific discourse relating to true changes to the biological body associated with human ageing. Growth is seen as a positive development by biologists in that a baby grows into a child who grows into an adult, but then, instead of *growing* into old age, the person *declines*. This scientific sanction perception is that that growth slows when a person reaches "old age" and is subsequently interpreted as decline rather than as change, which is taken for granted with earlier life-course transitions' (p 5). From some biological perspectives (and for some, but not all, species and organisms), growth is associated with early life, old age with decline. Although the issue of epistemological stances and their consequences within gerontology is addressed in the next chapter, it is worth noting that the decline view of aging, linked to physical and psychological change over time, has been and continues to be a prevailing view in the field, despite efforts to move away from it by focusing on concepts such as wisdom (Edmondson, 2009), resilience (Lipsitt & Demick, 2011), successful aging (Rowe & Kahn, 1997), progress narratives (Gullette, 1996) and others.

Once again, biological aging varies tremendously across individuals (and organisms). In addition, biological aging does not have a direct link to a specific chronological age (Hirshbein, 2000), although there are certainly general times in which some changes do occur. For example, in humans, there are time periods when crawling, puberty or menopause are initiated. Despite this, numbers of years, such as 60 or 65, have little meaning when looking at individuals and the accumulation of physical changes over time. One 65-year-old may be much more biologically aged than another 65-year-old. The first may have spent many years working in the sun and having little access to nutritional food. This person may therefore appear 'older' and may also have health-related challenges based on diet. The other may have had access to healthcare and nutritious food, may have engaged in work that was not physically demanding and may have other characteristics that make this person's experience of aging different than the first.

Chronological age

Although physical and functional changes can lead to one being labeled as 'old', chronological age is also a common way in which the status of 'old' is conferred. Bernice Neugarten, a pioneering figure in gerontology, observed, 'In all societies, age is one of the bases for the ascription of status and one of the underlying dimensions by which social interaction is regulated' (Neugarten, Moore, & Lowe, 1965, p 709). As mentioned earlier, chronological age is the way used by many countries to signify citizens' rights and obligations and access to benefit systems. These include age of legally recognized adulthood, age of retirement, age at which one can consume alcohol, the age of marriage and so on. Chronological age therefore takes on a social meaning. In the case of mandatory age-based retirement (for example, age 60 in Thailand), chronological age becomes associated with the social marker of required disengagement from work. 'Old', in this case, is a social or cultural construction, based on rules of the society rather than on the individual's ability to perform.

As with biological age, chronological age does not necessarily reveal much information about the person. Philosopher Jan Baars (2010) writes, 'The search for general ageing characteristics based on chronological age has produced much counterevidence, testifying to the many differences in ageing processes. This counterevidence hardly comes as a surprise when we try to imagine people with the same chronological age but living in very different circumstances' (p 110-111). Again, although there may be some common changes that occur with the passing of time – greying hair, wrinkles, increased risk for certain diseases – these do not universally occur at certain chronological ages. As Brian Sharkey (1987) has noted, 'While hair graying and skin elasticity correlate 0.72 and 0.60 with age, blood pressure, reaction time, and visual acuity are less related (r=0.52, 0.48, and -0.43, respectively)[1]' (p 175). Rather than being rooted in biological change, much of the meaning linked to chronological age is cultural or social.

The problem of chronological age and its association with 'old' isn't new. References to chronological age were used in antiquity, although accurate records of common people's ages were not generally kept until the late medieval period in Western countries, when 'time' took on new importance. Harold M. Stahmer (1984) points out that the use of the clock by the Benedictines in the 13th century helped them to regulate their time and therefore make better use of it. This, he argues, later spread to workers and the merchant class, who then linked time more directly with money. Such reliance on time would eventually give way to age categorization and segmentation of the working and social world by chronological age. Historian Pat Thane (2000) explains that historically, 'The ages of 60 and 70 have been used in official discourse in England to signify the onset of old age at least since medieval times. Sixty was long the age at which law or custom permitted withdrawal from public activities on grounds of old age, though old age as such was not legally defined' (p 24). Age 60 was also used in ancient Greece and Rome as the time at which certain obligations for men (for example, military service) ended (David, 1991; Thane, 2000). More recently, age has been used to define retirement eligibility. Axel von Herbay (2014) notes that age 70 was the original age for the pension scheme introduced by Otto von Bismarck in 1889. In 1916, the age was lowered to 65 years, an age that is still associated in many countries with entry into 'old age'.

Currently, many countries with pension systems have raised their retirement ages to better address the growing numbers of people who live in good health past official retirement ages. The United States, for example, has raised the Social Security retirement eligibility age from 65 to 67. Other places, such as the Philippines, have relatively low retirement ages (age 60) (SSA, 2014), while certain African countries use age 50 as the point when one is officially considered 'old' (Naidoo et al, 2010).

Functional Age

The concept of functional age addresses some of the limitations of biological and chronological age by recognizing that people experience the effects of aging at different rates. Functional age is especially important within perspectives aimed at measuring change over time or assessing current status or performance ability. Often used synonymously with physiologic age, functional age is determined through focus on a particular health component, such as maximal oxygen intake, and its changes over time (Sharkey, 1987). This, of course, leads back to the question: when does a person become old?

Cavan, Burgess, Havighurst and Goldhamer (1949), in defining the onset of old age, write: 'Old age commences when a person is no longer able to maintain some stated proportion of the achievements of the average adult in his [sic] culture' (p 8). An early version of functional age, this statement speaks to performance as an indicator, rather than chronology. Geriatrician Réjean Hébert (1997) describes 'functional autonomy' as involving the concepts of disability ('the consequences of impairment of an organ or system on the functioning of the individual in terms of limitation of functions or restriction of activities' (p 1038)) and handicap ('the gap between the person's disability and the material and social resources available to him or her to offset the disabilities (p 1038.)) As changes linked to biological aging ('primary aging') lead to impairments ('secondary aging'), people are placed at a social disadvantage (for example, limited access to resources) that may lead to further vulnerability. Functional change is, then, a result of both physical (and psychological) and social changes. Functional status is discussed in more detail in Chapter Four.

The stages of life

The previous section discussed different ways that age is conceptualized and measured. This section looks at how stages of life have been used historically, with special emphasis on later life. Although there are slight variations in the ways that stages of life have been defined, there are also remarkable similarities. As is the case with much gerontological thinking and many concepts (such as the human life span), surprisingly little seems to have changed.

Table 1.1: A historical overview of stages of life

Chronological stage				Functional stage		
Ancient Mesopotamia[a]	European Enlightenment[b]	Early gerontology[c]	Present gerontology[d]	Ancient Greece[e]	Early England[f]	Present gerontology[g]
50: short life	5th decade: 'the sun may not go higher'	55–75: young-old	55–75: young-old	Stasis	Green old age	
60: maturity	6th decade: 'makes the hair gray'	55–75: young-old	55–75: young-old			Third age
70: long life	7th decade: 'sorrow sees with joy child's children'	75 and over: old-old	75–85: old-old	Decline		
80: old age	8th decade: 'nothing by but sorrow'		85 and above: oldest old		Sad decrepitude	Fourth age
90: extreme old age	9th decade: 'one sees what one already was and will be'					
	100 years: 'shuts the eyes'					

Notes: [a] Harris (2000); [b] Cole (1992, p 28); [c] Neugarten (1974); [d] Suzman & Riley (1984); Suzman, Willis, & Manton (1995); [e] Cole (1992); [f] Thane (2000); [g] Gilleard & Higgs (2010, 2013); Higgs & Gilleard (2015).

Table 1.1 presents an overview of various stage schemas, which are broken down into two categories: chronological stages and functional stages. As the names suggest, chronological stages are those where actual ages have been ascribed. Functional stages are those based on performance abilities.

The first stage on the table comes from ancient Mesopotamia. Unlike the other stages in the chronological category, which are forward looking, the Mesopotamian stages look backward. In other words, the stage describes life stage in terms of a person's death. For example, someone who died before or in their 50s was considered to have had a short life. People dying in their 70s were considered to have lived a long life. Harris (2000) notes that middle age or 'mature adulthood' appears to have been the most valued life stage for the Mesopotamians, if one looks at who is depicted in their art. She notes that with few expectations, most men and women are shown as 'neither very youthful nor very old' (Harris, 2000, p 23). Although not present in the chronological category on Table 1.1, Aristotle also viewed middle age as the superior age. Thomas Cole (1992) writes: 'Since men at the height of their powers are neither too trusting or too cynical, he [Aristotle] claimed that the ideal ruler is neither young nor old, an argument often repeated in medieval writing' (p 6). Cole also cites artist Jan Houwen's depiction of life stages based on decade of life. In this, one's 70s appear to be the last decade before decline and 'sorrow'.

Bernice Neugarten (1974) classified the 'old' into two groups: the young-old (those aged 55 to 75) and the old-old (those aged 75 and over.) A third category, 'the oldest old'' (those aged 85 and over) was later added by Richard Suzman and Matilda White Riley (Suzman & Riley, 1984; Suzman, Willis, & Manton, 1995) in response to the growing number of people age 85 and older.

Examples of functional stages come from ancient Greece, early England and present gerontology. Aristotle described three stages of life: growth, stasis and decline (Cole, 1992, p 5). 'Growth' represents the majority of one's life. 'Stasis' describes middle age or what later would be called 'green old age' or the 'third age'. 'Decline', as the name implies, describes the period in which mental and/or physical health begins to diminish.

Similar to Aristotle's stages are stages from early modern England. Pat Thane (2000) writes that 'Commonly, old age has been divided into what in early modern England was called "green" old age, a time of fitness and activity with some failing powers, and the last phase of sad decrepitude' (p 4). More recently, the labels 'third' and 'fourth' age are used as a way of linking aging to functional status rather than chronological age. The third age is characterized by high function and independence. The fourth age describes a time of decline and dependence (West & Glynos, 2014; Higgs & Gilleard, 2015). Again, these stages bear remarkable similarity to each other despite decades of gerontological research. Looking at these historical stages of life provides an interesting way of seeing how past depictions influence current gerontological thinking.

Other ages

In addition to how age is measured – biologically, chronologically, functionally – there are several concepts in gerontology that describe how one can or should age. These include successful aging, active aging and productive aging. The following subsections provide a brief overview of each.

Successful aging

Many times, people use 'successful aging' when they mean that someone has aged well (however that is defined). Yet, successful aging does have a particular history in gerontology. The concept of successful aging was introduced in earlier gerontological discourse by Pressey and Simcoe (1950) through their description of the 'unsuccessfully aged' (Pressey & Simcoe, 1950). They recognized that not all older people aged in the same way. Some had relatively few signs of physiological or psychological change while others seemed to experience more difficulties. Later, Jeanette Baker (1959) introduced the idea of the 'unsuccessfully aged' to describe people who suffered from 'senile behavior' (p 570) due to unmet social needs. In the 1960s, Robert Havighurst (1963) proposed a broader concept of successful aging, stressing the importance of life satisfaction indices as essential correlates of any measures used. Havighurst defined successful aging as 'a statement of the conditions of the individual and social life under which the individual person gets a maximum of satisfaction and happiness *and* society maintains an appropriate balance among satisfactions for various groups which make up the old' (1963, p 1).

Paul and Margret Baltes (1993) defined 'successful ageing' from a developmental psychology perspective. They proposed that successful aging is 'an adaptive process involving the components of selection, optimization, and compensation' (pp 1–2). They add that 'a discussion of successful aging converges with the search for factors and conditions that help us to understand the potential of aging and, if desirable, to identify ways to modify the nature of human aging as it exists today' (p 4) For them, a combination of subjective and objective indicators are necessary.

In the 1980s and 1990s, Rowe and Kahn (Rowe & Kahn, 1987; Rowe & Kahn, 1997) redefined successful aging to distinguish between 'normal' aging, which includes physical and cognitive decline, and 'successful', which they define in terms of one's ability to maintain '1) low risk of disease and disease-related disability, or the absence of disease and risk factors for disease; 2) high mental and physical function, which means the ability to participate fully in all activities of daily living (of which there are well validated scales) such as shopping and bathing without assistance; 3) and active engagement with life,' (p 38) which Rowe and Kahn say includes 'maintaining relationships with others and participating in activities that are productive or that create goods or services or value' (p 38).

Recently, there has been growing criticism of Rowe and Kahn's use of successful aging because of its emphasis on the individual actor. In other words, it assumes that people have control over their own health outcomes, when in many cases this is not so. As will be discussed in later chapters, social location (for example, socioeconomic status, race, social class) can have a tremendous impact on one's aging, regardless of individual initiative (Harris, 2008; Rubinstein & de Medeiros, 2014).

Active aging

To move away from the negative outcomes often associated with later life and to stress the positive aspects of growing older, the World Health Organization (WHO) uses the phrase 'active ageing', which it defines as 'the process of optimizing opportunities for health, participation and security in order to enhance quality of life as people age. It applies to both individuals and population groups' (WHO, 2002). Active aging is an idea that has come as a response to 'successful aging' by stressing opportunity rather than performance, and focusing on quality of life.

Productive aging

Productive aging was introduced in the 1980s and still part of the gerontological discussion (Bass & Caro, 1993). According to Leonard Kaye and colleagues (Kaye, Butler, & Webster, 2003),

> Increased attention to the productive aspects of ageing is not solely an act of altruism toward current and future cohorts of elders. In fact, as a society, we have much to gain from greater participation of older persons in many walks of life. In particular, there are significant economic benefits to having swelling numbers of retirees spend their disposable income on travel, recreation, real estate, and consumer goods, as well as invest their assets in a variety of investment vehicles. 'Retirees' are also well suited to our contemporary economy, filling many of the emergent nontraditional jobs. (Kaye et al, 2003, p 202)

Kaye and colleagues continue to suggest employment realms that are 'considerably less attractive to younger workers' (such as caregiving) (Kaye et al, 2003, p 202).

Just as successful aging is fraught with controversy, so is productive aging. One of the controversies surrounding 'productive aging' is that much of the 'productivity' is without compensation. Using feminist arguments that identified unpaid domestic labor as a source of gender-based oppression, Neal King (2013) makes a similar case for productivity and older people. He writes that 'old people are pushed from realms of the paid workforce and thus used as a reserve *labor,* targeted by ads as *consumers*, and stigmatized as *dependents* on institutional support (p 53). King argues that ageist stereotypes of older people as less competent place older people in the position of performing tasks such as care work that are unpaid. 'Productivity', in this regard, requires older people to contribute to society, but without monetary compensation (King, 2013).

Overall, these depictions of aging present both possibilities and challenges. Successful aging is, on the one hand, a way to better identify positive performance aspects of later life. Uncovering specific reasons why some people maintain higher functional abilities than others could lead to targeted interventions. On the other hand, successful aging places emphasis on individual action without recognizing larger issues of social location. Active aging attempts to counter the decline discourse of aging by focusing on quality of life rather than performance. While conceptually this may seem a more favorable stance than successful aging, active aging as a construct may be difficult to measure and therefore not able to provide insight into processes and experiences of aging that can lead to the development of appropriate interventions. Finally, productive aging does not recognize marginalization that occurs when individuals are asked to work without compensation. Although volunteerism may be attractive to people (at any age in life), productive aging as an imperative can place older people in an economically compromised situation.

Summary

Gerontology is the study of later life and, as such, is focused on age. However, defining 'old age' is far more complicated than one might think. Despite the common use of chronological age to mark entry into various levels of social participation, chronological age itself is limited in the information it provides; there is great variability among people of the same chronological age. In addition to defining what 'old age' is, it is also helpful to look at how stages of life have been conceptualized over time, especially to see the similarities in both past and present depictions. Finally, concepts such as successful aging, active aging and productive aging are important to consider for several reasons, to include providing frameworks – good or bad – for how individual aging is viewed, and offering constructs through which aging can be measured. As will be illustrated throughout the book, definitions of and expectations for later life are central to the social, cultural and economic forces that shape aging.

Note

[1] R is the correlation coefficient which measures the strength and direction between two variables. The value of one means a perfect positive correlation; negative one means a perfect negative correlation. (Sharkey, 1987, p 175, note).

Further reading

Bond, J., Peace, S.M., Dittmann-Kohli, F., & Westerhof, G. (Eds.). (2007). *Ageing in society*. Thousand Oaks, CA: Sage.

Cruikshank, M. (2013). *Learning to be old: Gender, culture, and aging*. Landham, MD: Rowman & Littlefield Publishers.

Hayflick, L. (2007). Biological aging is no longer an unsolved problem. *Annals of the New York Academy of Sciences*, *1100*(1), 1–13.

Rowe, J. W., & R. L. Kahn (1997). Successful aging. *The Gerontologist*, *37*(4): 433–440.

References

Baars, J. (2009). Problematic foundations: theorizing time, age and aging. In: V. L. Bengston, M. Silverstein, N. M. Putney & D. Gans (Eds.), *Handbook of theories on aging* (2nd edn). New York: Springer Publishing, pp 87–100.

Baars, J. (2010). Philosophy of aging, time, and finitude. In: T. R. Cole, R. E. Ray, & R. Kastenbaum (Eds.), *A guide to humanistic studies in aging: What does it mean to grow old?* Baltimore, MD: Johns Hopkins University Press, pp 104–120.

Baker, J. L. (1959). The unsuccessful aged. *Journal of the American Geriatrics Society, 7*(7), 570–572.

Baltes, P. B., & Baltes, M. M. (1993). *Successful aging: Perspectives from the behavioral sciences* (Vol. 4). New York: Cambridge University Press.

Bass, S. A., & Caro, F. G. (1993). *Achieving a productive aging society.* London: Auburn House Publishing Co.

Bytheway, B. (1995). *Ageism.* Buckingham: Open University Press.

Cavan, R. S., Burgess, E. W., Havighurst, R.J., Goldhamer, H. (1949). *Personal adjustment in old age.* Chicago: Chicago Science Research Associates.

Cole,T. R. (1992). *The journey of life: A cultural history of aging in America.* New York: Cambridge University Press.

Cruikshank, M. (2013). *Learning to be old: Gender, culture, and aging.* Lanham, MD: Rowman & Littlefield Publishers.

David, E. (1991). *Old age in Sparta.* Amsterdam: Adolf m Hakkert.

Dolan, J. (2013). Firm and hard: popular culture, gendered stardom and the troubling embodiment of 'successful aging.' In: J.I. Prieto-Arranz, P. Bastida-Rodríguez, C. Calafat-Ripoll, M. Fernández-Morales, & C. Suárez-Gómez (Eds.), *De-Centring cultural studies: Past, present and future of popular culture.* Newcastle upon Tyne: Cambridge Scholars, pp. 217–246.

Edmondson, R. (2009). Wisdom: a humanist approach to valuing older people. In: R. Edmondson & H. J. von Kondratowitz (Eds.), *Valuing older people: A humanist approach to ageing.* Bristol: Policy Press, pp 201–216.

Gilleard, C., & Higgs, P. (2010). Aging without agency: theorizing the fourth age. *Aging & Mental Health, 14*(2), 121–128.

Gilleard, C., & Higgs, P. (2013). The fourth age and the concept of a 'social imaginary': a theoretical excursus. *Journal of Aging Studies, 27*(4), 368–376.

Goldman, M. (2012). Aging, old age, memory, aesthetics: introduction to special issue. In: M. Goldman, A. Charise, L. Hutcheon, and M. Hutcheon (Eds.), Special issue, *Occasion: Interdisciplinary Studies in the Humanities, 4,* 1–6.

Gullette, M. M. (1996). *Declining to decline.* Charlottesville, VA: University of Virginia Press.

Harris, P. (2008). Another wrinkle in the debate about successful aging: the undervalued concept of resilience and the lived experience of dementia. *The International Journal of Aging and Human Development, 67*(1), 43–61. doi: 10.2190/AG.67.1.c.

Harris, R. (2000). *Gender and aging in Mesopotamia: The Gilgamesh Epic and other ancient literature.* Norman, OK: University of Oklahoma Press.

Havighurst, R. J. (1963). Successful aging. *Processes of Aging: Social and Psychological Perspectives, 1*, 299–320.

Hayflick, L. (1988). Why do we live so long? *Geriatrics, 43*(10), 77.

Hayflick, L. (2000). The future of ageing. *Nature, 408*(6809), 267–269.

Hayflick, L. (2007). Biological aging is no longer an unsolved problem. *Annals of the New York Academy of Sciences, 1100*(1), 1–13. doi: 10.1196/annals.1395.001.

Hébert, R. (1997). Functional decline in old age. *Canadian Medical Association Journal, 157*(8), 1037–1045.

Higgs, P., & Gilleard, C. (2015). *Rethinking old age: Theorising the fourth age.* London: Palgrave.

Hirshbein, L. D. (2000). 'Normal' old age, senility, and the American Geriatrics Society in the 1940s. *Journal of the History of Medicine and Allied Sciences, 55*(4), 337–362.

Jones, R. L. (2006). 'Older people' talking as if they are not older people: positioning theory as an explanation. *Journal of Aging Studies, 20*(1), 79–91. doi: 10.1016/j.jaging.2004.12.003.

Katz, S. (2012). Embodied memory: aging, neuroculture, and the genealogy of mind. *Occasion: Interdisciplinary Studies in the Humanities, 4*(31), 1–14.

Kaye, L. W., Butler, S. S., & Webster, N. M. (2003). Toward a productive ageing paradigm for geriatric practice. *Ageing International, 28*(2), 200–213.

King, N. (2013). The lengthening list of oppressions: age relations and the feminist study of inequality. In: T.M. Calasanti & K.F. Slevin (Eds.), *Age matters: Re-aligning feminist thinking.* New York: Routledge, pp 47–74.

Kurnow, R. (2015). Intimacy international: transnational care as a challenge for age studies. Paper presented at Forum Age/ing Graz. Graz, Austria, https://forum-ageing-graz-2015.uni-graz.at/en/.

Leibing, A. (2005). The old lady from Ipanema: changing notions of old age in Brazil. *Journal of Aging Studies, 19*(1), 15–31.

Lipsitt, L. P., & Demick, J. (2011). Resilience science comes of age: old age, that is. *PsycCRITIQUES, 56*(26). doi: 10.1037/a0023900.

Löckenhoff, C. E., De Fruyt, F., Terracciano, A., McCrae, R. R., De Bolle, M., Costa Jr, P. T., ...Alcalay, L. (2009). Perceptions of aging across 26 cultures and their culture-level associates. *Psychology and Aging, 24*(4), 941.

Naidoo, N., Abdullah, S., Bawah, A., Binka, F., Chuc, N. T., Debpuur, C., ... Van Minh, H. (2010). Ageing and adult health status in eight lower-income countries: the INDEPTH WHO-SAGE collaboration. *Global Health Action, 11*, 8–11.

Neugarten, B. L. (1974). Age groups in American society and the rise of the young-old. *The Annals of the American Academy of Political and Social Science, 415*(1), 187–198. doi: 10.1177/000271627441500114.

Neugarten, B. L., Moore, J. W., & Lowe, J. C. (1965). Age norms, age constraints, and adult socialization. *American Journal of Sociology, 70*(6), 710–717.

Powell, J. L. (2006a). *Rethinking social theory and later life*. New York: Nova Science Publishers Incorporated.

Powell, J. L. (2006b). *Social theory and aging*. Lanham, MD: Rowman & Littlefield.

Pressey, S. L., & Simcoe, E. (1950). Case study comparisons of successful and problem old people. *Journal of Gerontology, 5*(2), 168–175.

Rowe, J. W., & Kahn, R. L. (1987). Human aging: usual and successful. *Science, 237*(4811), 143–149.

Rowe, J. W., & Kahn, R. L. (1997). Successful aging. *The Gerontologist, 37*(4), 433–440.

Rubinstein, R. L., & de Medeiros, K. (2014). 'Successful aging', gerontological theory and neoliberalism: a qualitative critique. *The Gerontologist, 55*(1), 34-42. doi: 10.1093/geront/gnu080

Salthouse, T. A. (2003). Memory aging from 18 to 80. *Alzheimer Disease & Associated Disorders, 17*(3), 162–167.

Sharkey, B. J. (1987). Functional vs chronologic age. *Medicine and Science in Sports and Exercise, 19*(2), 174–178.

SSA (Social Security Administration) (2014). *Social security programs throughout the world*, 2016, https://www.ssa.gov/policy/docs/progdesc/ssptw/2014.

Stahmer, H. M. (1984). Values, ethics and aging. *Frontiers in Aging Series, 4*, 26–40.

Suzman, R., & Riley, M. W. (1984). Introducing the 'oldest old'. *The Milbank Memorial Fund Quarterly. Health and Society, 63*(2), 177–186.

Suzman, R. M., Willis, D. P., & Manton, K. G. (1995). *The oldest old*. Oxford: Oxford University Press.

Thane, P. (2000). *Old age in English history: Past experiences, present issues*. Oxford: Oxford University Press.

von Herbay, A. (2014). Otto von Bismarck is not the origin of old age at 65. *The Gerontologist, 54*(1), 5. doi: 10.1093/geront/gnt111.

West, K., & Glynos, J. (2014). 'Death talk', 'loss talk' and identification in the process of ageing. *Ageing & Society, FirstView*, 1–15. doi:10.1017/S0144686X14001184.

WHO (World Health Organization) (2002). *Active ageing: A policy framework* (WHO/NMH/NPH/02.8). Geneva, Switzerland, http://www.who.int/ageing/publications/active_ageing/en/.

TWO

Gerontology:
a historical overview

Age, aging and gerontology were touched upon in the first chapter. This chapter will provide a more comprehensive look at gerontology's development. As mentioned earlier, gerontology can be broadly defined as the study of later life. The term itself is credited to Russian zoologist Elie Metchnikoff, who, in 1903 combined the Greek words 'geron' (old man) and 'logia' (study of) (Metchnikoff, 1903; Katz, 1996). Gerontology involves the structured pursuit of understanding the effects of the passage of time on individuals and society, as well as what the experience of time means. The term 'gerontology' is both a discipline and a descriptor used by people from various perspectives to describe their work pertaining to later life. Although gerontology began formally to take hold as an emerging discipline shortly after World War Two (Achenbaum, 1995), questions about how and why we age have been explored since antiquity. This chapter therefore provides an overview of the foundational components from which current gerontology was built and considers many explanatory stances both past and present used in examining later life.

The gerontological perspective

As noted in the Preface, to acknowledge the many ways that later life has been studied and considered, the *Short Guide* will use the term 'gerontological perspective'. The gerontological perspective describes the idea that the object of interest, through research, inquiry or practice, is older age, later life and/or older individuals themselves. As such, frameworks for best answering relevant research or critical questions are not limited by the boundaries of traditional academic disciplines or perspectives but, rather, driven by the object of interest. This is not to say that a gerontological perspective necessarily exists outside of traditional disciplines such as sociology or psychology. Instead, it acknowledges that the gerontological perspective is not restricted to the research methods, theories, epistemological stances or approaches within a given discipline, while also recognizing gerontology as a discipline in its own right.

This chapter will first explore how aging has been viewed in the ancient world and in the early development of gerontology. It will then examine gerontology's broader growth – from the formation of professional organizations, to perspectives. It will also examine some of the many major influences in the development of gerontology over time through examples of perspectives and key people who have shaped research and thought in the gerontological landscape. Note that there are many excellent books and journal articles that cover various aspects of gerontology's history, some of which are listed at the end of the chapter, and that can fill in many of the gaps here.

Old age and gerontology

As with all topics covered in the *Short Guide*, the history of old age itself could include multiple, lengthy volumes. This section will provide a brief look at some common themes in the ways that old age has been characterized and understood through history, early medicine, and social change. The latter half of the chapter will look specifically of the development of gerontology from the early 20th century until present.

History

This subsection provides a very brief overview of aging in the ancient world (Mesopotamia, Greece, Sparta and Rome) as well as brief mention of Eastern countries (Japan, Korea, China and Taiwan). (For rich accounts of aging in the medieval and premodern world, see Minois, 1989; Thane, 2000; Johnson and Thane 2002.) Historian Pat Thane (2010) and others point out that it is difficult to know how aging was perceived in the past, since many sources are limited to artistic renditions of older people (for example, sculpture, paintings), older characters in plays and literature, and laws affecting older citizens (Minois, 1989; Parkin, 2003). Since most of these sources were in the purview of wealthy men, much less is known about older women in particular, and the poor in general, than about privileged older men.

Rivkah Harris (2000) provides some insights into aging in ancient Mesopotamia. She mentions that, like other preindustrial societies, the Mesopotamians had little interest in chronological age although, as mentioned in the previous chapter, they did equate long life with the age of 70 and placed the human life span at 120 years. Harris writes, 'For the Mesopotamians, then, the appearance of gray hair was the distinguishing sign of old age as it is and has been for other societies ... the two most characteristic markers of old age in Mesopotamia were gray/white hair and a bent or stooped posture' (p 51). She mentions that, like the Egyptians, the Mesopotamians dyed their hair. In addition, like many other cultures, women were defined as old when they reached menopause. Overall, Harris describes the Mesopotamians as looking forward to longevity and that good health and happiness in old age were considered a gift from the gods. She also notes that 'length of years might also be accompanied by the increasing acrimony of long-grown sons, impatient to claim their inheritance and finally live economically independent lives' (p 66), a theme that is echoed across many other cultures.

Aging in ancient Greece had some similarities and differences to Mesopotamia. Georges Minois (1989) describes old age in ancient Greek society in very negative terms. He writes that old men 'attracted scorn, mockery and bad treatment: "A decrepit old man, with only three teeth left, scarcely sighted, who leans on four slaves to walk, whose nose distills a permanent drip, whose eyes are filled with rheum, insensible to all pleasure, a living sepulcher, an object of mockery for the young" is how Julian describes him' (p 62). Minois goes on to explain that there were charitable organizations that provided food for men who had provided services to the state. Thomas Falkner and Judith de Luce (1992) describe Greek women's lives in terms of their ability to reproduce. According to them, the female life cycle in ancient Greece consisted of (1) 'child not capable of motherhood', (2) 'the parthenos, sexually of age but not yet married', (3) 'mother-wife', and (4) 'no longer capable of motherhood (graia)' (p 5). In this schema, a woman ceased to be considered useful upon reaching menopause. For Greek men, there was, of course, no concept of retirement. It was common, however, for the Greek patriarch at around age 60 to hand over control of the house to his son at the son's marriage (usually at around age 30). In this way, the father would become relationally old but would still maintain some level of status.

In contrast to Greece, Sparta viewed age differently. Older wealthy men held power through the country's gerontocracy (David, 1991). Ephraim David (1991) writes, 'Unlike other Greek states, Sparta did not leave the decision over the future of the newly-born in the hands of the parents. It was typical of Spartan etatisme that the decision was an affair of state, and typical of Spartan gerontocracy that it was entrusted to "the eldest of the tribes"' (p 38). To serve on the gerousia or Council of Elders, one had to be age 60 and of noble birth. There were 28 council members who, once elected, served for life. According to David (1991) and others, the gerontocracy held great power in the sixth through fourth centuries BCE, gaining increasing strength over the years.

In ancient Rome, Tim Parkin (2003) explains that older people themselves are seldom mentioned and, when they are, it is usually under special circumstances, such as serving in a notable leadership role. He also explains that although Romans used the word 'senex' to refer to old age, 'senectus' was characterized by physical and mental function rather than chronological age. Senectus is also used rhetorically. For example, in the case of two generals in battle, both of the same age, the defeated one might be described in terms of senectus. This would be in contrast to the victor, who might be depicted as being in the 'flower of his youth' (Parkin, 2003, p 23). Senectus did not refer to one's age but, rather, to one's strength and abilities. Parkin adds that although there are accounts of mythical and historical figures who purportedly lived into advanced old age, they are generally celebrated for their accomplishments rather than their ages.

In Eastern countries such as Japan, Korea, China and Taiwan, Leng Leng Thang (2000) points to conflicting views of aging. On the one hand, the countries share a heritage of Confucianism, which stresses mutual respect for various categories of people (for example, parents, leaders) in society. On the other hand, Thang cites legends in Japan and Korea, obasuteyama and koryŏjang respectively, that describe abandoning elders on a mountain side or burying them alive when they became a burden to the family. Thang also points to the demonization of old women in Japan, especially older women who are childless. Or course, similar demonization of old women can be seen in numerous other countries of the world.

This brief history of ways in which the aged have been viewed points to some critical links to current gerontology. First is the social marginalization that old people have historically experienced. Second is the emphasis on appearance and function in determining who is old. Third is the way in which older women have been especially devalued, as compared to men. Arguably, these are also important issues in gerontology today.

Early gerontology

Moving away from the history of old age, this section focuses on the early development of gerontology. As Andrew Achenbaum (1995) points out, 'old age is one thing, gerontology another' (p 2). The early history of gerontology is one about the growing optimism of science and medicine, whereby aging was positioned as a disease that could potentially be cured, rather than as an inevitable part of the life cycle (Achenbaum, 1995; Katz, 1996). James Fries (1980) observed, 'Speculation about immortality is rooted in antiquity and in human hope. The bioscientific, medical model of disease, our prevalent model, assumes that death is always the results of a disease process; if there were no disease, there would be no death' (p 130). Books such as physician Ignatz L. Nascher's *Geriatrics: The diseases of old age and their treatment, including physiological old age, home and institutional care, and medico-legal relations* (Nascher, 1914) and psychologist G. Stanley Hall's *Senescence: The last half of life* (Hall, 1922) aimed to apply a structured and disciplined approach to addressing health and psychological issues associated with older age. In the United Kingdom, Marjory Warren is credited with the development of modern geriatrics in 1935 by introducing rehabilitation programs for people in the 'aged beds' and emphasizing the importance of motivation within older patients as a key step to healing and health (Morley, 2004).

Through the rigor of scientific method and procedures, as well as clearly conceptualized and seemingly attainable goals and outcomes (for example, treatments, explanatory models of function), the 'science' of gerontology seemed promising, even in the early 20th century (Achenbaum, 1987). In referencing Eli Metchnikoff, Ignatz Nascher and G. Stanley Hall, Andrew Achenbaum (1995) notes that 'all three men defined late life in dualistic terms; they distinguished between normal and pathological old age ... The trio believed that scientific advances in senescence would pave the way for more positive assessments of growing older; they expected science someday to make it possible for people to affix constructive meaning and purposes to later years' (p 49). Arguably, even more than 100 years later, gerontology is still seeking these same goals.

Social change and gerontology

While medicine and the bench sciences looked for answers about why and how we age, old age was increasingly recognized by others as a social problem. Fertility rates in Europe during the 1920s and 1930s declined and life expectancy at most ages and outward migration increased. In some countries, this led to government-sponsored incentives for women to have more children (Thane, 2010). Most European countries were aware of shifting demographics (Scharf, 2001; Thane, 2010). In Great Britain, the percentage of males age 65 and over and females age 60 and over were: 6.2% in 1901, 9.6% in 1931, 12% in 1941 and 13.5% in 1951 (Thane, 2000, p 333). Grace Leybourne, a British statistician, estimated that the population of Britain would begin to decline by around 2 million people in 1951 and would be around 32,700,000 by 1976. She, along with her contemporary Enid Charles, also predicted that 'the ageing of the population would perpetuate the female majority in the population if females continued to experience longer life expectancy than males' (Thane, 2000, p 336). The prospect of having a large aging female population was particularly troublesome for many.

In the United States, physician Edward Tuohy (1946), in the first issue of *Geriatrics* wrote, 'With increasing numbers of older people, humanity is faced with many serious problems. For these problems we are wholly unprepared. We do not know what to do with old people, and old people do not know what to do with themselves.' This concern of 'what to do with old people' was even more sharply addressed by B. B. Beard's (1946) article in the same issue of *Geriatrics*, where she describes a new 'army of the aged'. Among the challenges, according to her, was that this 'army' was forming a 'new societal increment in that they [the elderly] have no institutionalized place' (p 300).

Like Great Britain, the United States also became concerned about the shift in sex ratios of men and women. Edmund Vincent Cowdry (1947) wrote: 'In 1944, the excess of males over females was estimated at 6,105. Today, there are probably more females than males in the United States. It is a safe prediction that as the years roll by, this nation will become more and more female' (p 279). He added, however, that 'Before we reach the degree of female numerical excess typical of Tibet and some other countries, we may confidently expect to be able to control the sex of our offspring' (p 279). Reasons cited by Cowdry for the increase in females over males included greater decrease in women's mortality from major diseases compared to men (43%, compared 26% for men); greater privilege under the law, specifically alimony and death benefits payable to women but not to men; less 'occupational shock', since women did not need to give up their roles as caregivers and homemakers while men left their jobs; and, finally, that 'women are coming to hold the purse strings as never before' (p 280). All of these, for Cowdry, were distressing signs of change.

In response to these new and unprecedented social changes, there emerged a need for multi-disciplinary approaches to understanding aging. Andrew Achenbaum (1987) explains, 'precisely because old age was a problem of unprecedented scope, scholars and academic entrepreneurs had difficulty "fitting" gerontology into existing arrangements' (p 4). In other words, something as broad and encompassing as old age could not be easily addressed by existing, narrowly structured disciplines that existed in the developing stages of gerontology. In response, the Club for Research on Aging, which was formed in 1939, grew into the Gerontological Society of America (GSA), chartered in 1945 (Achenbaum, 1987; Morley, 2004). The GSA originally was organized around three sections – medical research, biological research and general. Later, it broadened its scope and renamed or created new sections to reflect its multi-disciplinary focus. Sections currently are: behavioral and social sciences; biological sciences; social research, planning and practice; and health sciences (Achenbaum, 1987).

In Britain, the Nuffield Foundation, thanks to the personal interest of Lord Nuffield, began supporting age-related research shortly after World War Two, well in advance of other major funding sources at the time (Welford, 1958). Allan Travis Welford (1958) notes that this research was practical for the country, since it focused on preventing older people from becoming a burden on society. The outcomes for older people themselves are less clear. Research supported by the Nuffield Foundation fell roughly into four categories: (1) social surveys to ascertain the welfare needs of older people in their homes; (2) work-related research to determine older people's work and retirement potential; (3) measurement of human capacity; and (4) 'the assessment of mental deteriorating in clinical senile states' (Welford, 1958, p 51). Environments and housing for older people, work and retirement, optimal physical functioning with age, and prevention of memory loss and poor cognitive performance are still major areas of research within gerontology, although there is now more focus on older people's experiences and perceptions, as opposed to performance and needs alone.

Travis Welford (1958) wrote that until the founding of the journals *Gerontologia* (in 1957) and *Vita Humana* (in 1958) academic scholars and researchers exploring topics in gerontology published their work in journals related to their specific disciplines. Welford (1958) optimistically wrote: 'Areas have already been identified in which practical action is needed and measures have been suggested which are likely to relieve some of the worst difficulties of older people. The results of any action taken need, however, to be carefully followed up; if resources and interest can be made available for this, the social investigations would seem to be capable of yielding insight into the "mechanisms" of individual and social relationships' (pp 63–64).

Gerontology was, of course, also developing in other parts of the world, although interest in gerontology was very much driven by need (for example, changes in population structure) and focused on response (such as pension and supports). The International Association for Gerontology and Geriatrics convened its first world congress on 9 July 1950 in Liège, Belgium, with 113 attendees and 14 countries represented (IAGG, 2016). Lucian Brull, a Belgian professor of clinical medicine, served as the first president. The first Chinese Gerontology and Geriatric Seminar was held in 1964. Argentina established the Argentinian Gerontological Conference in 1989 (Barca, 1994). Most countries now have a formal gerontological society to address issues and topics related to older age (IAGG, 2016).

Key people and ideas in gerontology

The final section in this chapter includes some of the major people and perspectives (Table 2.1) that have shaped gerontology. As with all of the topics in the *Short Guide*, this list is not meant to be exhaustive or all inclusive. Numerous books and articles have been written about perspectives and countless publications by and about the people mentioned tell rich stories about aging and aging research. What this section is meant to do is to show the breadth of perspectives, ranging from explanations of how older individuals cope in the face of challenges (for example, selective optimization with compensation), ideas that frame care philosophies (such as activity theory, continuity theory, learned dependency), explanations of how individuals interact with their environments (for example, congruence model of person–environment interactions, ecological theories of aging) and others (for example, generativity, wisdom). In addition, it is important to note that stances change and evolve over time. Some lose favor (for example, disengagement theory), others offer new potential for how we approach studies on age or understandings of social location (such as cumulative advantage/disadvantage, cumulative inequality.) Many of these stances will be revisited in later chapters.

Highly influential in gerontology's development, social psychologist Bernice Neugarten developed the idea of age norms. Along with colleagues Moore and Lowe, she observed that 'expectations regarding age-appropriate behavior form an elaborated and pervasive system of norms governing behavior and interaction, a network of expectations that is imbedded throughout the cultural fabric of adult life' (Neugarten, Moore, & Lowe, 1965, p 711). They went on to look at the structural ways that perceptions of age norms affected older people.

Other influential people include Robert J. Havighurst (Cavan, Burgess, Havighurst, & Goldhamer, 1949; Havighurst & Albrecht, 1953; Havighurst, 1963), whose work on the concept of successful aging was mentioned in Chapter One; Vern Bengston, George Maddox, Nathan Shock and many others (see Achenbaum & Albert, 1995).

Table 2.1: Examples of major perspectives and explanatory stances in gerontology

Structure	
Activity theory (Havighurst & Albrecht, 1953)	Posits that people desire to maintain the activities and attitudes of midlife throughout older age (Havighurst, 1963).
Congruence model of person–environment interaction (Kahana, 1982)	Proposes interrelationship of seven dimensions of congruence between personal life space and environmental influences: segregate, congregate, institutional control, structure, stimulation/engagement, affect and impulse control (Kahana, 1982; Rubinstein & de Medeiros, 2003).
Continuity theory (Atchley, 1989)	Assumption that people apply familiar strategies to maintain internal (for example, personal preferences) and external structures (for example, interacting with familiar physical or social environments) (Atchley, 1989).
Convergence theory (Goode, 1963)	Perspective that suggested that through industrialization, nuclear families would strengthen and ties to extended family would weaken (Goode, 1963).
Cumulative advantage/disadvantage (Dannefer, 1999, 2003)	Defined by Dannefer (2003) as the 'systematic tendency for interindividual divergence in a given characteristic (e.g., money, health, status) with the passage of time' (p 327).
Cumulative inequality (Ferraro & Shippee, 2009)	Specifies that 'social systems generate inequality, which is manifested over the life course via demographic and developmental processes, and that personal trajectories are shaped by the accumulation of risk, available resources, perceived trajectories, and human agency' (Ferraro & Shippee, 2009, p 334).
Disengagement theory (Cumming & Henry, 1961)	Describes a mutual yet adaptive social and psychological withdrawal of an individual from society and society from the individual as a person ages. Originally, 'disengagement' was believed to start at around age 50 (Baltes & Carstensen, 1999; Maddox, 1964).

Structure	
Ecological model of aging (Lawton & Nahemow, 1973; Parmelee & Lawton, 1990)	Explores the relationship between the individual and the environment based on levels of the individual's adaption in relation to environmental forces (that is, press) that are placed on the individual and his/her personal competence. (Lawton, 1983; Rubinstein & de Medeiros, 2003)
Learned dependency (Baltes, 1988)	A passive behavior that is learned to gain a desired outcome (for example, attention). Because of assumptions that older people are prone to dependency due to incompetence, over-protective environments are created whereby older people are 'rewarded' for adhering to dependency scripts (Baltes & Carstensen, 1999).
Lifecourse perspective (Elder & Rockwell, 1979; Settersten Jr, 1999)	Describes 'age-related role transitions that are socially created, socially recognized and socially shared' (Settersten Jr, 1999, p 6).
Modernization theory (Cowgill & Holmes, 1972)	Links changes in status of older individuals to changes from agriculture-based societies (high status) to industrial ones (low status) (Cowgill & Holmes, 1972; Fry, 1999) .
Political economy perspective (Estes, Swan, & Gerard, 1982)	According to Quadagno and Reid (1999), the political economy of aging framework 'recognizes old age as socially constructed, a product of struggles that result in the unequal distribution of societal resources. The central objective of the political economy of aging is to analyze the structure conditions that create inequality in old age and to emphasize the relevance of these struggles for understanding how the aged are defined and treated' (p 344).
Experience	
Compression of morbidity (Fries, 1980)	A hypothesis that suggests that the 'amount of disability can decrease as morbidity is compressed into the shorter span between the increasing age at onset of disability and the fixed occurrence of death' (Fries, 1980, p 248).
Generativity (Erikson, 1950; Erikson & Erikson, 1997)	The idea that people expend energy to guide the next generation or contribute to society in a way that will benefit future generations.

Structure	
Life review (Butler, 1963; Butler, 2002b)	Described by Butler (2002a) as 'a personal process by which a person evaluates his or her life as it nears its end' (p 1).
Selective optimization with compensation (Baltes, Baltes, & Baltes, 1990)	Describes three elements involved to response to changes: (1) selection, which requires directing resources to some domains while ignoring others; (2) optimization, which describes maximizing a behavior for a desired outcome; and (3) compensation, which means implementing new resources to achieve a goal (Baltes & Carstensen, 1996; Baltes et al, 1990).
Social convoy model (Antonucci & Akiyama, 1987)	'Convoy' describes the social network (for example, family, friends) that surrounds individuals over their life span and assists with changes and challenges over the lifecourse. It assumes 'basic norms of social relationships over time that help individuals maintain their well-being and cope with the stresses of life' (Antonucci & Akiyama, 1987, p 520). Although convoys may change in some ways, they remain relatively stable.
Social exchange theory (Dowd, 1975)	This refers to power balances that exist across age groups. According to Laura Carstensen (Carstensen, 1991), 'Social exchange theorists argue that limited resources in old age confine social relationships to a more narrow range than was available in youth, and an increased need for assistance undermines the equitable power balance necessary for mutually gratifying relationships' (p 205–206).
Socio-emotional selectivity theory (Carstensen, 1991; Carstensen, 1993)	Suggests that as people get closer to death, either with age or disease, they will increasingly choose to invest their time in meaningful relationships, as opposed to the acquisition of new knowledge or less-meaningful relationships.
Successful aging (Rowe & Kahn, 1997)	Defined by John Rowe and Robert Kahn (1997) in terms of one's ability to maintain 'low risk of disease and disease-related disability, high mental and physical function, and active engagement with life' (p 38). Earlier definitions include Havighurst (Havighurst, 1961) and Paul Baltes and colleagues (1990).

Structure	
Wisdom (Ardelt, 2003)	Monika Ardelt (2003) proposes three dimensions of wisdom: (1) a cognitive dimension, which 'refers to a person's ability to understand life, that is, to comprehend the significance and deeper meaning of the phenomena and event'; (2) a reflective dimension, which involves engaging 'in reflective thinking by looking at phenomena and events from many different perspectives to develop self-awareness and self-insight'; and (3) having 'diminished self-centeredness and a better understanding of people's behavior' (p 278).

This section looks at two of the general categories described in the Preface: structure and experience. Structure describes perspectives where the primary concern is about systems (for example, social, policy related) and their relationship to aging. Experience describes perspectives where the primary concern is the individual. The third framing concept mentioned in the Preface, 'care', is not included here for a few reasons. First, although perspectives such as disengagement theory (Cumming & Henry, 1961), the ecological model of aging (Lawton & Nahemow, 1973) or learned dependency (Baltes, 1988) might heavily influence how it is given and received, they do not directly address care. In addition, the vast literature on caregiving to include topics such as caregiver burden (Zarit, Todd, & Zarit, 1986; Baum & Page, 1991; Neal, Chapman, Ingersoll-Dayton, & Emlen, 1993; Neal, Wagner, Bonn, & Niles-Yokum, 2008) addresses issues associated with giving and receiving care, but not 'care' as a method or explanatory stance. In other words, care is part of structure and experience. One could argue that structure and experience also overlap. They do in many respects. Grouping them as separate categories is merely to facilitate thinking about how the object of interest (for example, persons, systems) is approached and understood rather than attempting to distinguish differences.

Structure

This subsection will look specifically at people and perspectives that focus on structural elements within societies, such as social location and policies, which influence aging. The subsection will be further divided into additional subcategories of social forces, policy and environments.

Social forces

Three related explanatory stances that address people's placement with societal structures are disengagement theory (Cumming & Henry, 1961), activity theory (Havighurst & Albrecht, 1953) and continuity theory (Atchley, 1989). Disengagement theory describes a mutual yet adaptive social and psychological withdrawal of an individual from society and society from the individual as he or she ages (at around age 50). Johanne Schroots (1996), in reflecting on the theory many years later, observes that 'Disengagement theory encouraged the development of an opposing theory of the aged, activity theory, which is based on the concept of developmental tasks' (p 744). Activity theory posits that people desire to maintain the activities and attitudes of midlife throughout older age. (Baltes & Carstensen, 1999). Baltes & Carstensen (1999) write, 'Activity theory considered inactivity a societally induced problem rooted in social norms, such as mandatory retirement and an indigenous ageism in our sociopolitical structures' (p 215). Carstensen (1991) adds that 'Activity theorists instead hold social and physical barriers to interaction accountable for declining rates of interaction' (p 205). Finally, continuity theory assumes that people apply familiar strategies to maintain internal (for example, personal preferences) and external structures (for example, interacting with familiar physical and social environments).

A pair of social theories that look at changing structures due to modernization are convergence theory (Goode, 1963) and modernization theory (Cowgill & Holmes, 1972). Convergence theory suggested that through industrialization, nuclear families would strengthen and ties to extended families would weaken. As is discussed in Chapter Five, this perspective no longer holds true. It did, however, provide the impetus for much research. The second explanatory stance, modernization theory, linked changes in the status of older individuals to changes from agricultural-based societies (high status) to industrial ones (low status) (Cowgill & Holmes, 1972). As discussed in Chapter Three, this stance also has been unsupported, although it still remains an important paradigm within gerontology.

A final grouping of explanatory stances based on social forces are the lifecourse perspective (Elder, 1975; Settersten, 1999), cumulative advantage/disadvantage (Dannefer, 1999, 2003) and cumulative inequality (Ferraro & Shippee, 2009). The first, the lifecourse perspective, is widely used in gerontology. It describes 'age-related role transitions that are socially created, socially recognized, and socially shared' (Settersten, 1999, p 6). The next, cumulative advantage/ disadvantage, describes the 'systematic tendency for interindividual divergence in a given characteristic (e.g., money, health status), with the passage of time' (p 327). In other words, people who start off with advantages in life (such as high social status) seem to accumulate more benefits as time goes on (for example, access to education and healthcare), while those with disadvantages (such as low socioeconomic status) accumulate additional disadvantages with time. All of these affect how one ages. The third, cumulative inequality, is similar to cumulative advantage/disadvantage, except the concepts of advantage and disadvantage are replaced with the notion of 'accumulation of risk, available resources, perceived trajectory, and human agency' (Ferraro & Shippee, 2009, p 334). In other words, personal choices along with access to and availability of resources accumulate over time and eventually affect how one ages.

Policy

As gerontology continued to progress, it began to include more social science disciplines that increasingly recognized later life as a time of marginalization. Subsequently, researchers began to explore imbalances in power structures based on categories such as gender and race, and the role that policy could play in trying to lessen older people's marginalization. An example of policy perspectives is the political economy of aging, which looked at the way social and economic forces could negatively affect older persons (Walker, 1981; Estes, Swan, & Gerard, 1982; Quadagno & Reid, 1999). As Alan Walker (1981) observed, 'A great deal of influential research in social gerontology has tended to treat elderly people as a detached minority, independent from economic and political systems, and "their problems" in terms of individual adjustment to ageing or retirement. Very little attention has been paid to the structural relationship between the elderly and the rest of society and the differential impact of social and economic institutions on elderly people' (p 88). When production is a valued outcome in a society, older persons may be either devalued or expected to 'produce' without compensation as was discussed in Chapter One.

Environments

Although environments have a direct effect on experience, there are also important structural elements within environments that should be considered. For example, Eva Kahana's (1982) congruence model of person–environment interaction proposes an interrelationship between seven dimensions of congruence between life space and environmental influences. These are: segregate, congregate, institutional control, structure, stimulation/engagement, affect and impulse control. Although some of these are personal (for example, stimulation/engagement), many are structural (for example, institutional control). One could argue that the structural will ultimately have a significant impact on the person. For example, if a person is restricted to only part of a facility, he or she becomes limited in the types of stimulation/engagement that are available.

Another important environmental perspective is Powell Lawton and Lucille Nahemow's ecological model of aging (Lawton & Nahemow, 1973). This model explores the relationship between the individual and environment based on levels of the individual's adaption in relation to the environmental forces (or 'press') (Lawton & Nahemow, 1973; Rubinstein & de Medeiros, 2003). Press can include physical structures of an environment such as the presence of stairs, or other factors such as proximity to transportation, noise level, privacy, and so on. In addition to influencing important work on place (see Chapter Seven), this model has also been important for studies on wellbeing in later life.

Another perspective that fits with the other two but is not uniquely related to environments is learned dependency (Baltes, 1988). Learned dependency describes a passive behavior that is learned to gain a desired outcome (for example, attention). Because of assumptions that older people are prone to dependency due to incompetence, over-protective environments are created whereby older people are 'rewarded' for adhering to dependency scripts. In this way, structure affects experience.

Demography

As mentioned earlier, gerontology emerged from the awareness that populations were shifting from predominantly 'young' to increasingly 'old'. Neil McCluskey and Edgar Borgatta (1981) argue that gerontology 'was born from demographic awareness of changes in population structure' (p 11). However, they continue by asking, 'But is this true? Isn't it more that gerontology has only become worthy of study because of demographics, that old age has always had a tenuous place in society?' (p 11).

Within the study of population characteristics emerged the study of cohorts and generation. Karl Mannheim (Mannheim, 1952), as cited by Kenneth Ferraro (2014), writes that 'individuals who belong to the same generation, who share the same year of birth, are endowed, to that extent, with a common location in the historical dimension of the social process' (Ferraro, 2014, p 128). For Mannheim, birth cohorts were important but birth year alone did not adequately capture experience. Rather, social location (for example, social class, religion) was also important.

Experience

Experience covers a wide number of topics. While 'structure' looked at larger forces that influence age, experience focuses more on the individual. Subcategories in this section include behavioral sciences' perspectives, and the humanities and cultural studies.

Of course, critical to understanding intra-individual variation in the experience of aging were the data from numerous longitudinal studies. Paul and Margret Baltes (1993) provide the following summary: 'Historically, the Kansas Studies of Adult Life conducted by Havighurst, Henry, Neugarten, and associates opened the way for a differential perspective. Subsequently, the Duke Longitudinal Studies, the Baltimore Longitudinal Study on Aging, the Bonn Longitudinal Study of Aging, and Schaie's Seattle Longitudinal Study of Intellectual Aging produced converging evidence. Each of these longitudinal studies documented that aging was not a general and uniform process. Instead, individuals were shown to age very differently' (p 9).

Behavioral sciences

Much of the earlier work involving experiences of aging come from perspectives within the behavioral sciences, specifically psychology. While many of these could arguably be framed around 'assessment' or 'performance', they are included here since they ultimately are tied with experiences of later life. This is not to neglect important work from the social sciences (for example, sociology, anthropology), which was also instrumental. In fact, Jon Hendricks and Andrew Achenbaum (1999) credit the 1949 publication *Personal adjustment in old age* (Cavan et al, 1949) and the 1953 publication *Older people* (Havighurst & Albrecht, 1953) as 'precursors to what in retrospect are regarded as the first theoretical statements in social gerontology' (p 31). In the first book, the authors discuss the concept of personal adjustment, which they define as 'change in behaviour in order to adapt successfully to a change in social situation' (1949, p 10). Relevant terms in their research include personal and social adjustment, changes in the situation (such as rural to urban, death of a spouse), mobility, level of achievement, level of aspiration, frustration, change in attitudes and what they call 'the reconstructed situation' (p 14), which refers to the reorganization of a social situation to better accommodate a person's interests or desires. They subsequently developed the Attitude Inventory, with 10 categories covering a variety of personal and social characteristics. The second book was described earlier with regard to activity theory.

Overall, the behavioral sciences' role in gerontology was initially concerned with understanding if and how older people differed in memory, intelligence, motor speed, abstract thinking and other areas. Anthropologist Francis Galton (1885) is credited with having visitors to an international health exhibit pay to participate in a series of psychomotor performance tests (Welford, 1958). His data showed little change with age and led to subsequent additional testing to distinguish between 'normal old people and those suffering from clinical senile conditions or between one type of clinical condition and another' (Welford, 1958, p 52).

As more behavioral scientists became interested in aging, the field began to rapidly expand. An early but unlikely contributor to gerontology was Erik Erikson (1950). His initial depiction of the life cycle focused mostly on childhood development. Later, as he himself began to age, his life cycle schema also expanded. An important perspective from Erikson that is still used in gerontology is 'generativity'. Generativity is the idea that people expend energy to guide the next generation or contribute to society in a way that will benefit future generations (Kotre, 1984). In essence, it describes ways in which people seek to invest themselves into the future through actions such as teaching the next generation, investing in projects that will outlive them, having children and others (Peterson & Stewart, 1996; Rubinstein, Girling, de Medeiros, Brazda, & Hannum, 2015).

Another important pioneer in the field was James Birren, who presented aging as a counterpart of development. According to Johannes Schroots (1996), 'The term "counterpart" is meant to express the idea that there are latent structures of behaviour (emotions, cognition, and motivations) carried forward from earlier experience. Counterpart theory advocates for positive late-life characteristics that embrace a wide range of complex biological (e.g., potential for long life) and behavioral (e.g., intelligence) characteristics' (p 744). From counterpart theory, one can see the development of other behaviorally based theories. Examples include socio-emotional selectivity theory (Carstensen, 1991; Carstensen, 1993), which suggests that as people get closer to death, they will choose to invest their time in meaningful relationships.

Also significant within gerontology is selective optimization with compensation (SOC) (Baltes, Baltes, & Baltes, 1990). SOC describes three elements involved in response to changes: (1) selection, which requires directing resources to some domains while ignoring others, (2) optimization, which describes maximizing a behavior for a desired outcome and (3) compensation, which means implementing new resources to achieve a goal (Baltes et al, 1990; Baltes & Carstensen, 1996). SOC is therefore concerned with the strategies that one employs in the face of change to achieve a particular end goal.

Moving away from the single individual, the social convoy model (Antonucci & Akiyama, 1987) describes social networks that surround an individual over his or her life span. Social convoys include various levels of social contacts such as family, friends, and acquaintances. Of particular interest in the social convoy model is the feeling of closeness that an individual has to various people within the social network. The underlying assumption is that stronger social support will lead to better functional outcomes. Another important perspective from the behavioral sciences is the 'life review' described by Robert Butler (1963) as the evaluation process a person goes on near the end of one's life. The concept of the life review was instrumental in shifting the previously held view of reminiscence in later life as a frivolous and potentially pathologic pastime, to instead recognizing the meaning that such a review might have. (This is discussed in more detail in Chapter Six.)

Other notable perspectives include social exchange theory (Dowd, 1975) and wisdom (Ardelt, 2003). Social exchange theory describes the shifts in power dynamics that occur in situations such as giving and receiving care. For example, the person providing care may have more power over the person receiving care, especially if care is uncompensated. The person receiving care may be dependent on the caregiver's schedule and therefore unable to choose when and how care is provided. Mechanisms to equalize power include, for example, paying for caregiving services.

'Wisdom' is a term that is often used in conjunction with later life. However, as Kathleen Woodward (2003) warns wisdom can be a euphemism or an empty label applied to older age. Wisdom, she argues, implies passive acceptance which in turn denies older people a social space for anger. In contrast, Monika Ardelt (2003) proposes three dimensions of wisdom: a cognitive dimension or the ability of a person to understand the deeper meaning of an event or phenomena; a reflective dimension or self-insight; and diminished self-centeredness.

The humanities and cultural studies

Work from the humanities and cultural studies are also critical to gerontology, although they are often overlooked in gerontological texts. The humanities and cultural studies ask questions about the meaning of older age rather than provide explanations about how and why aging happens. In the 1970s, David Van Tassel convened a conference entitled 'Human values and aging: New challenges to research in the humanities', as a way to stimulate humanities scholarship in aging (Van Tassel, 1979). Van Tassel writes, 'Clearly, twentieth-century civilization has discovered old age as a social, economic, and health problem of growing proportions. Old age as a problem has been studied by social and biological scientists through miles of questionnaires and computer printouts, laying bare in cold statistics the lives, the pains, and the hopes of the contemporary generation of elderly ... Yet few of these studies have been informed by a humanistic perspective drawn from the materials of the experience of mankind, which could and should be located, brought to life, and refined' (p ix). This led to the development of humanistic gerontology as a new way to understand age and aging (Cole & Gadow, 1987; Cole, Ray, & Kastenbaum, 2010). (See Cole et al., 2010 for a more complete discussion.)

Cultural studies draws on perspectives from the social sciences and humanities to explore symbolic communication and human expression. Julia Twigg and Wendy Martin (2015) note that there is no single definition of 'culture' used within cultural studies. Instead, they write 'Cultural is better understood here as a set of influences, containing contradictory definitions and theoretical approaches, while still sharing certain broad impulses or family resemblances. The element that unites the field however is concern with meaning, and the sense that the social world is constituted by such meanings' (p 354). Examples of topics of research in cultural gerontology include embodiment, subjectivity, and identity. (See Twigg and Martin (2015) for an overview of cultural gerontology.)

Summary

Old age is not something that has been newly discovered, nor did interest in the later part of life begin with the formal establishment of gerontology as a discipline. Knowing a bit about the past – how gerontology came to be, what some of the major issues being addressed were – can help to move gerontology forward. For example, the major issues in gerontology today seem, in many respects, to be the same ones that existed throughout time. Our thinking about the modern-day lifecourse is not that different from the lifecourse or life cycles depicted hundreds of years ago. What does seem to be different is the optimism that gerontology has today, not to 'cure' old age but, rather, to explore new ways to make meaning in the latter part of life.

Further reading

Achenbaum, W. A. (1995). *Crossing frontiers: Gerontology emerges as a science*. New York: Cambridge University Press.

Achenbaum, W. A., & Albert, D. M. (1995). *Profiles in gerontology: A biographical dictionary*. Westport, CT: Greenwood Press.

Bengtson, V., Gans, D., Putney, N., & Silverstein, M. (2009). *Handbook of theories of aging*. New York: Springer Publishing.

Cole, T. R., Ray, R. E., & Kastenbaum, R. (Eds.) (2010). *A guide to humanistic studies in aging: What does it mean to grow old?* Baltimore, MD: Johns Hopkins University Press.

Dannefer, D. (2010). *The SAGE handbook of social gerontology*. Thousand Oaks, CA: Sage Publications.

Katz, S. (1996). *Disciplining old age: The formation of gerontological knowledge*. Charlottesville: The University Press of Virginia.

Twigg, J., & Martin, W. (Eds.). (2015). *Routledge handbook of cultural gerontology*. London: Routledge.

References

Achenbaum, W. A. (1987). Reconstructing GSA's history. *The Gerontologist, 27*(1), 21–29.

Achenbaum, W. A. (1995). *Crossing frontiers: Gerontology emerges as a science*. New York: Cambridge University Press.

Achenbaum, W. A., & Albert, D. M. (1995). *Profiles in gerontology: A biographical dictionary*. Westport, CT: Greenwood Press.

Antonucci, T. C., & Akiyama, H. (1987). Social networks in adult life and a preliminary examination of the convoy model. *Journal of Gerontology, 42*(5), 519–527.

Ardelt, M. (2003). Empirical assessment of a three-dimensional wisdom scale. *Research on Aging, 25*(3), 275–324.

Atchley, R. C. (1989). A continuity theory of normal aging. *The Gerontologist, 29*(2), 183–190.

Baltes, M. M. (1988). The etiology and maintenance of dependency in the elderly: three phases of operant research. *Behavior Therapy, 19*(3), 301–319.

Baltes, P. B., & Baltes, M. M. (1993). *Successful aging: Perspectives from the behavioral sciences* (Vol. 4). Cambridge: Cambridge University Press.

Baltes, M. M., & Carstensen, L. L. (1996). The process of successful ageing. *Ageing and Society, 16*(4), 397–422.

Baltes, M. M. C., & Carstensen, L. L. (1999). Social-psychological theories and their applications to aging: from individual to collective. In: V. L. S. Bengston & K. Warner (Eds.), *Handbook of theories of aging* (1st edn). New York: Springer Publishing, pp 209–226.

Baltes, P. B., Baltes, M. M., & Baltes, P. B. (1990). Psychological perspectives on successful aging: the model of selective optimization with compensation. *Successful Aging: Perspectives from the Behavioral Sciences, 1*, 1–34.

Barca, R. (1994). Argentina. In: J. Kosberg (Ed.), *International handbook on services for the elderly*. Santa Barbara: Greenwood Publishing Group, pp 1–16.

Baum, M., & Page, M. (1991). Caregiving and multigenerational families. *The Gerontologist, 31*(6), 762–769. doi: 10.1093/geront/31.6.762.

Beard, B. B. (1946). The army of the aged: a sociomedical problem. *Geriatrics, 1*, 299–304.

Butler, R. N. (1963). The life review: an interpretation of reminiscence in the aged. *Psychiatry, 26*(1), 65–76.

Carstensen, L. L. (1991). Selectivity theory: social activity in life-span context. *Annual Review of Gerontology and Geriatrics: Behavioral Science & Aging, 11*, 195.

Carstensen, L. L. (1993). Motivation for social contact across the life span: a theory of socioemotional selectivity. Paper presented at the Nebraska symposium on motivation, vol. 40, February 1992, pp 209–254.

Cavan, R. S., Burgess, E. W., Havighurst, R. J., & Goldhamer, H. (1949). *Personal adjustment in old age*. Chicago: Chicago Science Research Associates.

Cole, T. R., & Gadow, S. A. (1987). *What does it mean to grow old? Reflections from the humanities*. Durham, NC: Duke University Press.

Cole, T. R., Ray, R. E., & Kastenbaum, R. (2010). *A guide to humanistic studies in aging: What does it mean to grow old?* Baltimore, MD: Johns Hopkins University Press.

Cowdry, E. V. (1947). The broader implications of aging. *Journal of Gerontology, 2*(4), 277–282. doi: 10.1093/geronj/2.4.277.

Cowgill, D. O., & Holmes, L. D. (1972). *Aging and modernization*. New York: Appleton-Century-Crofts.

Cumming, E., & Henry, W. E. (1961). *Growing old: The process of disengagement*. New York: Basic Books.

Dannefer, D. (1999). Neoteny, naturalization and other constituents of human development. In: C.D. Ryff & V.W. Marshall (Eds.), *The self and society in aging processes*. New York: Springer Publishing, pp 67–93.

Dannefer, D. (2003). Cumulative advantage/disadvantage and the life course: cross-fertilizing age and social science theory. *The Journals of Gerontology Series B: Psychological Sciences and Social Sciences, 58*(6), S327–S337.

David, E. (1991). *Old age in Sparta*. Amsterdam: Adolf m Hakkert.

Dowd, J. J. (1975). Aging as exchange: a preface to theory. *Journal of Gerontology, 30*(5), 584–594.

Elder, G. H. (1975). Age differentiation and the life course. *Annual Review of Sociology*, 1, 165–190.

Elder, G. H., & Rockwell, R. C. (1979). The life-course and human development: an ecological perspective. *International Journal of Behavioral Development, 2*(1), 1–21.

Erikson, E. H. (1950). *Childhood and society*. New York: W.W. Norton & Company.

Erikson, E. H., & Erikson, J. M. (1997). *The life cycle completed: Extended version with new chapters on the ninth state of development*. New York: W. W. Norton & Company.

Estes, C. L., Swan, J. H., & Gerard, L. E. (1982). Dominant and competing paradigms in gerontology: towards a political economy of ageing. *Ageing and Society, 2*(2), 151–164.

Falkner, T. M., & de Luce, J. (1992). A view from antiquity: Greece, Rome, and Elders. *Handbook of the humanities and aging*. New York: Springer, pp 3–39.

Ferraro, K. F. (2014). The time of our lives: recognizing the contributions of Mannheim, Neugarten, and Riley to the study of aging. *The Gerontologist, 54*(1), 127–133. doi: 10.1093/geront/gnt048

Ferraro, K. F., & Shippee, T. P. (2009). Aging and cumulative inequality: how does inequality get under the skin? *The Gerontologist, 49*(3), 333–343.

Fries, J. F. (1980). Aging, natural death, and the compression of morbidity. *New England Journal of Medicine, 303*(3), 130–135.

Fry, C. L. (1999). Anthropological theories of age and aging. In: V.L.S. Bengston & K. Warner (Eds.), *Handbook of theories of aging* (1st edn). New York: Springer Publishing, pp 271–286.

Galton, F. (1885). On the anthropometric laboratory at the late International Health Exhibition. *The Journal of the Anthropological Institute of Great Britain and Ireland*, 14: 205–221.

Goode, W. J. (1963). *World revolution and family patterns*. New York: Free Press of Glencoe.

Hall, G. S. (1922). *Senescence: The last half of life*. New York: Appleton.

Harris, R. (2000). *Gender and aging in Mesopotamia: The Gilgamesh Epic and other ancient literature*. Norman, OK: University of Oklahoma Press.

Havighurst, R. (1961). Successful aging: definition and measurement. *Journal of Gerontology, 16*(2), 134–143.

Havighurst, R. J. (1963). Successful aging. *Processes of Aging: Social and Psychological Perspectives, 1*, 299–320.

Havighurst, R. J., & Albrecht, R. (1953). *Older people.* New York: Longmans, Green Co.

Hendricks, J., & Achenbaum, A. (1999). Historical development of theories of aging. In: V.L.S. Bengston & K. Warner (Eds.), *Handbook of theories of aging.* New York: Springer Publishing, pp 21–39.

International Association for Gerontology and Geriatrics (IAGG) (2016). http://www.iagg.info/.

Johnson, P., & Thane, P. (2002). *Old age from antiquity to post-modernity.* London: Routledge.

Kahana, E. (1982). A congruence model of person–environment interaction. In: M.P. Lawton, P. Wendly, & T. Byerts (Eds.), *Aging and the environment: Theoretical approaches.* New York: Springer, pp 97–121.

Katz, S. (1996). *Disciplining old age: The formation of gerontological knowledge.* Charlottesville, VA: University of Virginia Press.

Kotre, J. (1984). *Outliving the self: Generativity and the interpretation of lives.* Baltimore, MD: Johns Hopkins University Press.

Lawton, M. P. (1983). Environment and other determinants of well-being in older people. *The Gerontologist, 23*(4), 349–357.

Lawton, M. P., & Nahemow, L. (1973). Ecology and the aging process. In: C. Eidsorfer & M.P. Lawton (Eds.), *The psychology of adult development and aging.* Washington, D.C.: American Psychological Association, pp 619–674.

Maddox, G. L. (1964). A critical evaluation. *The Gerontologist, 4*(2 Part 1), 80–82.

Mannheim, K. (1952). The problem of generations. *Karl Mannheim: Essays on the sociology of knowledge.* London: Routledge & Kegan Paul, pp 276–322.

McCluskey, N. G., & Borgatta, E. F. (1981). *Aging and retirement: Prospects, planning, and policy* (Vol. 43). Thousand Oaks, CA: Sage Publications, Inc.

Metchnikoff, E. (1903). *The nature of man: Studies in optimistic philosophy.* New York: G.P. Putnam's Sons.

Minois, G. (1989). *History of old age: From antiquity to the renaissance.* Chicago, IL: University of Chicago Press.

Morley, J. E. (2004). A brief history of geriatrics. *The Journals of Gerontology Series A: Biological Sciences and Medical Sciences, 59*(11), 1132–1152. doi: 10.1093/gerona/59.11.1132.

Nascher, I. L. (1914). *Geriatrics: The diseases of old age and their treatment, including physiological old age, home and institutional care, and medico-legal relations*. Philadelphia: P. Blakiston's Son & Company.

Neal, M. B., Chapman, N. J., Ingersoll-Dayton, B., & Emlen, A. C. (1993). *Balancing work and caregiving for children, adults, and elders* (Vol. 3). Thousand Oaks, CA: Sage Publications.

Neal, M. B., Wagner, D. L., Bonn, K. J. B., & Niles-Yokum, K. (2008). Caring from a distance. In: A. Martin-Matthews & J.E. Phillips (Eds.), *Aging and caring at the intersection of work and home life: Blurring the boundaries*. New York: Taylor and Francis, pp 107–128.

Neugarten, B. L., Moore, J. W., & Lowe, J. C. (1965). Age norms, age constraints, and adult socialization. *American Journal of Sociology, 70*(6), 710–717.

Parkin, T. G. (2003). *Old age in the Roman world: A cultural and social history*. Baltimore, MD: Johns Hopkins University Press.

Parmelee, P. A., & Lawton, M. P. (1990). The design of special environments for the aged. In: J.E. Birren & K. W. Schaie (Eds.), *Handbook of the psychology of aging* (3rd edn). San Diego: Academic Press, pp 464–488.

Peterson, B. E., & Stewart, A. J. (1996). Antecedents and contexts of generativity motivation at midlife. *Psychology and Aging, 11*(1), 21–33. doi: 10.1037/0882–7974.11.1.21

Quadagno, J., & Reid, J. (1999). The political economy perspective in aging. In: *Handbook of theories of aging* (1st edn). New York: Springer Publishing, pp 344–358.

Rowe, J. W., & Kahn, R. L. (1997). Successful aging. *The Gerontologist, 37*(4), 433–440.

Rubinstein, R. L., & de Medeiros, K. (2003). Ecology and the aging self. In: H.-W. Wahl, R. J. Schiedt & P. G. Windely (Eds.), *Annual review of gerontology and geriatrics* (Vol. 23). New York: Springer.

Rubinstein, R. L., Girling, L. M., de Medeiros, K., Brazda, M., & Hannum, S. (2015). Extending the framework of generativity theory through research: a qualitative study. *The Gerontologist, 55*(4), 548–558. doi: 10.1093/geront/gnu009.

Scharf, T. (2001). Social gerontology in Germany: historical trends and recent developments. *Ageing and Society, 21*(4), 489–505.

Schroots, J. J. F. (1996). Theoretical developments in the psychology of aging. *The Gerontologist, 36*(6), 742–748.

Settersten, R. A. (1999). *Lives in time and place: The problems and promises of developmental science*. Amityville, NY: Baywood Publishing Co.

Thane, P. (2000). *Old age in English history: Past experiences, present issues*. Oxford: Oxford University Press.

Thane, P. (2010). The history of aging and old age in 'Western' cultures. In: T. Cole, R.E. Ray & R. Kastenbaum (Eds.), *A guide to humanistic studies in aging: What does it mean to grow old?* Baltimore, MD: Springer Publishing, pp 33–56.

Thang, L. L. (2000). Aging in the East: comparative and historical reflections. In: T. Cole, R.E. Ray & R. Kastenbaum (Eds.), *Handbook of the humanities and aging* (2nd edn). New York: Springer Publishing, pp 183–213.

Tuohy, E. L. (1946). Geriatrics: the general setting. *Geriatrics, 1*, 17–20.

Twigg, J., & Martin, W. (2015). The challenge of cultural gerontology. *The Gerontologist, 55*(3), 353–359.

Van Tassel, D. D. (1979). *Aging, death, and the completion of being*. Pittsburg: University of Pennsylvania Press.

Walker, A. (1981). Towards a political economy of old age. *Ageing and Society, 1*(01), 73–94.

Welford, A. T. (1958). Psychological and social gerontology in Europe. *Journal of Gerontology, 13*(Suppl. 1), 51–67.

Woodward, K. (2003). Against wisdom: the social politics of anger and aging. *Journal of Aging Studies,* 17(1), 55–67.

Zarit, S. H., Todd, P. A., & Zarit, J. M. (1986). Subjective burden of husbands and wives as caregivers: a longitudinal study. *The Gerontologist, 26*(3), 260–266.

THREE

Myths and common assumptions about aging

The previous chapter looked at historical developments in gerontological perspectives. This chapter addresses some of the prominent cultural narratives that frame what we think about old age and how we study it. Unfortunately, discussions about old age and later life are very often clouded by myths, stereotypes and assumptions that can limit possibilities in later life.

A strong component of later life is its association with decline and death, which, despite historical changes, has formed a strong narrative across cultures and has spanned historical time. For example, Wendy Miller and Gene Cohen (2010), in describing Cohen's own experience at the end of life as well as his well-known research on creativity and aging, write: 'Even in good enough health, aging itself is a life experience that remains uncharted in many ways; not just for aging individuals and their families, but also for those planning programs and developing policies for this population. Here, too, confusion abounds, compounded by ignorance, myths and stereotypes that contribute to a dim view of what can make a difference in the lives of elders' (p 305). Such myths, stereotypes and ageist portrayal of older people in various cultural outlets have overshadowed the positive aspects of growing old and, in doing so, have contributed to misunderstandings about later life. The following myths will be addressed in this chapter.

- Myth 1: With the discoveries in modern medicine, people are living longer lives than ever before.
- Myth 2: Very few people survived into old age in the past.
- Myth 3: There was a golden age when older people were revered.
- Myth 4: There are still places in the world where elders are revered.
- Myth 5: Westerners used to care for their older family members at home but now abandon them to nursing homes.

As with many aspects of gerontology, the myths and assumptions presented in this chapter are neither entirely wrong nor entirely correct. Since they are so pervasive in the gerontological landscape it is important to discuss and debunk them so that attention can be placed on areas that will potentially benefit older adults, such as pensions and other forms of support (see Chapter Eight) and creative potential in later life (see Chapter Nine).

Myth 1: With the discoveries in modern medicine, people are living longer lives than ever before

In reality, more people are living into old age because they are not dying in childhood. The partial fallacy of this myth can be found in the misunderstanding of what is meant by life expectancy at birth versus life span. Life expectancy at birth is defined as 'the number of years a newborn infant would live if prevailing patterns of mortality at the time of its birth were to stay the same throughout its life' (Bank, 2015). According to the World Health Organization (WHO, 2015), the life expectancy for men and women born in 2013 globally was 71 years, with low-income countries having a life expectancy at birth of 62 years and high-income countries 79 years. In addition, the gap between men and women's life expectancy remained at around five years from 1990 to 2013, with women, on average, living longer than men in both developed and developing countries.

Often life expectancy at birth is mistakenly interpreted as the age at which most people die. For example, in 2013 average life expectancy at birth in Ghana was 61 years. In Japan it was 83 years. This does not mean that people in Ghana survive only into their 60s. Rather, lower life expectancy at birth is most likely related to high infant mortality rates, which bring the average down, and infectious diseases, such as malaria, which would also affect the average. The main reason behind increasing life expectancy at birth is not life prolongation through medical intervention at the end of life but, rather, public health interventions aimed at helping infants survive, such as vaccinations, clean water, sanitation (Alley & Crimmins, 2010) and disease prevention and treatment at all ages.

One statistic that can help to better understand the population breakdown of a country is median age. Median age describes 'the age that divides a population into two numerically equal groups; that is, half the people are younger than this age and half are older' (CIA, 2015). The median age for Ghana in 2013 was 20.9 years. In Japan it was 46.5 years. This shows two very different age structures, Ghana being a country with half its population under 20 years of age, as compared to Japan, where middle age is the half point. Median age is also useful in realizing that 'old people' are always a minority, despite their growing numbers.

Another helpful data point is life expectancy at age 60 (or 65). This, like life expectancy at birth, describes the average number of additional years that a person at age 60 could be expected to live if age-specific mortality rates remain unchanged. In Ghana, life expectancy at age 60 is 17 years; in Japan it is 26. That means that someone in Ghana who survives until age 60 could expect to live until around age 77; in Japan, until around age 86 (HelpAge International, 2014). Life expectancy at 60 provides a very different view of older age than one would see by looking at life expectancy at birth or median age alone.

In contrast to life expectancy is life span, which is 'the theoretical biological maximum length of life that could be achieved under ideal conditions' (Kunkel, Brown, & Whittington, 2014, p 91). The human life span is currently estimated to be 120 years. Interestingly, this figure is not one that has been newly discovered thanks to science. The ancient Mesopotamians identified the limit of human longevity as 120 years (Harris, 2000, p 5). Historian Andrew Achenbaum (2010) also notes that the Bible, Genesis 6.3, states that man's days will be 120 years, the age to which Moses was also said to have lived. Despite more than a century of gerontological research and advances in medical technology, the human life span has yet to change.

A concept that is important to note and one that is discussed in more detail in Chapter Four is compression of morbidity (Fries, 1980). James Fries (1980) first described this hypothesis in 1980. He noted that although the maximum human life span has not increased, there was a sharp reduction in premature death earlier in life. He argues that most premature death, in many countries throughout the world, occurs in later years as the result of chronic illness. He suggests that if chronic illness can be pushed into the last years of life, thereby compressing morbidity, the savings in human suffering and expense could be profound. More recent research (Crimmins & Beltrán-Sánchez, 2011) has questioned whether compression of morbidity is occurring as Fries hypothesized. Much has to do with how morbidity is defined and measured (see Chapter Four for a more detailed discussion on the topic).

Myth 2: Very few people survived into old age in the past

Myth two, that people rarely survived into old age in the past, is a slightly different version of myth one. This myth is not true, as there are many accounts of well-known figures from antiquity and later who survived into their 70s, 80s and even 90s. As mentioned with the first myth, part of the misunderstanding comes from misinterpretation of life expectancy numbers. Historian Georges Minois (1989) lists the supposed age of death for several Greek philosophers, ranging from Epicurus, who was said to have died at age 72, to Plato, who died at age 81, to Epicharmus, who was alleged to be 90 years old at his death. Certainly, one could question the accuracy of birth records, which is a legitimate concern. Yet, even if the exact ages are not entirely accurate, there is enough information to confirm that people (generally wealthy men) did survive well past the average life expectancy at birth.

Historian Pat Thane (2000) explains that because of the belief in the rarity of growing old in the past, older people are believed to have been granted a high status. She writes, 'It is widely believed that in the pre-industrial past it was rare to grow old. This is generally because life expectancy at birth is taken as evidence of survival to old age. Life expectancy at birth averaged around 35 years between the 1540s and 1800 and is unlikely to have been higher at any earlier time, but high infant and child mortality rates drastically pulled down such averages' (p 19). She further explains that those who survived childhood in medieval and early modern England had a good chance of living into their 50s or older and that death in one's 30s was not considered normal. In fact, nearly 10% of the population of pre-industrial England and Wales were aged 60 or over in the 17th and 18th centuries, a percentage that is greater than in many countries today. In 2014, for example, the percentage of people aged 65 and over was only around 5% in Bangladesh, around 8% in Serbia and around 3% in Kenya, according to the World Bank (World Bank, 2015).

Myth 3: There was a golden age when old people were revered

It is not uncommon to hear people talk about a past when older people held high status, as mentioned in the previous myth. Again, although there is some truth to this, a person's esteem had more to do with class, social position and male gender than with age alone. Minois (1989) describes the role and political rank of older men, especially in the context of kinship clans, as one of high privilege whereby such men would serve on elder councils or act as local judges for disputes. Older women's roles were generally more confined to positions within the household, whereby a woman with married sons would assume a controlling role over her daughters-in-law. Although this did grant older women a sense of domestic power, this power was not widely recognized outside of the home in many cultures.

Historian Thomas Cole (1992) notes that the Puritans in the American colonies held on to the idea that the young should venerate the old. He writes, 'Their images of aging and ideas of old age would seem to justify a rosy picture of old people in early America. But cultural ideals and social experience often diverge' (p 49). He adds that 'wealth, race and gender also structured the social experience of aging. Elderly slaves were the most vulnerable and powerless, while the aged poor – especially women without family – often became objects of scorn and abuse' (p 50). Although there was respect for the old in principle, such respect was not universally practiced.

Minois (1989) makes a similar point, also with regard to aging in early, non-industrial societies. He notes, however, that 'We must take care not to idealize. Where old age is concerned, primitive societies contain the same contradictions as our own, and they express these in a far cruder manner. They are not blind to decrepitude and ugliness' (p 10). He then provides examples of earlier cultures whereby words for old were the same as those for ugly, and cites examples of eldercide or the killing of older people (which is discussed in more detail in Chapter Six). Inheritance rights were a motivator for eldercide, as younger family members were eager to obtain property. There were even laws in Rome that explicitly prohibited the killing of one's parents, which suggests that eldercide was perhaps a big enough problem to have warranted legal rules (Minois, 1989).

Social class, status and value to the society, rather than age alone, appear to have been indicators of respect. Poor older people (poor people were the majority) were as likely to be devalued as younger poor people. Part of the belief in the status of older people in the past comes from Donald Cowgill and Lowell Holmes' (1972) modernization theory (mentioned in Table 2.1), which argued that the shift from agriculture-based to industrialized societies led to the devaluation of older people since their knowledge and skills were no longer needed (Cowgill & Holmes, 1972; Löckenhoff et al, 2009). However, as Corinna Löckenhoff and colleagues (2009) write, 'Although intuitively appealing, modernization theory has been criticized as an oversimplification (e.g. (Quadagno, 1982)). In particular, the theory ignores cross-cultural differences in values and belief systems that may shape the way in which a given culture responds to advanced socioeconomic development' (p 942). (See Chapter Seven, Social location and place and Chapter Eight, Financing old age.)

Myth 4: There are still places in the world where elders are revered

People often point to Asian countries as exemplars for respect of older people because of the concept of filial piety that is a core cultural component of most Asian societies (Ingersoll-Dayton & Saengtienchai, 1999; Sung, 2001). Japan, for example, enacted legislation in 1963 in Article 2 of the Law for the Welfare of the Aged. Yutaka Shimizu and Junko Wake (1994), in their translation, write: 'Article 2, Senior citizens shall be treated with dignity and respect as individuals who have contributed to the progress of our society for many years, and who possess a wealth of knowledge and experience. With this in mind, they shall be guaranteed a high quality of life that is sound and secure' (p 228–229). The Japanese also have a national holiday, called 'Respect of the Aged Day', which is celebrated on the third Monday in September. It was officially established in 1966 but is credited with beginning in 1947, when one province (Yachiyocho) began to celebrate 'Old Folks Day' on 15 September (Office Holidays, 2015). Although the day honors aged individuals, it does not necessarily mean that elders are revered, just like Mother's Day, as celebrated in the United States, does not mean that mothers are revered.

Berit Ingersoll-Dayton and Chanpen Saengtienchai (1999) explored attitudes toward older adults in four Asian countries – the Philippines, Singapore, Taiwan and Thailand – and found that traditional ways of respecting older adults had been changing over time, especially with regard to obedience toward older family members. They attributed this change to 'changes in family structure and function, education, income and modernization' (p 127). Migration of younger family members from rural areas to cities, differences in education between young and older members and declines in family size have meant that older people's roles within the family and proximity to other family members have changed. At first glance, this would seem to support modernization theory. However, as previously noted, modernization theory alone does not describe the complexities associated with a society's continued development. In addition, although change in obedience was noted, the authors stress that the deep values of respect still exist. (See Chapter Five for additional arguments against modernization theory in the context of family.)

Like other issues in aging, the issue of respect, is complicated and contradictory at times. For example, Löckenhoff and colleagues (2009) point to the dominance of 'respect' in the comparison studies of attitudes towards older people from Western versus Eastern perspectives. Western societies are portrayed as youth-centered and as having more negative views of older people than Eastern societies, which are influenced by Confucian values. However, the authors point out that the research literature has been unclear in establishing a clear delineation between views and that there is little empirical evidence for East–West differences (Ryan, Jin, Anas, & Luh, 2004; Cuddy, Norton, & Fiske, 2005).

There is also a growing literature on elder abuse around the world, to include Asian countries. Akekmi Soeda and Chineko Araki (1999), for example, explored abuse cases between daughters-in-law and their older mothers-in-law in Japan and found that although it was a phenomenon that was occurring, it was not widely researched. Overall, Soeda and Araki found that the types of abuse practiced by daughters-in-law were: neglect (51.6%), psychological abuse (41.9%), physical abuse (38.7%) and financial abuse (32.3%). Feelings of resentment and ultimately abuse were attributed to the strain of living within the same house and providing care. Reasons the authors cite as contributing to the lack of evidence include common assumptions that family care equaled good treatment. Also, there was fear within research and provider communities that asking about elder abuse in general would put families in a defensive position and potentially limit further contact with them. Finally, both perpetrators and victims go to great lengths to hide the abuse, making detection difficult. In 2000, Japan initiated its national Long-Term Care Insurance program, which required older people to undergo assessments for program eligibility (Nakanishi et al, 2009). These assessments uncovered evidence of elder abuse, which in turn led to the passage of an elder abuse prevention and caregiver support law in 2006 (Nakanishi et al, 2009).

Jinjoo Oh and colleagues (2006) cite similar reasons for lack of attention to elder abuse in Korea. They estimate that only 20% of elder abuse cases are actually reported. Other Asian countries, such as China, also experience elder abuse, although clear estimates of its prevalence are not available, due to suspected under-reporting. The presence of elder abuse, which is found throughout the world, is not meant to challenge the idea of respect toward older adults in Asian countries. Instead it is meant to point out that conditions of vulnerability differ and there are many complicated issues that should be considered.

Another part of the world where older people have been said to be held in high esteem is Africa (Kyobutungi, Egondi, & Ezeh, 2010). According to John Knodel and Minh Duc Nguyen (2015) and others, filial respect and financial support for older parents is a moral obligation deeply rooted in religious and cultural belief systems. Catherine Kyobutungi and colleagues (2010), in reporting qualitative findings from research in the Nairobi slums, found that, on the one hand, older people were considered fair arbitrators of disputes within families and communities and were sought for counsel and advice as well as functioning as heads of households and caregivers for grandchildren. Nearly 20% were caring for grandchildren whose parents had died from HIV/AIDS. However, they noted that older people were also increasingly more vulnerable. In their study, almost of quarter of the respondents lived alone and lacked social support. The older adults, many of whom were women, were therefore at risk of exploitation, violence, and other forms of abuse or neglect, since they had no means of protection.

Farzana Alli and Pranitha Maharaj (2013) note that although older people in Africa have traditionally been valued for their positions within the household and their knowledge, their position in society is being undermined by associations between older people, especially women, and witchcraft (see the section on eldercide in Chapter Six). They also note that health conditions facing older people are often viewed in non-health terms. They write: 'Information on the nature and occurrence of mental disorders are especially limited in Africa. In some countries, mental health disorders are perceived as bewitchment. An ethnographic study conducted in Ghana found that, in contexts where chronically mentally ill people had no access to medical treatment or support, they were subjected to immense suffering by families and healers resulting from chaining and beating' (pp 60–61). Overall, older people face many barriers to health care.

Ganzamungu Zihindula and Pranitha Maharaj (2013) note that African views of older people as spiritual healers and cultural educators have been replaced by emphasis on education and employment, from which older people are excluded. Natashya Pillay and Pranitha Maharaj (2013) write, 'In many parts of Africa, older people are making a valuable contribution to society – from providing care for sick and/or dying children and orphaned grandchildren to providing much needed financial support for the household' (p 12). Yet, they add, 'With the advent of modernisation, urbanisation, and migration, there has been a marked change in attitudes towards the elderly. The elderly have been largely ignored or excluded. Emphasis placed on the younger generation is to some extent justified as Africa is a relatively youthful continent, with more than 40% of its population below the age of 15 years. A youthful African population has meant that the elderly often do not feature in national policies' (p 12). According to the authors, older Africans do not receive the same levels of aid that younger people do because older people are still a relatively small minority, This further puts them at risk of poor health, due to lack of resources coupled with increased responsibility for caregiving.

As has been stressed throughout the *Short Guide,* attitudes toward old age cannot be simply summed up in terms of 'respect' or 'reverence'. Instead, the social location of older people, the ways in which care is delivered, how the care of older people is financed or not and many other surrounding issues should be considered in order to have a more holistic view of later life.

Myth 5: Westerners used to care for their older family members at home but now abandon them to nursing homes

The idea that Westerners once cared for older family members within their homes but now abandon them to nursing homes is another myth that is closely aligned with the previous one regarding the status of older people in the family. Contrary to popular belief, in-home family care was never the preferred practice in Western countries This is not to say that people didn't or still don't provide care for their family members in multigenerational households. Instead, the West has a long history of 'intimacy at a distance', or of providing care for family members but not necessarily within the same house or under the same roof.

Challenges associated with living with one's children in later life can be traced back to ancient Rome. Pat Thane (2000) writes, 'Old people [in Rome] were warned through a variety of channels of the danger of placing themselves at the mercy of the younger generation though this did not preclude co-residence of the old with the young if only for a short time before death' (p 43). As was mentioned in the previous myth, adult children eager to inherit property could pose a danger to a dependent parent, since they had an incentive to harm him or her in order to expedite the transfer of property and social position. Eagerness to obtain control of property is cited as a reason for many of the witch burnings occurring today that are discussed in Chapter Six.

Issues of position and authority within the household were also reasons against cohabitation. For example, Thomas Cole (1992) notes that in early industrial Europe, 'conventional wisdom held that old parents should avoid becoming dependent on their children' (p 50). He adds that older men often went to great lengths to legally specify a child's obligation for his and his spouse's care in the event that poor health required him to stop working and to relinquish his property to his heir. Plays such as Shakespeare's *King Lear* highlighted the problems of depending on children.

Pat Thane (2000) presents a similar position. She writes: 'Clearly, it was never the unquestioned custom in England, as in some other cultures, for families to be the main source of support to older people, and certainly not for the generations to share a home. In part, this was was unavoidable; about one-third of people in pre-industrial England had no surviving children when they reached old age, whereas almost all older persons had at least one surviving child in the late twentieth century' (p 11). Again, although people did reside in multigenerational households, it was not the preferred method of habitation.

Today in many Western countries, there is still a preference for adult children to live near but not with older parents (Kotlikoff & Morris, 1990; Jeffries & Konnert, 2002; He, Sengupta, Velkoff, & DeBarros, 2005). Many older people move to live closer to a child upon changes in their life circumstances (Kotlikoff & Morris, 1990; Longino Jr, 2001). Having a child has been found to greatly reduce the likelihood of institutionalization, because of help (for example, informal caregiving, financial support for formal caregiving services) provided by the child to the parent (Freedman, 1993; Brody, Litvin, Hoffman, & Kleban, 1995; Allen, Blieszner, Roberto, Farnsworth, & Wilcox, 1999; Pearlin, Pioli, & McLaughlin, 2001; Aykan, 2003). Such care is often reciprocated by help (for example, childcare), that parents offer to adult children. Although most older adults expect emotional support from their children, they prefer to maintain separate households rather than live together (Johnson, 2000). Research on racial and ethnic differences suggests that in the United States, older Blacks are more likely than older Whites to live with a relative (Johnson, 2000).

With regard to nursing homes in particular, many misunderstandings exist. Nursing homes, defined as 'a permanent residence for people who are too frail or sick to live at home or as a temporary facility during a recovering period' (Rowles & Teaster, 2015, p 460), are actually utilized by a very small percentage of people in the United States (less than 4% of people age 65 and over) (CDC, 2015). In looking at nine countries (Denmark, Iceland, Italy, Japan, the Netherlands, Sweden, Switzerland, the United Kingdom and the United States), Ribbe and colleagues (1997) found that between 2 and 5% of the population aged 65 and over lived in nursing homes. However, they noted that 'In most countries, 90–95% of elders remain at home, with many receiving formal and informal support services' (p 7). They also mentioned that around 6% of Japanese elders are institutionalized: two-thirds in hospitals and one-third in specialty care homes.

Summary

Myths about aging shape what a majority of people think about later life. Assumptions about care (or lack thereof), place, longevity and others can do much to harm our understanding of old age. For example, old age itself is not a new phenomenon; the number of people who are surviving into old age is. Life expectancy at birth has increased some, but the human life span remains at 120 years. There never really was a golden era when older people as such were revered. Instead, wealth, male gender and social class have long been determinants of such respect, even in countries where filial piety is a core cultural belief. Finally, nursing homes are not where the overwhelming proportion of older people reside in the Western world. Most live at home and prefer to live near to, but not with, their children.

Although not explicitly addressed in this chapter, there are implications of these myths. First, these myths lead to inaccurate perspectives about older people. Location in the world (for example, East, West) does not say a lot about the status of older people or their experience of aging. Rather, structures such as access to finances (addressed in Chapter Eight), experiences as a result of health and function (addressed in Chapter Four) and social location (addressed in Chapter Seven), and ability to receive and give appropriate care (addressed throughout the book) that matches the individual's expectations (for example, will care be provided by the family or by a healthcare professional?) will have much more influence on the experience of later life than location alone.

Further reading

Cole, T. R. (1992). *The journey of life: A cultural history of aging in America*. New York: Cambridge University Press.

Rowles, G. D., & Teaster, P. B. (2015). *Long-term care in an aging society: Theory and practice*. New York: Springer Publishing Company.

Thane, P. (2000). *Old age in English history: Past experiences, present issues.* Oxford: Oxford University Press.

References

Achenbaum, W. A. (2010). Past as prologue: toward a global history of ageing. In: D. Dannefer & C. Phillipson (Eds.), *The SAGE handbook of social gerontology.* Thousand Oaks, CA: Sage Publications, pp 20–32.

Allen, K. R., Blieszner, R., Roberto, K. A., Farnsworth, E. B., & Wilcox, K. L. (1999). Older adults and their children: family patterns of structural diversity. *Family Relations, 48*(2), 151–157.

Alley, D., & Crimmins, E. (2010). Epidemiology of ageing. In: D. Dannefer & C. Phillipson (Eds.), *The SAGE handbook of social gerontology.* Thousand Oaks, CA: Sage Publications, pp 75–95.

Alli, F., & Maharaj, P. (2013). The health situation of older people in Africa. In: P. Maharaj (Ed.), *Aging and health in Africa.* New York: Springer, pp 53–89.

Aykan, H. (2003). Effect of childlessness on nursing home and home health care use. *Journal of Aging & Social Policy, 15*(1), 33–53.

Brody, E. M., Litvin, S. J., Hoffman, C., & Kleban, M. H. (1995). Marital status of caregiving daughters and co-residence with dependent parents. *The Gerontologist, 35*(1), 75–85.

CDC (Centers for Disease Control) (2015). Nursing home care. Retrieved 15 December 2015, from http://www.cdc.gov/nchs/fastats/nursing-home-care.htm.

CIA (Central Intelligence Agency) (2015). *The World Factbook.* Retrieved 17 August 2015, from www.cia.gov/library/publications/the-world-factbook.

Cole, T. R. (1992). *The journey of life: A cultural history of aging in America.* New York: Cambridge University Press.

Cowgill, D. O., & Holmes, L. D. (1972). *Aging and modernization.* New York: Appleton-Century-Crofts.

Crimmins, E. M., & Beltrán-Sánchez, H. (2011). Mortality and morbidity trends: is there compression of morbidity? *The Journals of Gerontology Series B: Psychological Sciences and Social Sciences, 66B*(1), 75–86.

Cuddy, A. J., Norton, M. I., & Fiske, S. T. (2005). This old stereotype: the pervasiveness and persistence of the elderly stereotype. *Journal of Social Issues, 61*(2), 267–285.

Freedman, V. A. (1993). Kin and nursing home lengths of stay: a backward recurrence time approach. *Journal of Health and Social Behavior, 34*(2), 138–152.

Fries, J. F. (1980). Aging, natural death, and the compression of morbidity. *New England Journal of Medicine, 303*(3), 130–135.

Harris, R. (2000). *Gender and aging in Mesopotamia: The Gilgamesh Epic and other ancient literature.* Norman, OK: University of Oklahoma Press.

He, W., Sengupta, M., Velkoff, V. A., & DeBarros, K. A. (2005). *65+ in the United States, 2005.* Washington, DC: US Department of Commerce, Economics and Statistics Administration, US Census Bureau.

HelpAge International (2014). Life expectancy at 60. Retrieved 13 December 2015, from www.helpage.org.

Ingersoll-Dayton, B., & Saengtienchai, C. (1999). Respect for the elderly in Asia: stability and change. *The International Journal of Aging and Human Development, 48*(2), 113–130.

Jeffries, S., & Konnert, C. (2002). Regret and psychological well-being among voluntarily and involuntarily childless women and mothers. *The International Journal of Aging and Human Development, 54*(2), 89–106.

Johnson, C. L. (2000). Perspectives on American kinship in the later 1990s. *Journal of Marriage and Family, 62*(3), 623–639.

Knodel, J., & Nguyen, M. D. (2015). Grandparents and grandchildren: care and support in Myanmar, Thailand and Vietnam. *Ageing and Society, 35*(9), 1960–1988. doi: 10.1017/S0144686X14000786.

Kotlikoff, L. J., & Morris, J. N. (1990). Why don't the elderly live with their children? A new look. In: D.A. Wise (Ed.), *Issues in the economics of aging.* Chicago, IL: University of Chicago Press, pp 149–172.

Kunkel, S. R., Brown, J. S., & Whittington, F. J. (2014). *Global aging: Comparative perspectives on aging and the life course.* New York: Springer Publishing Company.

Kyobutungi, C., Egondi, T., & Ezeh, A. (2010). The health and well-being of older people in Nairobi's slums. *Global Health Action, 3*(Suppl. 2), 45–53.

Löckenhoff, C. E., De Fruyt, F., Terracciano, A., McCrae, R. R., De Bolle, M., Costa Jr, P. T., ... Alcalay, L. (2009). Perceptions of aging across 26 cultures and their culture-level associates. *Psychology and Aging, 24*(4), 941.

Longino Jr, C. F. (2001). Geographical distribution and migration. In: R.H. Binstock & L.K. George (Eds.), *Handbook of aging and the social sciences* (5th edn). San Diego: Academic Press, pp 103–124.

Miller, W., & Cohen, G. D. (2010). On creativity, illness, and aging. *Journal of Aging, Humanities, and the Arts, 4*(4), 302–311. doi: 10.1080/19325614.2010.529397.

Minois, G. (1989). *History of old age: From antiquity to the renaissance.* Chicago, IL: University of Chicago Press.

Nakanishi, M., Hoshishiba, Y., Iwama, N., Okada, T., Kato, E., & Takahashi, H. (2009). Impact of the elder abuse prevention and caregiver support law on system development among municipal governments in Japan. *Health Policy, 90*(2–3), 254–261. doi: http://dx.doi.org/10.1016/j.healthpol.2008.10.009.

Office Holidays (2015). Respect of the Aged Day. Retrieved 17 September 2015, from http://www.officeholidays.com/countries/japan/respect_the_aged.php.

Oh, J., Kim, H. S., Martins, D., & Kim, H. (2006). A study of elder abuse in Korea. *International Journal of Nursing Studies, 43*(2), 203–214.

Pearlin, L. I., Pioli, M. F., & McLaughlin, A. E. (2001). Caregiving by adult children: involvement, role disruption, and health. In: R.H. Binstock & L.K. George (Eds.), *Handbook of aging and the social sciences* (5th edn). San Diego: Academic Press, pp 238–253.

Pillay, N. K., & Maharaj, P. (2013). Population ageing in Africa. In: P. Maharaj (Ed.), *Aging and health in Africa.* New York: Springer, pp 11–51.

Quadagno, J. S. (1982). *Aging in early industrial society: Work, family, and social policy in nineteenth-century England.* New York: Academic Press.

Ribbe, M. W., Ljunggren, G., Steel, K., Topinkova, E., Hawes, C., Ikegami, N., ... Jónnson, P. V. (1997). Nursing homes in 10 nations: a comparison between countries and settings. *Age and Ageing, 26*(Suppl. 2), 3–12.

Rowles, G. D., & Teaster, P. B. (2015). *Long-term care in an aging society: Theory and practice.* New York: Springer Publishing Company.

Ryan, E. B., Jin, Y., Anas, A. P., & Luh, J. J. (2004). Communication beliefs about youth and old age in Asia and Canada. *Journal of Cross-cultural Gerontology, 19*(4), 343–360.

Shimizu, Y. and J. Wake (1994). Japan. In: J.I. Kosberg (Ed.), *International handbook on services for the elderly.* Westport, CT: Greenwood Press, 227–244.

Soeda, A., & Araki, C. (1999). Elder abuse by daughters-in-law in Japan. *Journal of Elder Abuse & Neglect, 11*(1), 47–58.

Sung, K.-t. (2001). Elder respect: exploration of ideals and forms in East Asia. *Journal of Aging Studies, 15*(1), 13–26.

Thane, P. (2000). *Old age in English history: Past experiences, present issues*. Oxford: Oxford University Press.

WHO (World Health Organization) (2015). *World health statistics 2015*. Geneva, Switzerland: World Health Organization.

World Bank, The (2015). Population ages 65 and above (% of total). Retrieved 26 July 2015, from http://data.worldbank.org/indicator/SP.POP.65UP.TO.ZS.

Zihindula, G., & Maharaj, P. (2013). Understanding the experiences of the elderly in rural areas in Rwanda. In: P. Maharaj (Ed.), *Aging and health in Africa*. New York: Springer, .

FOUR

Health and functional abilities in later life

This chapter provides an overview of some of the ways that health, disease, and wellbeing have been defined, conceptualized and studied in gerontology. Fears of decline in health and loss of function in later life have been linked to fears of aging. This could be seen in the stages of life that were introduced in Chapter Two, whereby 'green old age' or the Third Age and 'sad decrepitude' or the Fourth Age are distinguished by functional ability. Therefore, it is important to consider what is meant by health; historical perspectives of how to achieve a 'good old age'; health and the discourse of decline; distinctions between disease, normal aging and disability; morbidity and wellbeing; and social correlates of health. As has been highlighted throughout the *Short Guide*, health is rooted in the political and geographic. Structures such as social class, which affect one's access to nutrition, care and disease prevention, can ultimately play an important role in later life health. What constitutes 'health', how health is defined and what is viewed as 'normal' and 'pathological' aging will frame the beginning of this chapter. The latter part of the chapter will look more closely at concepts related to health measurement as well as the cognitive aspects of aging. It will not look at prevalence of individual diseases associated with older age, but instead will examine health and functioning from a broad context. Although social location and environmental determinants of health are discussed in more detail in Chapter Seven, they will also be briefly addressed here.

Health and the notion of 'aging well'

Aristotle used the word 'eugeria' to refer to 'a long and happy life in which independence was maintained and there was no pain or suffering' (Mulley, 2012). The key to a healthy long life, according to Lukian in the Macroboi, is 'climate, diet, occupation, physical fitness, and mental alertness' (Thane, 2000, p 37). Cicero, as cited by Patrick McKee (1982), came to a similar conclusion. Cicero wrote, 'But it is our duty, my young friends, to resist old age; to compensate for its defects by a watchful care; to fight against it as we would fight against disease; to adopt a regimen of health; to practice moderate exercise; and to take just enough of food and drink to restore our strength, not to overburden it' (p 31). These early frameworks for 'a good old age' have continued, more or less, until the present. For example, according to John Morley (2004), Roger Bacon, a Franciscan friar of the 13th century, suggested that 'old age could be warded off by eating a controlled diet, proper rest, exercise, moderation in lifestyle, good hygiene, and inhaling the breath of a young virgin' (p 1133). Today, most of these (except inhaling the breath of a young virgin) are still believed to be components of maintaining health into old age; there is a large body of research to support this (Burke et al, 2001; Houston et al, 2008; Chodzko-Zajko, 2014).

But what is health? Health, many have argued, can be an elusive concept, especially in a field like gerontology where such terms may carry different meanings depending on the perspective used. Farzana Alli and Pranitha Maharaj (2013) write that 'in its earliest conceptions, good health was viewed as a divine gift by the gods while poor health was viewed as a punishment' (p 54). Later, Susan J. Simmons (1989) argued that health was more of a generalized idea than a clearly defined one. She writes: 'The ancient Greek view of health, as formulated by Hippocrates in 400 B.C., stated that human well-being was influenced by the totality of environmental factors: living habits, climate, and the quality of air, water and food' (p 156). Eventually, the notion of health began to include other aspects of wellbeing beyond the physical. Since 1946, the World Health Organization (WHO) has defined health as 'a state of complete physical, mental and social well-being and not merely the absence of disease or infirmity' (WHO, 2015b). Chatterji and colleagues (2015) note that the WHO definition 'does not equate health with diseases or diagnostic classifications, but recognises a chain through which risk factors and environmental factors are determinants of diseases, and diseases and environmental factors, in turn, are determinants of health states' (p 565).

Parts of the WHO definition can be found in John Rowe and Robert Kahn's (1997) perspective on successful aging (see Table 2.1). They define successful aging as the ability to maintain 'low risk of disease and disease-related disability, high mental and physical function, and active engagement with life' (p 38). The body of research accompanying successful aging has been aimed at understanding why some individuals seem to age 'successfully' while others do not. Findings from the MacArthur Studies of Successful Aging (a series of studies based on Rowe and Kahn's definition) revealed several important components that seemed to be associated with function in later life. These included strong emotional support and better cognitive performance (Seeman, Lusignolo, Albert, & Berkman, 2001); social inequality and poorer health outcomes (Seeman et al, 2004); high levels of recreational activity and reduced inflammatory markers, which resulted in better health (Reuben, Judd-Hamilton, Harris, & Seeman, 2003); a nutritional diet and better physical function (Depp & Jeste, 2006), and many others. Interestingly, these findings are not all that different from what Cicero, Bacon and many others have suggested, although the structure of systematic research will hopefully provide better insight into why these outcomes occur rather than just the observation that these relationships between variables exist.

It should be noted that there are many criticisms of Rowe and Kahn's (1997) definition of successful aging and these were briefly mentioned in Chapter One. These criticisms include the focus on individual agency versus environmental and social factors that can lead to poor health (Rubinstein & de Medeiros, 2014); differences in definitions and measurement (such as what comprises 'high cognitive function' and what instruments are used to measure it) across studies (Depp & Jeste, 2006); and lack of personal assessments of whether one thinks he or she has aged 'successfully' (Montross et al, 2006). As noted in the earlier chapter, conceptualizations of successful aging that preceded Rowe and Kahn's (1997) placed more emphasis on an individuals' subjective assessment, on whether they considered themselves to be 'successfully aged', rather than by standardized performance levels (Havighurst, 1961; Havighurst, 1963). This difference in how successful aging is defined is an excellent example of how two different perspectives within gerontology may use the same terms or phrase but for two different reasons. Rowe and Kahn (1997), for example use successful aging as a construct through which to measure and compare health and function across groups of people. Havighurst (1963) and others use it as a term to describe one's personal assessment of one's life. In a similar way, health can be understood in terms of subjective evaluation (for example, 'I rate myself as healthy') or through outside determinants (for example, 'a person who performs at level x on a measurement of overall health is determined to be less healthy than a person who performs at level y'.) Topics related to determining health and disability status are discussed in further detail later in the chapter.

Health and challenging the discourse of decline

As was mentioned in Chapter Two, gerontology was founded as a way to learn more about how to avoid or remedy many illnesses associated with old age. The pathogenic (Greek 'pathos' or suffering) view of health sees health as 'the absence of disability, disease, and premature death' (Keyes, 2007, p 96). While on the one hand it is difficult to discuss concepts like health and function in later life without slipping into talk of decline and loss, ignoring the effects and experiences of disease in later life can lead to a 'discourse of denial', which is also problematic. There are several concepts that challenge the discourse of decline without overlooking the effects of disease and change which are under the large umbrella of salutogenic (from the Greek word 'salus' or health) models of health and aging (Antonovsky, 1996; Lindström & Eriksson, 2006; Keyes, 2007). These concepts include flourishing (Keyes, 2007;

Keyes, 2010), resilience (Werner & Smith, 1982; Wagnild & Collins, 2009; Lipsitt & Demick, 2011) and hardiness (Kobasa, Maddi, & Kahn, 1982). In contrast, there are other concepts that particularly look at decline – frailty and sarcopenia– as ways to better direct research and clinical efforts. Each is described in the following subsections, along with an explanation of the term 'functional abilities' that will be used throughout the chapter.

Salutogenic models

Aaron Antonovsky (1996) introduced the salutogenic model as a response to limits in health promotion that focused on disease and risk factors. He writes: 'When we look closely at the concept of "lifestyles" as it appears in the literature, however, what is found is a list of (generally well-documented) risk factors: smoking, other substance abuse, overnutrition, drunken driving, unsafe sex, exposure to injuries. We remain squarely in the realm of disease prevention' (p 13). He argues that rather than seeing health and disease as two dichotomous conditions, one should view all people as somewhere on a continuum. He adds that 'Salutogenic orientation, then, as the basis for health promotion, directs both research and action efforts to encompass all persons, wherever they are on the continuum' (p 14). Examples of salutogenic models relevant to aging include flourishing, resilience and hardiness. Corey Keyes (2002; Keyes, 2007) defines flourishing as the promotion and maintenance of mental health, rather than the absence of a condition. There are three broad positive dimensions of flourishing: emotions, psychological functioning and social functioning. 'Flourishing' captures the idea that health is not just the absence of disease, but a state of being in which a person positively functions.

The second salutogenic model, resilience, overlaps many of the concepts of flourishing. Werner Greve and Ursula Staudinger (2006) describe resilience in later life as 'a central concept for both the life span perspective on human development and for developmental psychopathology. It conveys the idea that individuals can avoid negative outcomes or decreasing trajectories of development despite the presence of significant risk factors in their environment or potentially harmful experiences during their lives' (p 797). Key to resilience is the concept of plasticity, which is a dynamic system of gains and losses that occurs across the life span and can act in a compensatory way in some individuals. Constructs of resilience propose that individuals can return to their initial level of function despite negative exposures because of their ability to act in a compensatory way.

Finally, the third salutogenic model is hardiness, which was described by Suzanne Kobasa, Salvatore Maddi and Stephen Kahn (1982) as a combination of commitment, control and challenge within an individual that allowed him or her to counter the effects of stressful life events without ill effects. The orienting idea in this approach was that stress produced negative health outcomes and that hardy individuals use a combination of resources (for example, social connections), personality and past experience through previous exposure to stressful situations or observing modelled coping behaviors by others to reduce the negative effects of a given exposure. Overall, these models suggest a continued, positive dynamic that can occur throughout one's life despite physical, emotional, financial and other changes.

Frailty and sarcopenia

On seemingly the flip side of salutogenic perspectives are two syndromes associated with decline in later life: frailty and sarcopenia. Frailty, has been described by Linda Fried and colleagues (2001) as 'a biologic syndrome of decreased reserve and resistance to stressors, resulting from cumulative declines across multiple physiologic systems and causing vulnerability to adverse outcomes' (p M146). This would appear to be the point in which resilience or other compensatory strategies are no longer effective. In their work, they found that the likelihood of frailty was more common in people with lower socioeconomic status and women, the latter possibly because of differences in muscle mass in women as compared to men.

The second syndrome, sarcopenia, is derived from the Greek roots 'sarx' (flesh) and 'penia' (loss) (Rosenberg, 1997), and describes a geriatric syndrome characterized by age-related decline in muscle mass and strength. Sarcopenia is sometimes considered within the frailty construct since loss of muscle mass is one of the systems that may decline. Prevalence estimates in the world range from 5 to 13% for people aged 60–70 years and from 11 to 50% for people aged 80 years and over (Cruz-Jentoft et al, 2010). Under- and overnutrition have been identified as risk factors. Returning to the 'stages of life' discussed in Chapter One, frailty and sarcopenia would be associated with the Fourth Age or periods in which one experiences decline and increased dependency. These are some of the negative aspects of aging that have led to fears of growing old.

Functional abilities

The term 'functional abilities' is being used here as a broad description to capture physical, cognitive and emotional changes that occur in later life. It is also a linguistic attempt to move away from the decline model by focusing on abilities rather than losses. 'Function' here includes the concepts of disease, health, disability and wellbeing, all of which are discussed in the sections that follow.

As with all aspects of aging, there are individual, societal, geographical and cultural factors to consider. For example, individuals may make choices about their health such as what to eat. However, those choices will be limited to what resources are available to purchase particular foods (societal), what foods can be grown (geographical), what is considered appropriate to eat or drink (cultural) and other factors that are beyond the control of individuals themselves. The same applies to encounters with health professionals. A person may want to seek medical attention but may not have access to appropriate services. He or she may not view a condition (for example, depression) as problematic or one for which to seek treatment. Although it is beyond the scope of the *Short Guide* to provide a full discussion of the range of issues affecting function, awareness of the complexities of function is important.

Disease, 'normal aging', health and disability

As mentioned earlier, gerontology's 'scientific' history is rooted in distinguishing 'aging' from 'disease' and 'normal' aging from 'unusual' aging. There are, of course, several challenges. The first is in the definition of disease. Merriam-Webster's dictionary defines disease as 'an impairment of the normal state of the living animal or plant body or one of its parts that interrupts or modifies the performance of the vital functions, is typically manifested by distinguishing signs and symptoms, and is a response to environmental factors (as malnutrition, industrial hazards, or climate), to specific infective agents (as worms, bacteria, or viruses), to inherent defects of the organism (as genetic anomalies), or to combinations of these factors' (Merriam-Webster, 2015). However, similar to challenges in defining health, Jackie Scully (2004) points out that although defining disease is at first straightforward, understanding what is really meant by 'disease' is actually difficult. Conditions which are labeled as 'disease' vary by context and culture and can change over historical time. Scully cites the example of osteoporosis, which was recognized as a disease by the WHO in 1994, thereby changing it from an 'unavoidable part of normal ageing to pathology' (p 650). Prior to that time, it was not considered to be a disease.

Kathy Charmaz (2000) distinguishes 'illness' from 'disease.' She writes, 'I define illness as the person's experience; disease constitutes a bodily disorder as agreed upon by physicians' (p 277). In this way, illness is an individual experience, while disease is a category that one's experience may be placed within. Finally, philosopher Christopher Boorse (1975) points to disease in contrast to health. He writes, 'The root idea of this account is that the normal is the natural. The state of an organism is theoretically health, i.e., free of disease, insofar as its mode of functioning conforms to the natural design of that kind of organism' (p 57). He adds that 'A disease is an illness only if it is serious enough to be incapacitating, and therefore is undesirable for its bearer, a title to special treatment, and a valid excuse for normally criticisable behaviour' (p 61).

Defining disease in contrast to health in this way can be problematic when considering aging and age-associated change.

Given the varying definitions of health and illness, there has been much criticism in the literature of how later life is linked to poorer health, especially when old age is framed as 'less than normal'. A great deal of research has been aimed at distinguishing 'normal' from 'pathological' aging. 'Normal aging' describes 'the underlying time-dependent biological process of aging in each species, which may involve functional loss or susceptibility to disease but is not in itself a disease' (Moody & Sasser, 2012, p 531). Normal aging is generally distinguished from 'pathological' aging, which would refer to functional loss that is not a part of the aging process. It is important to distinguish normal aging from pathological aging because while advancing age may increase one's risk of developing diseases and disorders such as dementia, types of cancers and others, age in itself is not the cause of such diseases and disorders; advanced age is, of course, associated with increased risk for disease and disability (Bochner, 2001; Debpuur, Welaga, Wak, & Hodgson, 2010). As Dawn Alley and Eileen Crimmins (2010) report: 'Age is one of the most important factors representing risk of poor health outcomes. Biological aging is associated with changes in the physical structures and physiological functioning of the body that affect viability ... About 85 per cent of the population survives to age 60, but exponentially increasing mortality risk leads to fewer and fewer survivors at old age' (p 76).

Types of disease

Moving away from questions of 'normal' and 'pathological', 'disease' and 'health,' this section will look specifically at disease. There are four basic disease groups: communicable and non-communicable, which describe transition; and acute and chronic, which describe duration. Communicable diseases are contagious and include HIV/AIDS, malaria and many others. Non-communicable diseases include disorders such as diabetes, heart disease, hypertension, cancers and others. Acute diseases have a relatively short course, often with severe consequences such as death. Chronic diseases are those that last three months or longer, often cannot be prevented (such as, dementia) and cannot be cured (CDC, 2015). The following is a more detailed discussion of all four.

Communicable

Communicable diseases such as HIV/AIDS and malaria have been identified as major causes of death, especially in sub-Saharan Africa (Lopez, Mathers, Ezzati, Jamison, & Murray, 2006). While these may not target older individuals in particular, the impact on aging is nonetheless great. One obvious impact is that premature death due to communicable disease will prevent many people from reaching old age. A second, which has been mentioned elsewhere in the book, is the need for grandparents or other carers to step in to provide care for children orphaned or otherwise affected by loss of family members due to disease.

Non-communicable

There is a general misconception that non-communicable diseases are more common in affluent countries than in poorer countries. While this is true for some types of non-communicable disease, such as various types of dementia, breast cancer and colorectal cancer, more than three-quarters of deaths from non-communicable diseases occur in non-developed countries (Di Cesare et al, 2013). The most common non-communicable disease deaths in non-developed countries include maternal, perinatal and nutritional disorders; diabetes; respiratory disease; and accidents. In addition, half of the deaths are in the 15–59 age group and are linked to low socioeconomic status and lack of access to treatment. For example, early childhood malnutrition can lead to cardiovascular and metabolic diseases later on. Pollution, including those from cooking and heating fuels, can lead to respiratory disease. High death rates from non-communicable disease in less-industrialized countries highlights the relationship between socioeconomic status and the availability of programs such as childhood nutrition and health initiatives that can influence the overall health of a region or group. Even in high-income countries, marginalized groups are far more likely to have higher rates of non-communicable disease than are non-marginalized groups (Di Cesare et al, 2013). Low levels of education, low income and neighborhoods deprived of resources, such as accessible health clinics, have all been linked to poorer health outcomes (Marmot, 2005; Stafford, Cummins, Macintyre, Ellaway, & Marmot, 2005; Marmot & Bell, 2016).

Acute

Africa currently bears the burden of acute disease, including: malaria, the major cause of mortality and morbidity in Africa, with close to 2 million deaths per year; AIDS, with two-thirds of the 30 million people with HIV/AIDS living in sub-Saharan African; and tuberculosis (Maharaj, 2013). AIDS is responsible for falling rates of life expectancy at birth since 1970 in six countries: Democratic Republic of the Congo (DRC), Lesotho, Swaziland, South Africa, Zambia and Zimbabwe (Li, 2013; Maharaj, 2013). In addition, strains placed on the healthcare systems because of these acute diseases mean that not only are older adults less likely to have access to treatments, but people who transition into old age are more likely to have chronic health impairments, putting them at further risk for poorer health (Kyobutungi, Egondi, & Ezeh, 2010).

HIV/AIDS and tuberculosis place a high burden on African countries in terms not only of medical resources used but also of caregiving needed. Older people currently provide care for their ill and dying children, and also for their grandchildren. This may mean that there will be a lack of caregivers for older people if should they fall ill or need assistance (Kyobutungi et al, 2010).

Chronic

Dementia, which is addressed in more detail in this chapter's section on cognition, is a chronic condition that is believed to contribute to more years spent with a disability than stroke, cardiovascular disease or cancer for people age 60 and over (Ballard et al, 2011). It is most burdensome in high-income countries since there are more people aged 70 and over who are at risk of developing a form of dementia. Other chronic diseases are mentioned later with regard to disability adjusted life years. In addition, osteoarthritis is a chronic condition that affects most people over age 65 and can contribute to loss in mobility.

With regard to the experience of chronic disease by older people in Africa, Farzana Alli and Pranitha Maharaj (2013) report that 'In Sub-Saharan Africa, studies on experiences of chronic illnesses show that these experiences are characterised by unhappiness, depression, spiritual distress, and suicidal tendencies' (p 62). In addition, stigma in many African countries associated with chronic conditions such as diabetes and cancer also compromises older adults' ability and willingness to seek and receive help and treatment (Alli & Maharaj, 2013).

Disability, compression of morbidity and healthy life expectancy

In addition to distinguishing types of disease, it is also important to address disability, compression of morbidity and health adjusted life years.

Disability

Disability is defined by the WHO (WHO, 2015a) as 'an umbrella term for impairments, activity limitations and participation restrictions. Disability is the interaction between individuals with a health condition (e.g. cerebral palsy, Down syndrome and depression) and personal and environmental factors (e.g. negative attitudes, inaccessible transportation and public buildings, and limited social supports).' This definition captures the idea that disability isn't about issues related to individual function alone but also about the ways in which the environment can help or hinder, thereby 'disabling' a person or creating unnecessary barriers. As noted by Pranitha Maharaj (2013), the Madrid International Plan of Action on Ageing in 2002 stressed that 'nations should take a holistic life course approach to ageing to enable older people to maintain their independence, productivity, and remain vital resources for their families, communities, and the economy; good health is crucial to achieve this' (p 1). This includes insuring accessibility, which, in turn, would decrease the ways in which environments can disable people.

Compression and expansion morbidity

Two competing views on the state of disease-related disability in later life are compression of morbidity and expansion of morbidity. As mentioned briefly in Chapter Three, compression of morbidity refers to the rectangularization of disability curves whereby, over time, disabilities begin to be pushed to the final years of life rather than occurring at earlier ages (Fries, 1980, 2003). James Fries (1980), originator of the compression of morbidity hypothesis, speculated that the same forces that lead to change in survival curves, which has made survival into old age quite common and nearly universal, would also lead to health promotion and other changes that would transfer into delaying the onset of chronic diseases later in life (Crimmins & Beltrán-Sánchez, 2010).

As Eileen Crimmins and Hiram Beltrán-Sánchez (2010) note, other views counter to the compression of morbidity hypothesis exist. For example, they write: 'Gruenberg (1977) felt that the decline in mortality from chronic disease would be met with increased prevalence. He did not think that the decrease in mortality would arise from lowered disease incidence rates but rather from higher survival of people with health problems, resulting in more disease in the population, which he termed the failure of success' (p 1); in other words, more people would survive chronic diseases such as cancer, thereby leading to increases in chronic disease rather than delays. This describes the second view of disease-related disability: expansion of morbidity, which is the opposite of the compression hypothesis. The expansion hypothesis, originally proposed by Ernest Gruenberg (1977), suggests that increases in life expectancy will lead to more people living longer with poorer health. People who would otherwise have died from diseases such as polio would now have the opportunity to survive into later life, but with the potential to acquire new chronic illnesses such as dementia. Gruenberg raises this issue not as a condemnation of medical progress, but as a call for research to address the new forms of disease-related disability that was likely to occur because of medicine's success.

Recently, Somnath Chatterji and colleagues (2015) explored which hypothesis was being realized at present: compression or expansion of morbidity. They reported some evidence for compression of morbidity in high-income countries, but inconclusive evidence for lower-income countries, mainly due to a lack of reliable data. Overall, however, they found that whether one hypothesis versus the other was supported depended on how disability was being measured. Differing types of data (such as data from longitudinal studies) and measurements (such as self-reported data versus performance-based data) led to different conclusions. In short, it is not yet clear whether compression or expansion is occurring, and whether particular diseases or types of disease are contributing to compression or expansion, or how compression or expansion differs according to the income status of a country (Chatterji et al, 2015).

Healthy life expectancy

One way that function is measured is through healthy life expectancy (HALE). HALE is defined as the 'average number of years that a person can expect to live in "full health" by taking into account years lived in less than full health due to disease and/or injury' (WHO, 2015, p 1). This concept considers what the personal and societal costs are for many chronic illnesses, which provides a very different picture than looking at mortality patterns (Gold, Stevenson, & Fryback, 2002). Mortality patterns provide only a very basic view of a region's health based on who has died, but they do not shed any light on who is ill or having difficulties with function (Gold et al, 2002). Although a heart attack may be a cause of death, living with osteoarthritis may affect one's health over the long run (WHO, 2015a). As Gold and colleagues (2002) explain, 'Health-adjusted life years (HALYs) are summary measures of population health that allow the combined impact of death and morbidity to be considered simultaneously' (p 116).

A slightly different measure of health is the disability adjusted life year (DALY). Unlike HALY, DALY measures the burden of premature death, injury and disease (Gold et al, 2002). DALY is calculated by adding years of life lost to years of life lost to disability. The conditions leading to greatest DALYs for people aged 60 and over globally include stroke, ischaemic heart disease, diabetes mellitus, chronic obstructive pulmonary disease and various types of cancers (depending on the region.) While trachea, bronchus and lung cancers contribute to high DALYs in most regions, other types of cancers such as stomach cancer are more common in Central and East Asian countries (WHO, 2015a). Also, DALYs do differ by age group. For example, 7,422,870 women age 70 and over in high income countries have DALY due to neurological disorders, as compared to 1,258,769 for women aged 60 to 69. While DALY and HALE are important ways of examining health, the data are only as good as the records that are being kept. Differences in how diseases and disorders are defined and recorded can contribute to inaccuracies in estimates.

Wellbeing and happiness

Another important component of health is wellbeing, one of many contested concepts in gerontology. How wellbeing is conceptualized depends on whether it is viewed as an outcome rather than a process. Some important challenges to wellbeing and happiness are depression and memory loss; this includes mild cognitive impairment and dementia, both of which are discussed later in the chapter.

Subjective wellbeing has been defined as 'positive evaluation of one's life associated with good feelings' (p 187) (Pinquart & Sörensen, 2000), 'the overall evaluation that people make about the quality of their inner experience, pertaining to their basic life aspects and positive mental health' (Shmotkin, 1990, p 201) or as 'a broad category of phenomena that include people's emotional responses, domain satisfactions, and global judgments of life satisfaction' (Diener, Suh, Lucas, & Smith, 1999, p 277). According to Margaret Gatz and Steven Zarit (1999), 'Other scholars have addressed the mechanisms by which mental health is achieved in old age. One of the most important achievements entails putting one's own life in context in order to realize contentment, congruence, self-acceptance, sense of purpose, and emotional regulation' (p 399). High levels of subjective wellbeing are considered to be an important aspect of aging well (Diener, 1984; Pinquart & Sörensen, 2000).

Ed Diener and colleagues (1999), in their review of subjective wellbeing over three decades, note that a 'happy' person was once thought to be a 'young, healthy, well-educated, well-paid, extroverted, optimistic, worry-free, religious, married person with high esteem, job morale, modest aspirations, of either sex and of a wide range of intelligence' (p 276). However, according to Natalia Melgar and Maximo Rossi (2013), there is a nonlinear relationship between happiness (which is often considered a part of subjective wellbeing) and age. They also report that there is 'a U-shaped relationship and that the minimum (when people are likely to be unhappiest) is found between 45 and 64 years of age' (p 355). This suggests that middle aged, not older people, are the most likely to be unhappy. In addition, work by Diener and Chan (2011) suggests that subjective wellbeing is something that can be improved in people across the life span, that high subjective wellbeing leads to reduced risk of some health disorders such as cardiovascular disease and that higher levels of subjective wellbeing are linked to longer life.

As mentioned Chapter Two with regards to the social convoy model, social networks have been found to have direct and indirect influences on subjective wellbeing. Specifically, being able to receive positive feedback has been cited as an important component of self-concept. Also, having supportive social relationships is believed to buffer some of the negative effects of stress on subjective wellbeing by positively influencing the coping process (Pinquart & Sörensen, 2000). Across age groups, married individuals have been found to have greater subjective wellbeing than never-married people; never-married people have higher subjective wellbeing than previously married individuals (divorced, separated, widowed) (Diener, Gohm, Suh, & Oishi, 2000). This has been attributed to companionship and buffers to stress that marriage may provide.

In the United States, there are racial and ethnic differences in subjective wellbeing relative to friends versus family networks. Subjective wellbeing has been reported to be more strongly associated with closeness to family rather than friends among African Americans, as compared to among European Americans, where friends rather than family are more strongly associated with subjective wellbeing (Johnson, 2000). Children have been reported as having a positive influence on the subjective wellbeing of their older parents when parents describe their relationship with their children as close (Connidis & McMullin, 1993). Distant parents (men and women) and older people without children have been found to have lower levels of subjective wellbeing.

Depression

Depression has been called the most common mental disorder in old age (Blazer, 2003) and a threat to wellbeing and happiness in later life. Prevalence rates for major depressive disorders for individuals aged 75 and over range from 4.6% to 9.3%, with women's rates (4.0–10.3%) exceeding men's (2.8–6.9%) (Luppa et al, 2012). When looking specifically at people aged 65 and over, prevalence of depressive symptoms is much greater than in the general population, with rates ranging from 5% to 27% depending on severity and diagnostic criteria (Glaesmer, Riedel-Heller, Braehler, Spangenberg, & Luppa, 2011; Luppa et al, 2012). Depression in older age is thought to be affected by situational demands, available coping resources and responses to stressers (Culbertson, 1997; Blazer, 2003; Blazer & Hybels, 2005; Djernes, 2006). Factors believed to contribute to depression in old age are traumatic events or events involving potential death, danger or harm to an individual or a person close to him or her; loss, including personal loss of abilities and/or resources and loss of social and/or emotional support; events described as adjustment disorders, such as change in financial or marital status; daily hassles like heavy traffic commute; decreases in physical abilities; or illness, both physical and mental, and changes in locus of control (Roberts et al, 1997; Barusch et al, 1999; Blazer, 2003; Blazer & Hybels, 2005). Some studies have suggested that external presentation of depression may have a cohort effect, specifically, that adults born in the earlier part of the 20th century may have a negative view of sadness or depression and may therefore alter their affect to appear positive despite actually being depressed (Gallo & Rabins, 1999; Hybels, Blazer, & Pieper, 2001). Consequently, depressed older persons who do not exhibit a corresponding sadness are not likely to be identified or treated and are therefore at greater risk for negative health outcomes.

Memory

Memory is important to consider in old age, since overall age-related memory decline is estimated to occur in one in seven people aged 65 and over (Grady & Craik, 2000; Ball et al, 2002). Memory in particular is equated with one's sense of self. Threats to memory therefore are often experienced and viewed as threats to the self, especially in the extreme cases of dementia. As is discussed later, while some gradual memory loss is considered to be a part of 'normal' aging, profound memory loss, as in the case of dementia, is not.

For 'healthy' older persons, the primary complaint with regard to changes in memory is name recall. This fear of memory decline in general has led to prolific research on improving various components of memory in older adults using formal memory-training strategies (for example, mnemonics), games (such as, crossword puzzles, online memory tools) and others. In mnemonic strategies, such as method of loci, participants learn techniques for effectively encoding and retrieving new information, such as remembering a new word by visually associating that word with a physical location – a specific room inside a house, for example (Hampstead et al, 2012). To date, most studies have found that improvements to memory apply only to the specific task for which someone was trained (for example, remembering a list of words), that improvements do not transfer to memory in everyday life (for example, recalling the location of the car keys) and that the effects do not have long-term impact (Rebok et al, 2007. Some have speculated that difficulty in remembering the memory strategy itself and loss of interest due to the unappealing nature of the memory tasks have contributed to lack of success in many memory-training strategies. It has also been suggested that tasks that have personal meaning have more potential to improve memory performance (Hampstead et al, 2012), and that semantic elaboration improves subsequent memory.

Some researchers have also found that memory performance is directly tied to one's belief about his or her own memory (Bottiroli, Cavallini, & Vecchi, 2008; Troyer, Murphy, Anderson, Moscovitch, & Craik, 2008). For example, Angela Troyer and colleagues (2008) found that although it was possible to train people to change their memory beliefs, lasting improvement in memory did not often occur until people believed their memories could be improved. In this important example, the predominant narratives of decline work to prevent many people from realizing their potential with regard to memory if they buy into the notion that memory decline is inevitable and unalterable.

Mild cognitive impairment and dementia

Two extreme forms of memory loss and cognitive decline are mild cognitive impairment and dementia. Mild cognitive impairment is defined as 'cognitive decline greater than expected for an individual's age and education level but that does not interfere notably with activities of daily living' (Gauthier et al, 2006, p 15). Someone with mild cognitive impairment would likely be able to function independently but would experience more difficulty with name recall or other age-related memory loss. The prevalence range in people aged 65 and over is estimated to be between 3% and 19%. Mild cognitive impairment is believed to increase one's risk of Alzheimer's dementia, although this is a relatively new area of clinical research that is still not well understood.

Dementia is a general word to describe progressive cognitive and/ or behavioral symptoms that affect one's ability to function due to inability to remember or acquire new information; poor judgment or poor reasoning; problems with visuospatial abilities such as recognizing common objects or people; impairment with language; and/or changes in personality or behavior (McKhann et al, 2011). Alzheimer's disease is the most common type of dementia and is characterized by the presence of amyloid plaques and neurofibrillary tangles that are believed to interrupt and damage neurotransmitters, leading to cognitive decline and other challenges highlighted above (Ballard et al, 2011). In 2006, there were estimated to be 26.6 million cases of Alzheimer's disease worldwide, although some sources place the range of estimated cases as between 11.4 million to 59.4 million) (Brookmeyer, Johnson, Ziegler-Graham, & Arrighi, 2007). In the United States, one in nine people aged 65 and over is believed to have Alzheimer's disease. This number increases to one in three for people over age 85 (Alzheimer's Association, 2013). Nearly half of the new cases of Alzheimer's disease are expected to be in Asia due to the rapid increase of the percentage of people reaching older age, as increasing age is the major risk factor. There is currently no effective treatment or means of prevention.Other dementia types include vascular dementia and dementia with Lewy bodies. There is debate as to which of these two is the second most common dementia (Román, Erkinjuntti, Wallin, Pantoni, & Chui, 2002; Hanson & Lippa, 2009). Vascular dementia is caused by damage in the brain due to impaired blood flow (Román et al, 2002). Hypertension, which can then lead to arteriolosclerosis, is a major risk factor. Lewy body dementia is the result of alpha-synuclein, a protein, in the brain's nerve cells. It is also associated with the beta-amyloid and tau tangles found in Alzheimer's disease. Both vascular dementia and Lewy body dementia can co-occur with Alzheimer's disease. Overall, dementia (of all types) was estimated to contribute 11.2% of years spent with a disability in people aged 60 and over (Ballard et al, 2011).

Summary

Health encompasses more than the absence of disease and includes social wellbeing. One of the challenges in gerontology has been disassociating older age with decline and instead focusing on new opportunities. Yet, to ignore physical, psychological and social changes that occur in later life is to present an unrealistic and inaccurate picture: just as inaccurate as assuming that all older people are ill, have significant functional loss and are unhappy. To better understand a population's health, HALE and DALY are helpful. Although acute disease is far more prevalent in lower-income countries, most countries share some disorders of later life such as diabetes, stroke and others that contribute to disability in later life. Other important considerations include wellbeing and happiness, which may be affected by social networks, emotional health and perceived memory. More specifically, depression can affect wellbeing as can the belief that extreme memory loss is an inevitable part of aging. Although risk of mild cognitive impairment and dementia do increase with age, they are not a part of 'normal' aging. Overall, health is a multi-dimensional concept that can be viewed as a public outcome or an individual experience and can be heavily influenced by surrounding political, economic, and social structures.

Further reading and resources

World Bank, The, http://data.worldbank.org/indicator/SP.POP.65UP. TO.ZS.

WHO (World Health Organization) (2015a). *World health statistics 2015.* Geneva, Switzerland: WHO. http://www.who.int/gho/publications/ world_health_statistics/en/.

WHO (2015b). *World report on ageing and health.* Geneva, Switzerland: WHO.

References

Alley, D., & Crimmins, E. (2010). Epidemiology of ageing. In: D. Dannefer & C. Phillipson (Eds.), *The SAGE handbook of social gerontology.* London: Sage Publications, pp 75–95.

Alli, F., & Maharaj, P. (2013). The health situation of older people in Africa. In: P. Maharaj (Ed.), *Aging and health in Africa.* New York: Springer, pp 53–89.

Alzheimer's Association (2013). 2013 Alzheimer's disease facts and figures. *Alzheimer's & Dementia, 9*(2), 208–245.

Antonovsky, A. (1996). The salutogenic model as a theory to guide health promotion. *Health Promotion International, 11*(1), 11–18.

Ball, K., Berch, D. B., Helmers, K. F., Jobe, J. B., Leveck, M. D., Marsiske, M., . . . Willis, S. L. (2002). Effects of cognitive training interventions with older adults: a randomized controlled trial. *Journal of the American Medical Association, 288,* 2271–2281.

Ballard, C., Gauthier, S., Corbett, A., Brayne, C., Aarsland, D., & Jones, E. (2011). Alzheimer's disease. *The Lancet, 377*(9770), 1019–1031. doi: http://dx.doi.org/10.1016/S0140-6736(10)61349-9.

Barusch, A., Rogers, A., & Abu-Bader, S. (1999). Depressive symptoms in the frail elderly: physical and psychosocial correlates. *International Journal of Aging and Human Development, 49*(2), 107 –125.

Blazer, D. G. (2003). Depression in late life: review and commentary. *The Journals of Gerontology Series A: Biological Sciences and Medical Sciences, 58*(3), M249–M265.

Blazer, D. G., & Hybels, C. F. (2005). Origins of depression in later life. *Psychological Medicine, 35*(9), 1241–1252.

Bochner, A. P. (2001). Narrative's virtues. *Qualitative Inquiry, 7*(2), 131–157.

Boorse, C. (1975). On the distinction between disease and illness. *Philosophy & Public Affairs, 5*(1), 49–68.

Bottiroli, S., Cavallini, E., & Vecchi, T. (2008). Long-term effects of memory training in the elderly: a longitudinal study. *Archives of Gerontology and Geriatrics, 47*(2), 277–289.

Brookmeyer, R., Johnson, E., Ziegler-Graham, K., & Arrighi, H. M. (2007). Forecasting the global burden of Alzheimer's disease. *Alzheimer's & Dementia, 3*(3), 186–191.

Burke, G.L., Arnold, A.M., Bild, D.E., Cushman, M., Fried, L.P., Newman, A., Nunn, C., & Robbins, J., 2001. Factors associated with healthy aging: the cardiovascular health study. *Journal of the American Geriatrics Society, 49*(3), 254–262.

CDC (Centers for Disease Control) (2015). Chronic disease prevention and health promotion. Retrieved 16 December 2015, from http://www.cdc.gov/chronicdisease/.

Charmaz, K. (2000). Experiencing chronic illness. In: G.L. Albrecht, R. Fitzpatrick, & S.C. Scrimshaw (Eds.), *Handbook of social studies in health and medicine*. Thousand Oaks. CA: Sage Publications, pp 277–292.

Chatterji, S., et al. (2015). Health, functioning, and disability in older adults—present status and future implications. *The Lancet* 385(9967), 563-575.

Chodzko-Zajko, W. J. (2014). Exercise and physical activity for older adults. *Kinesthiology Review, 3*(1), 1–3.

Connidis, I. A., & McMullin, J. A. (1993). To have or have not: parent status and the subjective well-being of older men and women. *The Gerontologist, 33*(5), 630–636.

Crimmins, E. M., & H. Beltrán-Sánchez (2010). Mortality and morbidity trends: is there compression of morbidity? *The Journals of Gerontology Series B: Psychological Sciences and Social Sciences, 66B*(1), 75–86.

Cruz-Jentoft, A. J., Baeyens, J. P., Bauer, J. M., Boirie, Y., Cederholm, T., Landi, F., ... Schneider, S. M. (2010). Sarcopenia: European consensus on definition and diagnosis. Report of the European Working Group on Sarcopenia in Older People. *Age and Ageing, 39*(4), 412–423.

Culbertson, F. M. (1997). Depression and gender: an international review. *American Psychologist, 52*(1), 25.

Debpuur, C., Welaga, P., Wak, G., & Hodgson, A. (2010). Self-reported health and functional limitations among older people in the Kassena-Nankana District, Ghana. *Global Health Action, 3*(Suppl. 2), 54–63.

Depp, C. A., & Jeste, D. V. (2006). Definitions and predictors of successful aging: a comprehensive review of larger quantitative studies. *The American Journal of Geriatric Psychiatry, 14*(1), 6–20.

Di Cesare, M., Khang, Y.-H., Asaria, P., Blakely, T., Cowan, M. J., Farzadfar, F., ... Msyamboza, K. P. (2013). Inequalities in non-communicable diseases and effective responses. *The Lancet, 381*(9866), 585–597.

Diener, E. (1984). Subjective well-being. *Psychological Bulletin, 95*(3), 542–575. doi: 10.1037//0033-2909.95.3.542.

Diener, E., & Chan, M. Y. (2011). Happy people live longer: subjective well-being contributes to health and longevity. *Applied Psychology: Health and Well-Being, 3*(1), 1–43.

Diener, E., Gohm, C. L., Suh, E., & Oishi, S. (2000). Similarity of the relations between marital status and subjective well-being across cultures. *Journal of Cross-cultural Psychology, 31*(4), 419–436.

Diener, E., Suh, E. M., Lucas, R. E., & Smith, H. L. (1999). Subjective well—being: three decades of progress. *Psychological Bulletin, 125*(2), 276–302.

Djernes, J. (2006). Prevalence and predictors of depression in populations of elderly: a review. *Acta Psychiatrica Scandinavica, 113*(5), 372–387.

Fried, L. P., Tangen, C. M., Walston, J., Newman, A. B., Hirsch, C., Gottdiener, J., ... Burke, G. (2001). Frailty in older adults evidence for a phenotype. *The Journals of Gerontology Series A: Biological Sciences and Medical Sciences, 56*(3), M146–M157.

Fries, J. F. (1980). Aging, natural death, and the compression of morbidity. *New England Journal of Medicine, 303*(3), 130–135.

Fries, J. F. (2003). Measuring and monitoring success in compressing morbidity. *Annals of Internal Medicine 139*(5 Part 2), 455–459.

Gallo, J. J., & Rabins, P. V. (1999). Depression without sadness: alternative presentations of depression in late life. *American family physician 60*(3), 820–826.

Gatz, M., & Zarit, S. H. (1999). A good old age: paradox or possibility. In: V.L.S. Bengston & K. Warner (Eds.), *Handbook of theories of aging* (1st edn). New York: Springer Publishing, pp 396–416.

Gauthier, S., Reisberg, B., Zaudig, M., Petersen, R. C., Ritchie, K., Broich, K., ... Winblad, B. (2006). Mild cognitive impairment. *The Lancet, 367*(9518), 1262–1270. doi: 10.1016/s0140-6736(06)68542-5.

Glaesmer, H., Riedel-Heller, S., Braehler, E., Spangenberg, L., & Luppa, M. (2011). Age- and gender-specific prevalence and risk factors for depressive symptoms in the elderly: a population-based study. *International Psychogeriatrics, 23*(8), 1294–1300.

Gold, M. R., Stevenson, D., & Fryback, D. G. (2002). HALYs and QALYs and DALYs, oh my: similarities and differences in summary measures of population health. *Annual Review of Public Health, 23*(1), 115–134. doi: 10.1146/annurev.publhealth.23.100901.140513.

Grady, C. L., & Craik, F. I. (2000). Changes in memory processing with age. *Current Opinion in Neurobiology, 10*(2), 224–231.

Greve, W., & Staudinger, U. M. (2006). Resilience in later adulthood and old age: resources and potentials for successful aging. In: D. Cichetti and D. Cohen (Eds.), *Developmental psychopathology, vol 3, Risk, disorder and adaptation*. Hoboken, MJ: John Wiley & Sons, Inc., pp 796–840.

Gruenberg, E. M. (1977). The failures of success. *The Milbank Memorial Fund Quarterly. Health and Society, 55*(1), 3–24.

Hampstead, B. M., Sathian, K., Phillips, P. A., Amaraneni, A., Delaune, W. R., & Stringer, A. Y. (2012). Mnemonic strategy training improves memory for object location associations in both healthy elderly and patients with amnestic mild cognitive impairment: a randomized, single-blind study. *Neuropsychology, 26*(3), 385.

Hanson, J. C., & Lippa, C. F. (2009). Lewy body dementia. *International Review of Neurobiology, 84,* 215–228.

Havighurst, R. (1961). Successful aging: definition and measurement. *Journal of Gerontology, 16*(2), 134–143.

Havighurst, R. J. (1963). Successful aging. *Processes of Aging: Social and Psychological Perspectives, 1,* 299–320.

Houston, D. K., et al. (2008). Dietary protein intake is associated with lean mass change in older, community-dwelling adults: the Health, Aging, and Body Composition (Health ABC) Study. *The American Journal of Clinical Nutrition, 87*(1), 150–155.

Hybels, C. F., Blazer, D. G., & Pieper, C. F. (2001). Toward a threshold for subthreshold depression. An analysis of correlates of depression by severity of symptoms using data from an elderly community sample. *The Gerontologist, 41*(3), 357–365.

Johnson, C. L. (2000). Perspectives on American kinship in the later 1990s. *Journal of Marriage and Family, 62*(3), 623–639.

Keyes, C. L. M. (2002). The mental health continuum: from languishing to flourishing in life. *Journal of Health and Social Behavior,* 43(2), 207–222.

Keyes, C. L. M. (2007). Promoting and protecting mental health as flourishing: a complementary strategy for improving national mental health. *American Psychologist, 62,* 95–108.

Kobasa, S. C., Maddi, S. R., & Kahn, S. (1982). Hardiness and health: a prospective study. *Journal of Personality and Social Psychology, 42*(1), 168.

Kyobutungi, C., Egondi, T., & Ezeh, A. (2010). The health and well-being of older people in Nairobi's slums. *Global Health Action, 3*(Suppl. 2), 45–53.

Li, Y. (2013). *Global aging issues and policies: Understanding the importance of comprehending and studying the aging process.* Springfield, IL: Charles C. Thomas Publisher, Inc.

Lindström, B., & Eriksson, M. (2005). Salutogenesis. *Journal of Epidemiology and Community Health, 59*(6), 440–442.

Lindström, B., & Eriksson, M. (2006). Contextualizing salutogenesis and Antonovsky in public health development. *Health Promotion International, 21*(3), 238–244.

Lipsitt, L. P., & Demick, J. (2011). Resilience science comes of age: old age, that is. *PsycCRITIQUES, 56*(26). doi: 10.1037/a0023900.

Lopez, A. D., Mathers, C. D., Ezzati, M., Jamison, D. T., & Murray, C. J. L. (2006). Global and regional burden of disease and risk factors, 2001: systematic analysis of population health data. *The Lancet, 367*(9524), 1747–1757.

Luppa, M., Sikorski, C., Luck, T., Ehreke, L., Konnopka, A., Wiese, B., ... Riedel-Heller, S. G. (2012). Age-and gender-specific prevalence of depression in latest-life – systematic review and meta-analysis. *Journal of Affective Disorders, 136*(3), 212–221.

Maharaj, P. (2013). *Aging and health in Africa.* New York: Springer Publishing.

Marmot, M. (2005). Social determinants of health inequalities. *The Lancet, 365*(9464), 1099–1104.

Marmot, M., & Bell, R. (2016). Social inequalities in health: a proper concern of epidemiology. *Annals of Epidemiology, 26*(4), 238–240.

McKee, P. L. (1982). *Philosophical foundations of gerontology.* New York: Human Sciences Press, Inc.

McKhann, G. M., Knopman, D. S., Chertkow, H., Hyman, B. T., Jack Jr, C. R., Kawas, C. H., ... Mayeux, R. (2011). The diagnosis of dementia due to Alzheimer's disease: recommendations from the National Institute on Aging–Alzheimer's Association workgroups on diagnostic guidelines for Alzheimer's disease. *Alzheimer's & Dementia, 7*(3), 263–269.

Melgar, N., & Rossi, M. (2013). Happiness among the elderly, the Latin American case. In: Y. Li (Ed.), *Global aging issues and policies: Understanding the importance of comprehending and studying the aging process.* Springfield, IL: Charles C. Thomas Publisher, Ltd., pp 354–370.

Merriam-Webster.com (2015). http://www.merriam-webster.com

Montross, L. P., Depp, C., Daly, J., Reichstadt, J., Golshan, S., Moore, D., ... Jeste, D. V. (2006). Correlates of self-rated successful aging among community-dwelling older adults. *The American Journal of Geriatric Psychiatry, 14*(1), 43–51.

Moody, H. R., & Sasser, J. R. (2012). *Aging: Concepts and controversies.* Los Angeles: Sage.

Morley, J. E. (2004). A brief history of geriatrics. *The Journals of Gerontology Series A: Biological Sciences and Medical Sciences, 59*(11), 1132–1152. doi: 10.1093/gerona/59.11.1132.

Mulley, G. (2012). A history of geriatrics and gerontology. *European Geriatric Medicine, 3*(4), 225–227. doi: http://dx.doi.org/10.1016/j.eurger.2012.06.007.

Pinquart, M., & Sörensen, S. (2000). Influences of socioeconomic status, social network, and competence on subjective well-being in later life: a meta-analysis. *Psychology and Aging, 15*(2), 187.

Rebok, G. W., Carlson, M. C., & Langbaum, J. B. (2007). Training and maintaining memory abilities in healthy older adults: traditional and novel approaches. *The Journals of Gerontology Series B: Psychological Sciences and Social Sciences, 62*(Special Issue 1), 53–61.

Reuben, D. B., Judd-Hamilton, L., Harris, T. B., & Seeman, T. E. (2003). The associations between physical activity and inflammatory markers in high-functioning older persons: MacArthur studies of successful aging. *Journal of the American Geriatrics Society, 51*(8), 1125–1130.

Roberts, R., Kaplan, G., Shema, S., & Strawbridge, W. (1997). Prevalence and correlates of depression in an aging cohort: the Alameda county study. *Journal of Gerontology: Social Sciences, 52B*(5): S252–S258.

Román, G. C., Erkinjuntti, T., Wallin, A., Pantoni, L., & Chui, H. C. (2002). Subcortical ischaemic vascular dementia. *The Lancet Neurology, 1*(7), 426–436.

Rosenberg, I. H. (1997). Sarcopenia: origins and clinical relevance. *The Journal of Nutrition, 127*(5), 990S–991S.

Rowe, J. W., & Kahn, R. L. (1997). Successful aging. *The Gerontologist, 37*(4), 433–440.

Rubinstein, R. L., & de Medeiros, K. (2014). 'Successful aging', gerontological theory and neoliberalism: a qualitative critique. *The Gerontologist, 55*(1), 34–42. doi: 10.1093/geront/gnu080.

Scully, J. L. (2004). What is a disease? *EMBO Reports, 5*(7), 650–653. doi: 10.1038/sj.embor.7400195.

Seeman, T. E., Crimmins, E., Huang, M.-H., Singer, B., Bucur, A., Gruenewald, T., ... Reuben, D. B. (2004). Cumulative biological risk and socio-economic differences in mortality: MacArthur studies of successful aging. *Social Science & Medicine, 58*(10), 1985–1997.

Seeman, T. E., Lusignolo, T. M., Albert, M., & Berkman, L. (2001). Social relationships, social support, and patterns of cognitive aging in healthy, high-functioning older adults: MacArthur studies of successful aging. *Health Psychology, 20*(4), 243.

Shmotkin, D. (1990). Subjective well-being as a function of age and gender: a multivariate look for differentiated trends. *Social Indicators Research, 23*(3), 201–230.

Simmons, S. J. (1989). Health: a concept analysis. *International Journal of Nursing Studies, 26*(2), 155–161.

Stafford, M., Cummins, S., Macintyre, S., Ellaway, A., & Marmot, M. (2005). Gender differences in the associations between health and neighbourhood environment. *Social Science & Medicine, 60*(8), 1681–1692. doi: http://dx.doi.org/10.1016/j.socscimed.2004.08.028.

Thane, P. (2000). *Old age in English history: Past experiences, present issues.* Oxford: Oxford University Press.

Troyer, A. K., Murphy, K. J., Anderson, N. D., Moscovitch, M., & Craik, F. I. (2008). Changing everyday memory behaviour in amnestic mild cognitive impairment: a randomised controlled trial. *Neuropsychological Rehabilitation, 18,* 65–88.

Wagnild, G. M., & Collins, J. A. (2009). Assessing resilience. *Journal of Psychosocial Nursing & Mental Health Services, 47*(12), 28–33. doi: 10.3928/02793695-20091103-01.

Werner, E. E., & Smith, R. S. (1982). *A longitudinal study of resilient children and youth.* New York: McGraw-Hill.

WHO (2015a). *World health statistics 2015.* Geneva, Switzerland: WHO.

WHO (2015b). *World report on ageing and health.* Geneva, Switzerland: WHO.

FIVE

Rethinking family and family structures

Families are a source of affective bonds, of shared responsibilities such as caregiving for young and old and of intergenerational transfers of wealth and experience. Family structures and kinship relationships can determine power structures and how power is transferred when one ages and dies. As was discussed in Chapter Three, families can also be sources of violence, of abuse and of oppression, although the topic of abuse is seldom discussed in the context of family. How 'family' is conceptualized, both formally and informally, is an important topic in gerontology. Understanding old age within family and kin structures and practices (for example, marriage, number of children) adds insight into role expectations in later life, including older people's positions within families, expectations for care both by and for older and younger members and expectations about living arrangements.

In thinking about families and aging, it is important to understand how family and kin have been defined and how those definitions have changed over time. This chapter will therefore begin with an overview of the family and kin structure with regard to later life, including trends in marriage and other partnered relationships, sibling and later life, and grandparenting. It will then briefly address misconceptions about the family. Finally, it will look at living arrangements (place and aging are discussed in detail in Chapter Seven) and will briefly cover caregiving in the family context. Overall, the chapter will highlight ways in which gerontology's assumptions about 'productivity' and social connectedness based on family roles have led to overlooking many important aspects to be considered with regard to age and kin.

Family, kin, aging and the life course

Until fairly recently, 'family' in the research literature has commonly been defined and conceptualized in terms of the nuclear unit of father, mother and children under the legal age of independence (for example, 18 years) (Malinowski, 1930; Fox, 1967; Baum & Page, 1991; Bould, 1993). This has led to what many have called a narrow view of family and missed opportunities to understand the complexities embedded within the concept. Addressing this shortcoming, Rosemary Blieszner and Victoria Bedford (2012) offer the following definition of family: 'a set of relationships determined by biology, adoption, marriage and, in some societies, social designation and existing even in the absence of contact or affective involvement, and, in some cases, even after the death of certain members' (p 4). This definition is meant to capture conceptions of family that go beyond legal definitions, that otherwise exclude older members (for example, nuclear family) or that fail to recognize new types of partnerships, such as same-sex couples, that comprise 'family'.

Other concepts related to family include extended family, multigenerational family and kin networks. 'Extended family' describes 'a relational experience involving a group of people who are kin related in some way, regardless of how they are organized in terms of living arrangements' (Vicente & Sousa, 2009, p 29) or a 'social system made of various independent but interacting (nuclear and/or multigenerational) family units' (Vicente & Sousa, 2009, p 29). Although extended family is often used interchangeably with 'multigenerational family', there is a difference. 'Multigenerational family' describes a living arrangement containing three or more generations or 'people connected by family ties who live together, made up of several generations' (Vicente & Sousa, 2009, p 29). In other words, extended family refers to relationships, while multigenerational family refers to who lives with whom.

Finally, kinship originally referred to networks among people defined by 'blood' relationship (Malinowski, 1930; Fox, 1967; Wolf, 1988). The concept of kin, however, has been expanded to include friends and other non-blood relatives who are recognized by another as being family despite the lack of a legal or sanguine bond (Weston, 2013) – a bond sometimes referred to as 'fictive kin' (Ibsen & Klobus, 1972; MacRae, 1992; Chatters, Taylor, & Jayakody, 1994; Taylor, Chatters, Hardison, & Riley, 2001).

Although families have changed over time, most notably in overall size and geographical proximity of members, Blieszner and Bedford (2012) observe that 'most people around the world grow up and grow old in the context of family life, a pattern that has not changed over the centuries' (p 4). When thinking about aging and families, it is important to consider two aspects: (1) aging individuals and their relationships with family and (2) families and the role of aging individuals within them. Both aspects support the idea of 'linked lives' embedded in the lifecourse perspective (Elder, 1975; Settersten Jr, 1999). Bengston and colleagues (2012) describe the lifecourse as 'a sequence of age-linked transitions that are embedded in social institutions and history.' (p 10). The lifecourse affects the individual and the family since individuals have roles within families that change over time, and families in turn shape those roles and responsibilities. On the positive side, changes in family structure, the roles of individuals within families and the roles of families within communities can lead to new potential and previously undefined roles and opportunities. On the negative side, such changes can lead to uncertainty about the position of older people in relation to other family members and of families in relation to their older members (Phillipson, 2013). To better look at the positives and negatives of changing families, the following subsections will address individuals and relationships within families and the roles of aging individuals within families. These include marriages and other partnered relationships, relationships with siblings, adult children and parents, and grandparents.

Marriage

Marriage is a relationship with social and legal distinction that confers particular rights, benefits and obligations (Bookwala, 2012). Although marriage was exclusively applied to heterosexual couples in the past, in 2001 the Netherlands became the first country in the world to grant same-sex couples the full legal rights of marriage, followed by Belgium (Smith, 2006). Given the relative newness of this status, most datasets currently include same-sex couples in categories other than 'married', which can complicate research findings relative to things such as health and marital status. Although this oversight will certainly change in future research, it is important to be aware of it when reading the research literature.

According to the United Nations (United Nations, 2013), 64% of people aged 60 years and over were married in 2012 in less-developed regions in the world, as compared to 60% in more-developed regions. In both areas, approximately 80% of men age 60 and over were married, as compared to around 60% of women. The percentage of married men in least-developed countries is higher than the world average, while the percentage of married women in the same regions is substantially lower (United Nations, 2013). In Africa, 85% of men aged 60 and over were married, as compared to only 38% of women. In 2008, around 40% of women aged 65 and over were widowed, as compared to around 20% of men (Kinsella, Wan, & US Bureau of the Census, 2009). There is a well-established link between better health and wellbeing for older married men, although this link is not so clear for women. There are also links between higher rates of loneliness and depression and widowhood for women (Kinsella et al, 2009). With regard to marital satisfaction and older age, some research findings mirror findings regarding happiness (discussed in Chapter Four) and loneliness in later life (discussed in Chapter Six), whereby satisfaction has a U shape: higher levels of satisfaction are found in younger and older adults, as compared to middle-aged adults (Carstensen, Gottman, & Levenson, 1995; Henry, Berg, Smith, & Florsheim, 2007). Happiness, as discussed in Chapter Four, is greatest for younger and older people. Loneliness, as discussed later, is greatest among middle-aged adults, as compared to younger and older people, although loneliness may increase for people aged 80 and over (Newall et al, 2009). The reasons for these levels of marital satisfaction may be due to marriages ending in middle age rather than later life, or other reasons not yet fully understood.

Studies suggesting that marriage holds unique mortality benefits as compared to cohabitation include a large Finnish study by Seppo Koskinen and colleagues (Koskinen, Kaisla, Tuija, & Pekka, 2007). In this study, the researchers found that working-age and older people who were married had lower mortality rates than people who were living alone, cohabitating with another or living with someone other than a partner. In addition, having no children was associated with increased mortality in all groups. Recent research in the United States has come to similar conclusions. Theodore Fuller (2010), for example, found that cohabitating persons had poorer health status than either married or single counterparts, although lacking a live-in partner seemed to have greater negative effects on women than on men. Although it is important to consider cohabitation with regard to healthcare outcomes, marital trends in cohorts who are aged 65 and over suggest that cohabitation is not likely to have an effect for some years to come.

Other partnered relationships

Other partnered relationships include legal recognition of civil unions, cohabitating relationships where couples choose to live without marriage and 'living apart together' (LAT) relationships. LAT relationships are ones 'in which a couple does not share the same household but the two individuals define themselves and are defined by their social network as a couple' (Bookwala, 2012, p 92). Jamila Bookwala, citing works by Marion Willetts (2006), suggests a similar U-shaped relationship between age and relationship satisfaction for heterosexual couples in long-term cohabitating relationships, similar to the work by Carstensen and colleagues (1995) and other discussed earlier (Henry et al, 2007). Although there is a lack of research on same-sex older couples, US survey data comparing gay and lesbian cohabitating couples with heterosexual married couples in their 30s and 40s found little difference in satisfaction between the two groups

(Kurdek, 2004). An interesting finding from Lawrence Kurdek's work was that same-sex couples negotiated household issues such as cleaning and family rituals on grounds that did not involve gender roles (for example, based on availability rather than gender).

Siblings

Siblings can include offspring of the same parents or one of the same parents (biological and adopted), or those who do not legally share a parent (that is, quasi-siblings such as foster children). Within families, sibling ties have longer durations than others (Van Gaalen, Dykstra, & Flap, 2008; Bedford & Avioli, 2012). In addition, the more siblings within a family, the less the interaction that adult children have with their older parents (Van Gaalen et al, 2008). Female siblings, those who have never married (compared to siblings who have married) and siblings living nearby (compared to those living far away) are the most likely to provide instrumental support to parents (Bedford & Avioli, 2012; Baum & Page, 1991). Siblings have also been found to be an important part of family for people who do not have children, which will be discussed later in the chapter (Wenger, Scott, & Patterson, 2000).

Adult children and parents

The topic of adult children and their older parents has formed the majority of the literature on family relationships and aging, especially with regard to caregiving. Adult children can be an important source of instrumental support, caregiving and affective bonds. As mentioned in Chapter Three, older adults in Western industrialized cultures typically prefer living independently from their adult children, although they may receive social, caregiving and other types of support (for example, financial) and there is a long, historical tradition for this (Cole, 1992; Thane, 2010). Historically, adult children did, however, provide support and in some cases in medieval and early modern Europe were required to by law (Crowther, 1982; Thane, 2010).

In contrast, many cultures in Africa, Asia and Latin America practice co-residence, whereby older adults do have an expectation of support and care from their children in later life. In developing countries in these geographical areas, households, which include extended families, are the primary source of financial support and caregiving (Apt, 2002; Bongaarts & Zimmer, 2002). Part of the relationship between adult children and parents in non-Western countries is guided by deeply rooted values of filial piety (Knodel & Nguyen, 2015) or 'unconditional material and emotional support for parents' (Cheung & Kwan, 2009, p 180). Support includes financial support, caregiving, showing respect and obedience. Some countries such as China have included filial obligations by adult children to their older parents in legislation (Bongaarts & Zimmer, 2002; Cheung & Kwan, 2009). In countries with a patrilineal family structure, sons and their wives are responsible for care (for example, China, India) (Bongaarts & Zimmer, 2002). In countries with a bilateral family system, daughters play an important role in care and support (for example, Thailand, Cambodia) (Knodel & Nguyen, 2015). Despite a culturalized notion of care embedded in the value of filial piety, abuse does occur, as mentioned in Chapter Three (Soeda & Araki, 1999; Oh, Kim, Martins, & Kim, 2006). Therefore it important not to simply view family support as always positive but to consider risk factors for abuse, regardless of the cultural setting.

Grandparents

Although the position of 'grandparent' within a family is not dependent on chronological age it can serve as a marker for one to acquire the social label of being 'old', as mentioned in Chapter One. As such, there has been extensive research in gerontology on grandparents, with much of the focus on grandmothers in particular. To date, there have been few studies on lesbian, gay, bisexual or transgendered grandparents (see Orel & Fruhauf, 2013 for a review).

The function of grandparents has been described as supporters and carers of the younger generation (Timonen & Arber, 2012). Just after World War Two, when housing was scarce and unemployment was high for returning soldiers, Hans Von Hentig (1946) wrote: 'Again the grandmother in countless cases stands ready to shelter the divorcee and her children, to receive children and grandchildren in her home when apartments cannot be found, or the man is out of work. The lower mobility of the older generation renders her more shock-proof to the contingencies and fortunes of industrial life. The rural habitat of grandmothers is another asset in war and the postwar crisis' (p 391). Grandmothers were looked upon to provide assistance by providing housing during a time of housing shortages, and in the form of care for grandchildren to further alleviate financial burden and provide a needed service. Von Hentig goes on to write, 'She [the grandmother] assumes – temporarily at least – a vital role in the life of the family, a primitive, but effective mechanism of group survival' (p 392). Despite competing discourses of panic at the growing percentage of aging women in many developing countries, the function that grandmothers could potentially serve was viewed positively.

This 'productive' role of grandmothers in particular later gained support in biological research. George C. Williams (1957), in writing about the biological underpinnings of senescence, made an observation that would later become the 'grandmother hypothesis'. In short, when contemplating why certain mammals should survive past their reproductive capabilities (for example, female primates), Williams concluded the following:

> At some time during human evolution it may have become advantageous for a woman of forty-five or fifty to stop dividing her declining faculties between the care of extant offspring and the production of new ones. A termination of increasingly hazardous pregnancies would enable her to devote her whole remaining energy to the care of her living children, and would remove childbirth mortality as a possible cause for failure to raise these children. Menopause, although apparently a cessation of reproduction may have arisen as a reproductive adaptation to a life-cycle already characterized by senescence, unusual hazards in pregnancy and childbirth, and a long period of juvenile dependence. (p 408)

The grandmother hypothesis, which continues to attract research interest, asserts that grandmothers serve an evolutionary function, supplementing care to young members of the family to insure their survival. Since men can theoretically continue to reproduce throughout their lives and yet tend to live shorter lives than women, they are not part of this proposed evolutionary imperative.

In less-developed countries, the role of grandparents has taken on an increasingly important role with regard to child rearing as a result of migration and chronic disease. In many places in Asia and Africa, migration of parents from rural to urban areas has meant that care for the children has been delegated to the grandparents, usually the grandmother (Knodel & Nguyen, 2015). In many African countries, devastation caused by the HIV/AIDS epidemic has also led to increased care of grandchildren by their grandparents, due to the death of parents or inability of parents to provide care for their young children (Duflo, 2003; Mwanyangala et al, 2010; Pillay & Maharaj, 2013; Zihindula & Maharaj, 2013). As mentioned later in the subsection on skip-generation households, grandparents raising grandchildren is also becoming more widespread in developed countries (Baugh, Taylor, & Bates, 2016).

Overall, grandparents continue to play an important role in family life throughout the world. Given that much of the focus has been on grandmothers, future research would benefit by taking a closer look at grandfathers and their contributions to the family (Thompson, 2007; Thompson, 1999) as well as at whether grandparent contributions differ by social location factors such as social class.

Misconceptions about family

It is a commonly held belief that families have deteriorated over time, contributing to social instability. John Bongaarts and Zachary Zimmer (2002), Edward Thompson (1999), Isobella Aboderin (2004), Sarah Harper (2006) and many others point to the myths surrounding 'family', its alleged decline and assumptions about older people based on these misconceptions, many of which are based on non-contextualized demographic, economic and living arrangement data. As discussed earlier, misinterpretation of data (for example, marriage statistics) can obscure other important interactions between family members.

One example that challenges the 'decline of family' view comes from John Bongaarts and Zachary Zimmer (2002), who challenge modernization and convergence theory. In referencing William Goode's (1963) convergence theory of family structure, Bongaarts and Zimmer (2002) explain that Goode had predicted that as economies expanded through industrialization, the nuclear family would become more of an independent unit as ties to extended family members (for example, older members) weakened. In many respects, this echoes Donald Cowgill and Lowell Holmes' (1972) modernization theory (discussed in Chapters Two and Three), since both the convergence and modernization theories suggest that older members became devalued with the onset of industrialization. However, modernization and convergence theories make assumptions that may not actually be realized. First, in the case of convergence theory, there is an assumption that physical proximity is necessary for instrumental and emotional support among family members. Bongaarts and Zimmer's data point to strong ties between family members, despite distance. Also challenged is the notion that older people lose their status within the family when societies become modernized. Given the importance of grandparents (specifically grandmothers) as primary caregivers for their grandchildren, the modernization theory is challenged.

Edward Thompson (1999) also addresses the myth of the decline in the extended family. Referencing texts from his early training in sociology, Thompson writes that major scholars 'asserted that in the past most human beings had lived in extended family households, and the nuclear family was a modern development, a functional adaptation to the needs of modern Western industrial societies' (p 472). This myth, he explains, was later refuted by historical demographers in the 1960s, who found that nuclear families had been dominant since the Middle Ages. Pat Thane (2000) has a similar observation, writing that 'the tenacity of the belief that in the past families were the mainstay of older people is matched only by the conviction that in the late twentieth century such support is dwindling and vanishing, propelled by greater ease of movement, by the demand of paid work on sons, and especially daughters, and growing divorce rates' (p 12).

Thompson (1999) provides an overview of ways in which the discourse on the declining extended family has been revived and countered into the present, often with government policy being enacted as a means to 'preserve the family'. Yet, as he points out, what may be behind the myths of declining family is the misuse or misunderstanding of data. He uses the example of births outside of marriage to illustrate this point, arguing that one cannot assume that children born outside of traditional marriage are somehow not part of extended family networks or that care for these children is not being provided by grandparents or other family members. In short, data outside of the larger social context can easily be misread.

Isabella Aboderin (2004) addresses another misconception about family based on modernization theory. She cites the origin of what later became Cowgill and Holmes' (1972) theory in work by Ernest Burgess (1960). Using demographic and anecdotal data from five countries – the United Kingdom, the United States, France, Italy and the Netherlands – Burgess linked rising divorce rates and overall increased poverty to declining familial support of older family members, thereby creating a need for government assistance. Citing an extensive literature, she argues that what has been overlooked is that industrialization led to new forms of poverty, making it such that families could no longer afford to care for themselves, let alone additional members. It is therefore an issue not of want or value but, in many cases, of economic necessity. Although older people's status hasn't changed, families' abilities to provide monetary support for older family members may have. Also embedded in this assumption is that older people need to be supported by their families. As Pat Thane (2000) has observed, historically, the needs of older people have changed. She writes: 'Older people more often lead generally independent lives, less dependent upon families for sociability or care, if at all, until later in life, than in earlier generations' (p 12). Finally, Sarah Harper (2006) argues that the myth of families as 'loose, multigenerational collections of individuals, experiencing more emotional strain, as fewer children are available to take care of elderly parents' (p 22) is not entirely true. Instead, she writes that 'rather than the demise of the family, however, more heterogeneous forms of family are emerging from the reality of population aging. These alternative structures include multigenerational relationships and members not formerly defined as kin' (pp 24–25). According to Harper, families aren't fractured, they're just evolving or changing into new types of units. Divorce, for example, doesn't mean isolation of one part of the family from another but, rather, can lead to new opportunities for expanded family networks, to include remarriage, development of closer social ties with extended family or cohabitation with others to form new family types. Nana Apt (2002), for example, notes that 'the most striking feature of traditional care systems in Asia, Latin America and Africa is that they are rooted in complex family systems that include reciprocal care and assistance among the generations, with older people not only on the receiving end but also fulfilling an active, giving role. This pattern is changing. Nevertheless, and in spite of the cultural imbalance in modern times, developing country observers would agree that the emotional ties and economic support among family members remain relatively strong, certainly in comparison with industrialized countries' (p 41). This supports Thompson's (1999) and Aboderin's (2004) arguments that change in families does not equate to negative outcomes for older people.

People without children

The phrase 'people without children' is being used in lieu of 'childless' or 'childfree', since both imply values related to having children. In addition, it should be noted that data on people without children is available only for women and is gathered through historical censuses, survey data or vital registrations (Dykstra, 2009). The Organisation for Economic Cooperation and Development (OECD, 2011) reports an increase in women without children who were born in the 1960s or later, as compared to those born in the 1950s. However, other evidence suggests that rates of women without children are not increasing among younger cohorts (those born between 1960 and 1964), as compared to earlier cohorts (Dykstra, 2009) and that the pattern of having children takes on a U shape. For example, in Australia, 31% of women born between 1900 and 1910 did not have children, as compared to 16% for those born between 1960 and 1964. In Finland, 26% of women born between 1905 and 1909 did not have children, as compared to

19% for those born between 1960 and 1964 (Dykstra, 2009). Reasons for the difference could be due to inaccurate records, in both the past and the present. The important aspect of considering people without children is that they are a group who have only recently begun to be the focus of robust research and are not a group often considered in the public discourse about family.

Even when they are studied, people without children are generally limited to women since men's fertility is more complicated to ascertain. Although research on men without children is lacking, G. Clare Wenger and colleagues (2000), in their study of older people in England who did not have children, found that older men and married couples experienced a negative impact on their social networks. Single women, in contrast, had robust social networks. Since women with higher levels of education are more likely to not have children than are women with lower levels of education, their social networks may be positively affected (OECD, 2011).

Assumptions about familial care, including programs and policies directed at family caregiving, may need to be reconsidered, since many assume a nuclear family model based on child–parent care. Siblings and other friends and relatives as potential sources for instrumental care and social networks among older adults who don't have children have only recently begun to gain attention (Rubinstein, 1987; Koropeckyj-Cox, 2002; Koropeckyj-Cox & Call, 2007; Dykstra, 2009; Albertini & Mencarini, 2014).

Families and living arrangements

This section will provide more discussion on living arrangements, including changes over time, types of living arrangements and key considerations. Several people have pointed out that ideas about family often overlap with living arrangements, which can lead to false assumptions about who comprises family and how families operate. For example, if research emphasis is placed on family members who live together, the roles of non-cohabitating family are not well understood. Another challenge has been looking at proximity of family as a proxy to outcomes such as loneliness or social connectivity (Teachman, Tedrow, & Crowder, 2000; Russell, 2009; Blieszner & Bedford, 2012; Bookwala, 2012). Assumptions based on both living arrangements (for example, living alone) and proximity (for example, adult child living far away) have been critiqued as supporting stances that people who live alone are lonely and that those who do not live close to family do not receive social or other forms of support. These will be discussed briefly later in the chapter.

Living arrangements describes the people with whom one lives (such as, spouse, family members, friends, no one) (Foley, 1980). Living arrangements may be culturally dictated (for example, living with extended family), the result of economic status (for example, publicly subsidized housing, living in one's own home), individually selected and managed and so on. As mentioned earlier, living arrangements alone do not provide a full picture of aging or the experience of the older person with regard to family and social network.

Cohabitation and living alone

Living independently (alone or with a spouse) is preferred by many older adults, especially in Western countries. The United Nations (United Nations, 2013) estimates that 40% of the world's population aged 60 and over live independently. In more developed countries, around 75% of older adults live independently, as compared to only 10% in least-developed regions. In Africa, around 78% of males aged 65 and over live with a spouse, as compared to only 24% of females. These percentages are roughly similar for Asia and Latin America: 78% of men and 32% of women lived with a spouse in Asia and 70% of men and 34% of women lived with a spouse in Latin America (Bongaarts & Zimmer, 2002).

Living alone in later life is common in Western countries, although it is relatively rare in many Asian countries (Ng & Northcott, 2015). In Canada, around 30% of people aged 65 and over live alone, compared to only around 5% who live with families (Ng & Northcott, 2015). For older people living with others, the majority of the time (85% for men, 69% for women) they are the head of the household (United Nations, 2013).

Living alone has been thought to contribute to increased loneliness, since it is assumed that maintaining one's social connectedness is contingent on a person's ability to visit others (for example, proximity to friends and families, access to transportation). Others suggest, though, that it is not living alone per se that contributes to loneliness but, rather, the lack of having an intimate partner (Russell, 2009) or social networks (Stephens, Alpass, Towers, & Stevenson, 2011). (See Chapter Six.)

Currently, most older people who live alone are female, partially due to women's greater longevity and cultural customs of marrying older men. This is true for many places in the world. For example, Natashya Pillay and Pranitha Maharaj (2013) write: 'What is striking in selected African countries is the disparity between older men and women who live alone. For instance, in Egypt, older women (16%) are four times more likely than older men (4%) to live alone. In Ethiopia, older women (10%) are five times more likely than older men (2%) to live alone, and in Sudan and Nigeria more than twice as many older women live alone than men' (p 47). They note that women who live alone are far less advantaged than men, since they likely lack financial support, may be at security risk and may lack social ties, depending on their situations.

Multi-generation households

As mentioned earlier, co-residence with an adult child in a multigenerational household is determined by kin structures (that is, patrilineal or bilateral) (Bongaarts & Zimmer, 2002). Cultural expectations of living arrangements in later life are believed to have a strong relationship with health beliefs. For example, Hoang Van Minh and colleagues (2010) found that in Vietnam, having more people living in the same family had positive impacts on the health beliefs of the older members. This was due to the expectation that one should live in a multi-generation house. A person who expects to live in a multigenerational household but ends up living alone is likely to face more negative outcomes, such as loneliness. This would not likely be the case for someone who expected and preferred to live alone.

Skip-generation households

One important phenomenon is that of the skip-generation household. Skip-generation households are households composed of grandparents and grandchildren, where the grandchildren's parents are absent (Zimmer, 2009; Knodel & Nguyen, 2015). In sub-Saharan Africa, it has been estimated that one in four grandparents live with a grandchild whose parents are absent, mostly attributable to HIV/AIDS-related mortality of the middle generation (Zimmer, 2009). In the United States, more than 2.5 million grandparents reported being the head of the household and responsible for their grandchildren (Baugh et al, 2016).

Caregiving

Some aspects of care practices within families were addressed in the earlier sections on individuals and relationship within families, such as grandparents and adult children. This section will briefly address caregiving within families. Contrary to popular belief, most older people are not in need of substantial help with care. In the United States, for example, fewer than 7% of non-institutionalized people aged 65 and over needed help with personal care (CDP, 2015). Fewer than 4% of people aged 65 and over live in nursing homes in the United States and in most countries of the world (Ribbe et al, 1997; CDC, 2015). (See Chapter Seven for a definition of 'nursing home' and other housing types.) In Thailand, 88% of survey respondents aged 60 and over reported not needing any help with personal care or with climbing steps or walking (Knodel, Chayovan, & Prachuabmoh, 2011). Need greatly increases with age, with people aged 85 years and over much more likely to need help with the activities of daily living (such as bathing, eating, dressing, toileting, and transferring from a bed to a chair) than those between the ages of 65 and 84 years.

Most care (for example, help with activities of daily living and others) is provided by women, regardless of the age of the care recipient. Even paid caregiving jobs are predominantly occupied by women, usually at low wage. For older people, most direct care is provided by wives, daughters and daughters-in-law (Hequembourg & Brallier, 2005), although sons may provide financial support for such care. In contrast to government support, family members contribute the most to caring for older people throughout the world. According to Klaus Haberkern, Tina Schmid and Marc Szydlik (2015), families provide 80% of care work in Southern and Eastern European countries, 64% in Germany and 40% in Denmark. Because women on average live longer than men, women are often providers of care for their spouse (if they are married) but do not see that care reciprocated. Relocation of children, increasing numbers of women who do not have children, loss of children due to illness or accident, or other reasons therefore put older women in the position of increased risk of needing non-familial caregiving. Suhita Chatterjee and colleagues (2008) point out that even in Japan, which has traditionally espoused strong ideals of familial piety, caregiving is increasingly being outsourced from families to paid caregivers.

Another important caregiving phenomenon is that of the 'sandwich generation'. This describes family members who are caring for younger children and aging family members (Neal, Chapman, Ingersoll-Dayton, & Emlen, 1993; Neal, Hammer, Pines, Bodner, & Cannon, 2013). Often, these family members are also in the formal workforce, which may add to burden and stress.

Caregiving has received extensive coverage in the research literature, although generally from the perspective of the caregiver rather than the care recipient. Topics such as caregiver burden (Pinquart & Sörensen, 2003) and health risks associated with providing care are among the most common, especially in the context of dementia. It is beyond the scope of the *Short Guide* to review the caregiving literature, since much of it falls within the scope of nursing, social work or allied professions. However, it should be noted that, despite the abundance of caregiving literature, the perspectives of older people who receive care are surprisingly lacking.

Summary

Although the idea of family may seem straightforward at first, there are many considerations with regard to how family is defined, how families are studied and what expectations exist within family networks. Defining 'family' strictly in terms of sanguine or blood relationships overlooks the many types of non-kin yet familial bonds that exist, including non-biological children, partners and close friends who may be providing instrumental and emotional support to people in later life. Broadening definitions of family can also expose false assumptions based on changes in family structure, such as termination of marriages or declining numbers of married couples. Looking at these figures alone can provide a false outlook on the status of family, pointing to a decline, when such a decline in the broader notion of family may not exist.

Other important areas of family include relationships of adult children and parents, including older adults' views of their relationships rather than research focused on support only. As the role of grandparents increases around the world, it is important to include the perspective of grandfathers as well as grandmothers and to critically consider the role of grandparents in the family life cycle. Additional considerations include families and living arrangements, which, on the surface, may also be misinterpreted. For example, the assumption that people residing in multigenerational families are less lonely than people living alone has not been demonstrated in the research literature. Instead of viewing living arrangements alone, it is important to include the larger cultural context of individual expectations and relationships with family members. As family compositions and definitions continue to evolve, understanding families from a comprehensive perspective will become increasingly important.

Further reading

Bedford, V. H., & Blieszner, R. (2012). *Handbook of families and aging* (2nd edn). New York: Praeger.

Bongaarts, J., & Zimmer, Z. (2002). Living arrangements of older adults in the developing world an analysis of demographic and health survey household surveys. *The Journals of Gerontology Series B: Psychological Sciences and Social Sciences, 57*(3), S145–S157.

Harper, S. (2004). *Families in ageing societies: A multi-disciplinary approach*. New York: Oxford University Press.

Weston, K. (2013). *Families we choose: Lesbians, gays, kinship*. New York: Columbia University Press.

References

Aboderin, I. (2004). Modernisation and ageing theory revisited: current explanations of recent developing world and historical Western shifts in material family support for older people. *Ageing and Society, 24*(1), 29–50. doi: 10.1017/S0144686X03001521.

Albertini, M., & Mencarini, L. (2014). Childlessness and support networks in later life new pressures on familistic welfare states? *Journal of Family Issues, 35*(3), 331–357.

Apt, N. A. (2002). Ageing and the changing role of the family and the community: an African perspective. *International Social Security Review, 55*, 39–47.

Baugh, E. J., Taylor, A. C., & Bates, J. S. (2016). Grandparents raising grandchildren. In C. Sheehan (Ed.), *The Wiley Blackwell encyclopedia of family studies* (Vol. 4). Madison, WI: Wiley Blackwell, pp. 993–1001.

Baum, M., & Page, M. (1991). Caregiving and multigenerational families. *The Gerontologist, 31*(6), 762–769. doi: 10.1093/geront/31.6.762.

Bedford, V.H. & Avioli, P. S. (2012). Sibling relationships from midlife to old age. In: V. H. Bedford, & R. Blieszner (Eds.), *Handbook of families and aging* (2nd edn). New York: Praeger, pp 125–151.

Bengston, V. L., Elder Jr, G. H., & Putney, N. M. (2012). The life course perspective on ageing: linked lives, timing, and history. In: J. Katz, S. Peace & S. Spurr (Eds.), *Adult lives: A life course perspective*. Bristol: Policy Press, pp 9–17.

Blieszner, R., & Bedford, V. H. (2012). The family context of aging. In: V. H. Bedford & R. Blieszner (Eds.), *Handbook of families and aging* (2nd edn). New York: Praeger, pp 3–8.

Bongaarts, J., & Zimmer, Z. (2002). Living arrangements of older adults in the developing world: an analysis of demographic and health survey household surveys. *The Journals of Gerontology Series B: Psychological Sciences and Social Sciences, 57*(3), S145–S157.

Bookwala, J. (2012). Marriage and other partnered relationships in middle and late adulthood. In: V. H. Bedford, & R. Blieszner (Eds.), *Handbook of families and aging* (2nd edn). New York: Praeger, pp 91–125.

Bould, S. (1993). Familial caretaking a middle-range definition of family in the context of social policy. *Journal of Family Issues, 14*(1), 133–151.

Burgess, E. W. (1960). *Aging in western societies*. Chicago, IL: University of Chicago Press.

Carstensen, L. L., Gottman, J. M., & Levenson, R. W. (1995). Emotional behavior in long-term marriage. *Psychology and Aging, 10*(1), 140.

CDC (Centers for Disease Control) (2015). Nursing home care. Retrieved 15 December 2015, from http://www.cdc.gov/nchs/fastats/nursing-home-care.htm

CDP (Center for Disease Prevention) (2015). *Older persons' health*. Atlanta, GA: CDP.

Chatterjee, S. C., Patnaik, P., & Chariar, V. M. (2008). *Discourses on aging and dying*. New Delhi, India; Thousand Oaks, CA: SAGE Publications.

Chatters, L. M., Taylor, R. J., & Jayakody, R. (1994). Fictive kinship relations in black extended families. *Journal of Comparative Family Studies, 25*(3), 297–312.

Cheung, C.-K., & Kwan, A. Y.-H. (2009). The erosion of filial piety by modernisation in Chinese cities. *Ageing and Society, 29*(2), 179–198.

Cole, T. R. (1992). *The journey of life: A cultural history of aging in America*. New York: Cambridge University Press.

Cowgill, D. O., & Holmes, L. D. (1972). *Aging and modernization*. New York: Appleton-Century-Crofts.

Crowther, M. A. (1982). Family responsibility and state responsibility in Britain before the welfare state. *The Historical Journal, 25*(01), 131–145.

Duflo, E. (2003). Grandmothers and granddaughters: old-age pensions and intrahousehold allocation in South Africa. *The World Bank Economic Review, 17*(1), 1–25.

Dykstra, P. A. (2009). Childless old age. In: P. Uhlenberg (Ed.), *International handbook of population aging*. New York: Springer, pp 671–690.

Elder, G. H. (1975). Age differentiation and the life course. *Annual Review of Sociology*, 1, 165–190.

Foley, D. L. (1980). The sociology of housing. *Annual Review of Sociology*, 6, 457–478.

Fox, R. (1967). *Kinship and marriage: An anthropological perspective*. Cambridge: Cambridge University Press.

Fuller, T. D. (2010). Relationship status, health, and health behavior: an examination of cohabiters and commuters. *Sociological Perspectives*, 53(2), 221–246.

Goode, W. J. (1963). *World revolution and family patterns*. New York: Free Press Glencoe.

Haberkern, K., Schmid, T., & Szydlik, M. (2015). Gender differences in intergenerational care in European welfare states. *Ageing and Society*, 35(2), 298–320. doi: 10.1017/S0144686X13000639.

Harper, S. (2004). *Families in ageing societies: A multi-disciplinary approach*. New York: Oxford University Press,.

Harper, S. (2006). Mature societies: planning for our future selves. *Daedalus*, 135(1), 20–31.

Henry, N. J. M., Berg, C. A., Smith, T. W., & Florsheim, P. (2007). Positive and negative characteristics of marital interaction and their association with marital satisfaction in middle-aged and older couples. *Psychology and Aging*, 22(3), 428.

Hequembourg, A., & Brallier, S. (2005). Gendered stories of parental caregiving among siblings. *Journal of Aging Studies*, 19(1), 53–71. doi: http://dx.doi.org/10.1016/j.jaging.2003.12.001.

Ibsen, C. A., & Klobus, P. (1972). Fictive kin term use and social relationships: alternative interpretations. *Journal of Marriage and Family*, 34(4), 615–620.

Kinsella, K. G., Wan, H., & US Bureau of the Census (2009). *An aging world: 2008*. Washington, DC: US Department of Commerce, Economics and Statistics Administration, US Census Bureau.

Knodel, J., & Nguyen, M. D. (2015). Grandparents and grandchildren: care and support in Myanmar, Thailand and Vietnam. *Ageing and Society*, 35(9), 1960–1988. doi: 10.1017/S0144686X14000786.

Knodel, J., Chayovan, N., & Prachuabmoh, V. (2011). Impact of population change on the well-being of elderly in Thailand. In: G. Jones & W. Imem (Eds.), *The impact of demographic change in Thailand,* report 48. UNFPA, Thailand, pp. 35–63.

Koropeckyj-Cox, T. (2002). Beyond parental status: psychological well-being in middle and old age. *Journal of Marriage and Family, 64*(4), 957–971. doi: 10.1111/j.1741–3737.2002.00957.x.

Koropeckyj-Cox, T., & Call, V. (2007). Characteristics of older childless persons and parents – cross-national comparisons. *Journal of Family Issues,* 1362–1414. doi: DOI 10.1177/0192513X07303837.

Koskinen, S., Kaisla, J., Tuija, M., & Pekka, M. (2007). Mortality differences according to living arrangements. *International Journal of Epidemiology, 36*(6), 1255–1255.

Kurdek, L. A. (2004). Are gay and lesbian cohabiting couples really different from heterosexual married couples? *Journal of Marriage and Family, 66*(4), 880–900.

MacRae, H. (1992). Fictive kin as a component of the social networks of older people. *Research on Aging, 14*(2), 226–247.

Malinowski, B. (1930). 17. Kinship. *Man, 30,* 19–29. doi: 10.2307/2789869.

Mwanyangala, M. A., Mayombana, C., Urassa, H., Charles, J., Mahutanga, C., Abdullah, S., & Nathan, R. (2010). Health status and quality of life among older adults in rural Tanzania. *Global Health Action, 3*(Suppl 2), 36–44.

Neal, M. B., Chapman, N. J., Ingersoll-Dayton, B., & Emlen, A. C. (1993). *Balancing work and caregiving for children, adults, and elders* (Vol. 3). Thousand Oaks, CA: Sage Publications.

Neal, M. B., Hammer, L. B., Pines, A. M., Bodner, T. E., & Cannon, M. L. (2013). Working Caregivers in the 'Sandwiched Generation'. In: J. Field, R.J. Burker, & C. Cooper (Eds.), *The SAGE handbook on aging, work and society.* Los Angeles: Sage Publications, pp 329–347.

Newall, N. E., Chipperfield, J. G., Clifton, R. A., Perry, R. P., Swift, A. U., & Ruthig, J. C. (2009). Causal beliefs, social participation, and loneliness among older adults: a longitudinal study. *Journal of Social and Personal Relationships, 26*(2–3), 273–290.

Ng, C. F., & Northcott, H. C. (2015). Living arrangements and loneliness of South Asian immigrant seniors in Edmonton, Canada. *Ageing and Society, 35*(3), 552–575. doi: 10.1017/S0144686X13000913.

OECD (2011). *Doing better for families*. Paris: OECD.

Oh, J., Kim, H. S., Martins, D., & Kim, H. (2006). A study of elder abuse in Korea. *International Journal of Nursing Studies, 43*(2), 203–214.

Orel, N. A., & Fruhauf, C. A. (2013). Lesbian, gay, bisexual, and transgender grandparents. In: A.E. Goldberg & K.R. Allen (Eds.), *LGBT-parent families: Innovation in research and implications for practice*. New York: Springer, pp 177–192.

Phillipson, C. (2013). *Ageing*. Cambridge: Polity.

Pillay, N. K., & Maharaj, P. (2013). Population ageing in Africa. In: P. Maharaj (Ed.), *Aging and health in Africa*. New York: Springer, pp 11–51.

Pinquart, M., & Sörensen, S. (2003). Associations of stressors and uplifts of caregiving with caregiver burden and depressive mood: a meta-analysis. *The Journals of Gerontology Series B: Psychological Sciences and Social Sciences, 58*(2), P112–P128.

Ribbe, M. W., Ljunggren, G., Steel, K., Topinkova, E. V. A., Hawes, C., Ikegami, N., ... Jónnson, P.V. (1997). Nursing homes in 10 nations: a comparison between countries and settings. *Age and Ageing, 26*(Suppl. 2), 3–12.

Rubinstein, R. L. (1987). Childless elderly: theoretical perspectives and practical concerns. *Journal of Cross-cultural Gerontology, 2*(1), 1–14.

Russell, D. (2009). Living arrangements, social integration, and loneliness in later life: the case of physical disability. *Journal of Health and Social Behavior, 50*(4), 460–475.

Settersten Jr, R. A. (1999). *Lives in time and place: The problems and promises of developmental science*. Amityville, NY: Baywood Publishing Co.

Smith, S. D. (2006). Global families. *Families in Global and Multicultural Perspective, 2*, 3–24.

Soeda, A., & Araki, C. (1999). Elder abuse by daughters-in-law in Japan. *Journal of Elder Abuse & Neglect, 11*(1), 47–58.

Stephens, C., Alpass, F., Towers, A., & Stevenson, B. (2011). The effects of types of social networks, perceived social support, and loneliness on the health of older people: accounting for the social context. *Journal of Aging and Health*, 23(6), 887–911. doi: 0898264311400189.

Taylor, R. J., Chatters, L. M., Hardison, C. B., & Riley, A. (2001). Informal social support networks and subjective well-being among African Americans. *Journal of Black Psychology, 27*(4), 439–463.

Teachman, J. D., Tedrow, L. M., & Crowder, K. D. (2000). The changing demography of America's families. *Journal of Marriage and Family, 62*(4), 1234–1246.

Thane, P. (2000). *Old age in English history: Past experiences, present issues*. Oxford: Oxford University Press.

Thane, P. (2010). The history of aging and old age in 'Western' cultures. In: T. Cole, R.E. Ray, & R. Kastenbaum (Eds.), *A guide to humanistic studies in aging: What does it mean to grow old?* Baltimore: Johns Hopkins University Press, pp 33–56.

Thompson, E. H. (2007). Older men as invisible men in contemporary society. In: B.A. Arrighi (Ed.), *Understanding inequality: The intersection of race/ethnicity, class, and gender*. London: Rowman & Littlefield Publishers, Inc., pp 289–298.

Thompson, P. (1999). The role of grandparents when parents part or die: some reflections on the mythical decline of the extended family. *Ageing and Society, 19*(4), 471–503.

Timonen, V., & Arber, S. (2012). Introduction: a new look at grandparenting. *Contemporary grandparenting: Changing family relationships in global contexts*. Bristol: Policy Press.

United Nations, Population Division (2013). *World population ageing 2013,* Department of Economic and Social Affairs, ST/ESA/SER.A/348, New York: United Nations.

Van Gaalen, R. I., Dykstra, P. A., & Flap, H. (2008). Intergenerational contact beyond the dyad: the role of the sibling network. *European Journal of Ageing, 5*(1), 19–29.

Van Minh, H., Byass, P., Chuc, N. T. K., & Wall, S. (2010). Patterns of health status and quality of life among older people in rural Vietnam. *Global Health Action, 3*(Suppl. 2), 64–69.

Vicente, H., & Sousa, L. (2009). The multigenerational family and the elderly: a mutual or parasitical symbiotic relationship? In: L. Sousa (Ed.), *Families in later life: Emerging themes and challenges*. New York: Nova Science Publishers, pp. 27–48.

Von Hentig, H. (1946). The sociological function of the grandmother. *Social Forces*, 24(4), 389–392.

Wenger, G. C., Scott, A., & Patterson, N. (2000). How important is parenthood? Childlessness and support in old age in England. *Ageing and Society, 20*(2), 161–182.

Weston, K. (2013). *Families we choose: Lesbians, gays, kinship*. New York: Columbia University Press.

Willetts, M. C. (2006). Union quality comparisons between long-term heterosexual cohabitation and legal marriage. *Journal of Family Issues, 27*(1), 110–127.

Williams, G. C. (1957). Pleiotropy, natural selection, and the evolution of senescence. *Evolution, 11*(4), 398–411. doi: 10.2307/2406060.

Wolf, D. A. (1988). Kinship and family support in aging societies. In: *Social and economic consequences of population aging*. New York: UN Department of International Economic Social Affairs.

Zihindula, G., & Maharaj, P. (2013). Understanding the experiences of the elderly in rural areas in Rwanda. In: P. Maharah (Ed.), *Aging and health in Africa*. New York: Springer, pp 197–209.

Zimmer, Z. (2009). Household composition among elders in sub-Saharan Africa in the context of HIV/AIDS. *Journal of Marriage and Family, 71*(4), 1086–1099.

SIX

Death, grief, loss and loneliness

How death is viewed – its social meaning – is as much of a cultural construction as are other aspects of the lifecourse (Platt & Persico, 1992). For example, is death a disease to be overcome, the final point in the lifecourse, the start of a new spiritual journey (Chatterjee, Patnaik, & Chariar, 2008)? As mentioned in previous chapters, old age is often associated with death; death is taboo in many Western cultures. As Robert Butler (1974) wrote some 40 years ago, 'Western man's [sic] consummate dream of immortality if fulfilled by religion while integration of the aging experience into his life process remains incomplete. Increasing secularization produces a frightening void which frequently is met by avoiding and denying the thought of one's own decline and death and by forming self-protective prejudices against old people' (p 530).

Of course, death is not universally viewed as a final ending. Some cultural beliefs see death as the start of another phase (Tilak, 1989; Chatterjee et al, 2008), a transition that holds important meaning. It may not be the death in itself that becomes problematic in some cultures but, rather, the timing of death. For example, Stephen Sapp

(2010) addresses death in the Indian context. In referencing the Vedic roots of modern Hinduism in Indian culture, he argues that although many of the Vedic views have changed over time, 'the association of old age with a good life – or more properly that untimely or premature death is still viewed in a negative light' (p 124). He describes how death before age 60 was considered '*akal mrityu* or "untimely death"', understood to be a result of bad *karma* – of past sins … In addition, dying "young" prevents one both from reaching the stage of life in which enlightenment is most likely to be reached and from satisfying the accumulated debt of karma, which will then carry over into subsequent incarnations' (p 124). Death, therefore, marks the passage from one incarnation to another. The longer one lives, the more able he or she is to work toward a more favorable incarnation in the next life.

In contrast to the Hindu view, John Vincent (2003) and others argue that age is viewed so negatively *because* of its ties to illness and death (West & Glynos, 2014). Since old age always ends in death, the meaning of old age is tied to death. Also, since death in modern society is now concentrated in older age, as compared to other historical periods, the meaning of old age has become increasingly connected to the postponement of death and pro-longevity movements (Vincent, 2003).

Presenting yet another view, Gene Cohen (2009) addresses loss in later life not as the start of irreversible decline leading toward death, but as a motivation for change. He writes, 'There is nothing romantic about loss, but it is part of the human condition that when we experience a decline in a capacity that we cannot restore, we often attempt to transcend this loss by tapping into or developing new strategies' (p 427). According to Cohen, loss, including the death of another, can lead to positive change within, a notion that is further elaborated in Chapter Nine, on narratives and creativity in later life. In addition, the anticipation of loss can also lead one to invest one's self into the future. In the context of generativity (see Table 2.1), generative acts can be thought of as ways to preserve aspects of the self through investments in future generations (Charmaz, 1999; de Medeiros, 2009).

Despite these positives, gerontology has struggled with disentangling itself from the fear of death, of loss of self and of changes in external identity that may come with advancing age (West & Glynos, 2014). Gary Kenyon, Jan-Eric Ruth and Wilhelm Mader (1999) have written about the importance of separating death from aging. They write that 'the first important point about death, then, is that is must be distinguished from the aging process. This point may be generally understood in the gerontological community, namely, that aging is not dying and not death' (p 48).

Yet, separating death from aging leads to additional challenges. More specifically, despite the fact that (or perhaps because) aging is implicitly paired with loss, many books on gerontology do not address death, grief and loneliness as well as other forms of loss. When chapters about death are addressed in gerontology texts, they often appear at the end of the book. This is perhaps likely due to overzealous efforts, described earlier, to combat the image of aging as a time of decline, by overly stressing the positive aspects of growing old. The fact that grief and loss are part of aging, however, makes these topics important ones to address.

Although meanings and rituals associated with death have played an important role in anthropology (Kaufman, 2000; Kaufman & Morgan, 2005) and in the development of thanatology (or the study of death and dying) (Meagher & Balk, 2013), death in gerontology is generally limited to two areas: planning end-of-life (Carr & Khodyakov, 2007; West & Glynos, 2014) and suicide (Pearson & Conwell, 1996; Cattell, 2000; Kjølseth, Ekeberg, & Steihaug, 2010). Walter (2008) has suggested that

> social scientists know far more about communication with middle-aged cancer patients than with old people suffering from dementia; far more about premature bereavement than elderly bereavement; far more about counselling services frequented by middle-class clients than about working-class styles of coping; far more about adjustment to death and loss by privileged Westerners than by sub-Saharan Africans. Such are the biases that have dominated death studies. Researchers, like Western societies at large, have ignored their own elderly, their own poor, the poor half of the world, and those made

stateless by exile or war – all of whom experience death and loss disproportionately often. (pp 329–330)

This chapter begins with a brief overview of how death, grief and loss became structured and problematized in older age to the point where they are not often addressed in gerontology. In contrast, a term often associated with the experiences of death, such as late-life loss – loneliness – has remained a topic of concern perhaps because effective interventions can potentially be used, making loneliness a 'problem' that can potentially be fixed. The chapter will then examine two other death-related topics – suicide and eldercide. Overall, the chapter argues for more research and attention to be paid to death and its surrounding issues.

The problem of death and aging

As the satirical online journal *The Onion* (1997) noted, 'despite the enormous efforts of doctors, rescue workers and other medical professionals worldwide, the global death rate remains constant at 100 percent' (Onion, 1997). As has been well noted in the literature, death at home was common in most countries prior to industrialization in the 19th century and the rise of the hospitals and payment systems for such services. Recent writing about death and aging has therefore been focused more on end-of-life care – with special emphasis on dying in hospitals – than on death itself (West & Glynos, 2014). Karen West and Jason Glynos (2014) argue that 'contemporary "talk about death" is all too readily assimilated to "talk about control over the end of life", rather than opening up to "talk about losses" that accompany the ageing process in the flow of life itself' (p 2). This is true for gerontology as well. This chapter will therefore not address end-of-life care but instead will focus on other aspects of death and related loss.

A major issue related to death and dying, and perhaps the reason it is often overlooked in gerontology, is due to anxiety about death. Adrian Tomer and Grafton Eliason (2000) define death anxiety as 'a negative emotional reaction provoked by the anticipation of a state in which the self does not exist' (p 4). This is similar to Kathy Charmaz's (1999) description of suffering as the loss of self. In proposing a model of death anxiety, Tomer and Eliason list the following components. They first describe three determinants of death anxiety: past regret, future regret and the meaningfulness of death. The first two types of regret refer to goals that haven't been fulfilled, either in the past or future, because of death. The meaningfulness of death describes whether the person makes sense of death (such as, Is death senseless? Is there a purpose to death?). According to their model, one can modify death anxiety into death salience by: '1) directly activating feelings of regret and thoughts concerning the meaningfulness of death, 2) by affecting the determinants by modifying one's beliefs about the self and/or the world'; and 'by activating a variety of coping mechanisms such as the life review, ... identification with one's culture' and others (p 6).

This model points to some interesting perspectives within gerontology that are often not explicitly linked to death. These include the life review (Butler, 1963; Butler, 2002b), which was mentioned in Tomer and Eliason's (2000) death anxiety model, generativity (Erikson, 1950; Erikson & Erikson, 1997) and socio-emotional selectivity theory (Carstensen, 1991; Carstensen, 1993), all of which were briefly introduced in Table 2.1. The life review describes 'a personal process by which a person evaluates his or her life as it nears its end' (Butler, 2002a, p 1). The life review was first identified by Butler as a positive coping mechanism used by older adults as they approached death. It involves recalling and possibly resolving past conflicts, but not to an obsessive point to where one becomes burdened with guilt about the past. Instead, the life review can lead to death salience if one is able to come to peace with past conflicts in a way that makes sense within that person's belief system (Tomer & Eliason, 2000).

Generativity, or the idea of investing oneself into the future, can be a way of lessening death anxiety by first placing some meaning on one's life (for example, I have done something that will benefit future generations) and establishing a sense of permanency in the face of death. It can be a way of staving off the perception of a total loss of self and instead bring in a restorative element (Erikson, 1950; de Medeiros, 2009; Rubinstein, Girling, de Medeiros, Brazda, & Hannum, 2014). The last perspective, socio-emotional selectivity theory, hypothesizes that people nearing the end of life choose to invest in activities that are emotionally salient (for example, personal relationships) rather than activities that are not (Carstensen, 1993). Investment in emotionally important relationships can add the component of meaningfulness that, in the model, influences death salience.

Culture also plays an important part in how death is viewed and experienced. For example, fear of having a spirit linger after death is very real for many and such beliefs can have great effect on the experience of the dying (Lamb, 1997; Sapp, 2010). In contrast to the view that death marks a new beginning, a lingering spirit can also be problematic. Sarah Lamb (1997), for example, points out that in North India,

> After death, there is also the considerable danger that a person with too many attachments will cling on to his or her former habitat and relations in the form of a lingering ghost or *bhut*. People said that if a person has not been able to "cut" the ties of *maya* before dying, then his or her soul may continue to hang around his former home and relations, unable to leave. Several told of the suffering of such ghosts: how they become confused, hungry, and trapped, and painfully long to be reunited with their former households. (p 286)

In this case, how one dies has implications not only in the present but also in the future. Dying without the proper closure could result in unnecessary suffering in the afterlife.

Overall, talk about death is missing in gerontology, with most focus being on how people die (for example, end-of-life care and planning) rather than on personal views about the meaning of death (Carr & Khodyakov, 2007). Given the high likelihood of death anxiety, which could possibly be remediated or at least lessened by life reviews and personally important interactions with others, death is an important area for gerontology to be concerned with.

Bereavement, grief and mourning

The problem of death also extends to the emotions surrounding death, such as bereavement, grief and mourning. As Neil Small, Jeanne Katz, and Jennnifer Hockey (2001) write, 'Within Anglophone Western societies, the late twentieth century saw much attention being given to grief and mourning as mental health "problems" that could be "solved". This is often thought to represent an attitudinal shift in these areas' (pp 1–2). Following is a brief discussion of each of these three concepts and how they apply to our understanding of older age.

Bereavement

Bereavement is defined by Small and colleagues (2001) as

> the state of being bereaved or deprived of something; that is, bereavement identifies the objective situation of individuals who have experienced a loss. Both the noun bereavement and the adjective bereaved derive from a less-familiar root verb, reave, which means 'to despoil, rob or forcibly deprive' (OED, 1989, vol 13, p 295) . In short, a bereaved person is one who has been deprived, robbed, plundered or stripped of something. (Small et al, 2001)

Grief

Grief differs from bereavement in that grief is a response to loss, whereas bereavement refers to the person who has experienced that loss. Charles Corr and colleagues (1997), as cited by Small et al (2001), define grief as 'the response to loss. When one suffers a loss, one grieves. The word grief signifies one's reaction, both internally and externally, to the impact of loss ... The term grief is often defined as "the emotional response to loss"' (Small et al, 2001, p 5). Carolyn Jacobs and colleagues (2000) define grief as 'a form of attachment behavior that occurs in the circumstances of a death. Grief includes the emotional, cognitive, and somatic aspects of a person's response to a death' (p 186). Small and colleagues (2001) write:

The opening lines of Douglas Dunn's poem "December" bid the reader to write their grief into their poetry until there is none left, a task which may take many years. His lines indicate a sea change in the attitudes of the English speaking Western world to grief and mourning. It reflects an emergent postmodern view that grief can accompany what remains of a lifetime. The message here is clear, that grief is work, and that this is not necessarily bad, nor time limited. On the contrary it suggests that it might fruitfully occupy the time of mourners and even be productive in some way. The explicit expression of this perspectives (the assumption that grieving could be productive and indeed constitute legitimate creativity) is something of a departure from the popular assumption that grieving should be time limited and that one can expect to recover from loss. (p 1)

Although they are not referring to old age in particular, they describe grief in terms of an action rather than a passive emotion. In other words, one doesn't passively experience loss; one reacts to it (grieves).

Mourning

Mourning is the social expression of grief (Stroebe & Schut, 1998). It is the process through which one copes with grief and loss. Mourning is not the same as grief, but it is associated with grief (Small et al, 2001). It is how grief is made known. Culture, including familial norms and societal expectations – as has been stated throughout the book – forms the ways in which grief is expressed, and the supports available to and attitudes toward the grieving person are shaped by familial and societal expectations (Platt & Persico, 1992).

With regard to bereavement, grief and mourning and aging, the major focus has been on whether grief leads to depression and, if so, how grief should be clinically treated. Margery Hegge and Cheryl Fischer (2000) report conflicting research on grief and depression in widowed older adults in particular. As they mention, early literature suggested that older widows were better able to cope with loss because of having many age-related role models. Other literatures cited older adults as being at higher risk of depression because of losses that have cumulated over their lifetime, making the loss of a spouse or friend even more difficult for an older person than for a younger one. There has been surprisingly little research on grief in general in older adults since 2005, with many studies linked specifically to widowhood, grief in the context of the bigger topic of depression or links between grief and morbidity (Stroebe & Schut, 1998; Jacobs, 2000).

Loneliness

Although death is a topic often avoided in the gerontological literature, loneliness is one that receives much attention, to the point where loneliness is assumed to be a part of later life. Loneliness is commonly defined as 'a subjectively experienced aversive emotional state that is related to the perception of unfulfilled intimate and social needs' (Luanaigh & Lawlor, 2008, p 1213). Christina Victor and colleagues (2005) describe a sense of loneliness as being 'associated with an individual's evaluation of their overall level of social interaction, and describes a deficit between the actual and desired quality and quantity of social engagement' (p 359). Loneliness is often linked to changes in social networks through loss over time as well as changes in social location and place (discussed in Chapter Seven). Older people are commonly believed to experience loneliness at higher levels than their younger counterparts do. In addition, loneliness has also been linked to negative health consequences such as major depression and cardiovascular disease (Pinquart & Sörensen, 2001; Alli & Maharaj, 2013). However, as mentioned in Chapter Five, work by Newall and colleagues (2009) suggests loneliness in relation to age has a U-shaped pattern with younger and older people reporting lower levels of loneliness than middle-aged people.

Martin Pinquart and Silvia Sörensen (2001) make some important distinctions with regard to definitions and ideas surrounding loneliness. First, they point out that loneliness is generally defined in one of two ways: (1) distress due to the perceived absence of social interactions and (2) a disconnect between the social relationships a person believes he or she has and the type of relationships that person is seeking. In the latter, one could be surrounded by people and have an extensive social network yet still feel lonely. How loneliness is defined will have a direct relationship to how it is studied.

Connor Luanaigh and Brian Lawlor (2008) cite prevalence rates of loneliness in British community studies to between 5% and16% for people aged 65 and over. They mention that others studies have found a median rate of 9–10% (Luanaigh & Lawlor, 2008). In terms of risk for loneliness, they report that females are lonelier than men; non-married men and women have higher rates of loneliness than married men and women. Bereavement is also believed to be a risk for loneliness, due to loss of a spouse or close friend. Finally, according to their research, people aged 75 and over are more likely to report being lonely than people aged 65 to 74 (Luanaigh & Lawlor, 2008).

Christina Victor and colleagues (2005) also examined the prevalence of loneliness. In their study, 7% of their survey responders (all of whom were aged 65 or over) described themselves as being often or always lonely, a figure they described as stable when compared to earlier studies. In other words, prevalence of loneliness had not increased for people in this age group as compared to the same age groups in earlier studies. In addition, they also examined risk factors for loneliness in later life in Great Britain and came to three conclusions that differed slightly from the research literature. First, they found that loneliness in later life mirrored loneliness patterns from earlier life. People tended to have long-established patterns of feeling lonely that stayed with them into old age; people who were lonely at earlier ages continued to be lonely in later ages. Also, they did not find an association between loneliness and social networks, which had been reported in other large studies (Pinquart & Sörensen, 2001). Second, they did find a subgroup of people aged 75 and over who reported loneliness in response to the loss of a friend or spouse or declining health. Finally, they found a subgroup whose loneliness declined over time rather than increased, which can challenge previously established assumptions about loneliness in older people. Overall, they conclude that there are different types of loneliness with different pathways of onset (such as old-age onset, which occurs in response to losses) and the continuation of life-long patterns of loneliness. Regardless of cause, loneliness does have implications for quality of life.

Like grief and bereavement, loneliness is also very culturally and contextually based. For example, Nana Apt (2013), in reference to several studies on African countries, reports that the migration of working-age children to urban areas has created a new loneliness for the older people left behind in rural areas and that this is creating a new health problem for older people who already are disadvantaged in many ways. Most authors do agree that a better understanding of loneliness, and possible interventions, are needed.

Care at the end of life

As mentioned in the beginning of the chapter, much of the gerontological literature on death is related to end-of-life care and death practices (for example, euthanasia, physician-assisted suicide, suicide), which are considered in the next section. As with many topics in the *Short Guide*, there is a vast research literature on care at the end of life. Many of the concerns with end-of-life care involve inadequate treatment of pain and fear of suffering, discussions of life-extending treatments that compromise overall wellbeing, and end-of-life planning. These will be briefly discussed in this section but are not the focus of the chapter.

A big issue associated with end-of-life care, one that relates to physician-assisted suicide and other forms of death, involves pain. Pain has been described as 'an experience of the body, though most people will also experience emotional pain' (de Medeiros & Black, 2015, p 181). Herta Flor (2001) defines pain as 'unpleasant sensory and emotional experience associated with actual or potential tissue damage or described in terms of such damage' (p 1099). Lucia Gagliese and colleagues (Gagliese & Melzack, 1997; Gagliese, 2009) have argued that pain in older adults differs from pain in younger adults particularly because of the higher likelihood of poorer health outcomes and increased co-morbid conditions in older versus younger adults. In addition, Gagliese (2009) suggests that 'given the increased vulnerability associated with aging it is reasonable to expect that pain would differ with age in important, clinically relevant ways ... The processes of aging, in interaction with the biopsychosocial substrates of pain, result in an experience – geriatric pain – that is sufficiently different from that of younger people' (p 344). Pain is also highly personal. One person's level of pain is not necessarily the same as another's with the same condition. Assessing pain can therefore pose unique challenges (Mao, 2009).

Pain is important in the context of death, since avoidance of pain is cited by many as a reason behind wishes to die and is an indirect goal of end-of-life planning, namely to avoid unnecessary pain through invasive interventions that will prolong life (Lynn & Adamson, 2003; Lorenz et al, 2008). Pain operates almost in opposition to death anxiety. Fear of pain could lead someone to choose death over pain, despite fear of death. Fear of pain could also lead people to better planning. For example, Deborah Carr and Dmitry Khodyakov (2007) found that people who have survived the painful death of a loved one were more likely to have some formal directions regarding end-of-life care in place than those who did not. Also influencing end-of-life-care planning were gender (females are more likely to do formal planning), increasing age, higher education level and married status (Carr & Khodyakov, 2007).

Suicide and eldercide

Suicide is another important topic related to death and aging. Suicide is often associated with younger ages. However, suicide in older people is increasing. Suicide rates for people aged 55 and over have been reported to be higher than for younger people in many industrialized countries in the world (Waern, Rubenowitz, & Wilhelmson, 2003). Margda Waern and colleagues (Waern et al, 2003) report that by 2020, suicide is expected to be the tenth most common cause of death. Men tend to have higher suicide rates than women. Also, loss and bereavement are often causally attributed to increased suicide, although many studies have not supported this. In a qualitative study based on friends of suicide victims in Norway, Ildri Kjølseth and colleagues (Kjølseth et al, 2010) found that informants reported that feelings that life wouldn't improve, due to bodily decline, or that part of themselves had disappeared were linked to men's suicides.

Table 6.1 presents the number of deaths through intentional harm for several countries for three age groups: 15–24 years, 55–74 years and 75+ years. Although none of the countries show more suicides in the 75+ group, Japan, the Republic of Korea, the Russian Federation and the United States all have much higher numbers of suicides in the 55 to 74 age group than in the younger one. The reasons for the higher suicide rates are not clear. Some studies cite untreated depression as an underlying cause (Blair-West & Mellsop, 2001; Waern et al, 2003). Other studies point to changes in support systems (for example, access to care) and family changes (such as loss of a spouse), although this is still an area that is not well understood.

Suicide is important to consider in the context of gerontology for several reasons. As stated, little is known about the reasons why people in some countries commit suicide at higher rates. It is unclear, for example, whether fear of aging, fear of pain, untreated depression, fear of dependency or other issues are driving these decisions. When thinking back on the broader topic of health and subjective wellbeing, one can argue that suicide represents a missing component and should be the focus of more research.

Eldercide and death hastening

Although there has been some attention paid to suicide in older people, eldercide or the purposeful killing of older people, is not an issue that is often discussed. Eldercide can include death through neglect (for example, failure to provide food) or violence. Although often thought of as a 'pre-modern' activity linked to competition for food and other essential resources, eldercide is still openly practiced in some areas of the world, and more covertly practiced in others.

Work done in the 1980s by Anthony Glascock and Susan Feinman (1981) reported that half of the societies they analyzed practiced death-hastening of 'decrepit' older people: 38% abandoned them, 19%

denied them food and 23% denied all support. These societies tended to be non-agricultural and located in harsh climates. In contrast, the other half of the societies they examined were supportive of their older citizens (Glascock, 1990).

Table 6.1: A comparison of 2009 suicide rates by age groups for selected countries

Country	15–24 years	55–74 years	75+ years
Argentina	773	546	202
Australia	276	465	178
Brazil	1,613	1,572	353
Canada	479	872	228
Czech Republic	97	415	177
Denmark	28	217	96
Germany	564	3,066	1,729
Japan	1,931	10,803	3,865
Norway	69	150	43
Republic of Korea	1,009	4,177	1,926
Russian Federation	5,471	7,156	2,667
Saudi Arabia	21	3	0
South Africa	113	42	7
United States	4,371	8,726	2,941

Source: http://apps.who.int/healthinfo/statistics/mortality/whodpms/.

Perhaps the most obvious form of eldercide today is the practice of 'witch burning' in several socioeconomically deprived regions. Edward Miguel (2005), for example, examined witch killings in Tanzania and reported that 3,072 accused witches were killed during the years 1970 to 1988. This amounts to over two-thirds of all murders for that time period. In addition, 80% of the victims were women whose median age was between 50 and 60 years. Killing older women who are accused of witchcraft has also been documented in Kenya, Mozambique, Uganda, Zimbabwe, Andean regions in South America and in India (Miguel,

2005). Cott Van and Donna Lee (2000) also report that killing older people who are considered to be a burden is practiced in some Andean regions in Bolivia and Colombia, although it is technically against the law in both countries.

Although elder abuse is a topic that is gaining recognition, eldercide is not. Estimates of eldercide are difficult for several reasons. Since death is most common in later life, the death of an older person is generally not questioned, especially if there are no visible signs of violence. It can be culturally taboo to question a family with regard to the death of older members, since such questions may imply a level of guilt on the part of the family member. Finally, some have argued that because of older people's generally lower social status, they are not in positions that garner much attention in order to raise suspicion.

Summary

The topic of death is often not addressed in gerontology for several reasons. Fear of death has been cited as a reason why there is a general fear of aging. In order to combat fear of aging, death – with the exception of end-of-life planning and causes – is generally not discussed or studied in the context of aging overall. Yet, death and its correlates bereavement, grief and mourning are part of the aging process, as older people will encounter cummulative losses over their lifetimes. Another important concept is loneliness, which many assume is to be expected with age but may actually be misunderstood. Research has pointed to loneliness more as a lifetime experience, not as one associated with age alone. Reduced social networks and other losses may certainly contribute to loneliness in older individuals, but loneliness is not an inevitable part of aging. Finally, suicide and eldercide have had mixed attention. Suicide has gained some research interest, although there is no clear understanding with regard to why many older people put an end to their lives at high rates in some countries. Also not well understood or reported is eldercide; its prevalence rate is unknown. Overall, if death is the last part of the lifecourse, it deserves a more prominent place within the gerontological literature.

Further reading

Luanaigh, C. Ó., & Lawlor, B. A. (2008). Loneliness and the health of older people. *International Journal of Geriatric Psychiatry, 23*(12), 1213–1221.

Small, N., Katz, J., & Hockey, J. (2001). *Facing death: Grief, mourning and death ritual.* Philadelphia: Open University Press.

West, K., & Glynos, J. (2014). 'Death talk', 'loss talk' and identification in the process of ageing. *Ageing & Society, FirstView*, 1–15. doi:10.1017/S0144686X14001184.

References

Alli, F., & Maharaj, P. (2013). The health situation of older people in Africa. In: Pranitha Maharaj (Ed.), *Aging and health in Africa.* New York: Springer, pp 53–89.

Apt, N. (2013). Older people in rural Ghana: health and health seeking behaviours. In: Pranitha Maharaj (Ed.), *Aging and health in Africa.* New York: Springer, pp 103–119.

Blair-West, G. W., & Mellsop, G. W. (2001). Major depression: does a gender-based down-rating of suicide risk challenge its diagnostic validity? *Australian and New Zealand Journal of Psychiatry, 35*(3), 322–328. doi: 10.1046/j.1440-1614.2001.00895.x.

Butler, R. N. (1963). The life review: an interpretation of reminiscence in the aged. *Psychiatry, 26*(1), 65–76.

Butler, R. N. (1974). Successful aging and the role of the life review. *Journal of the American Geriatrics Society, 22*(12), 529–535.

Butler, R. N. (2002a). Age, death, and life review. In: J. Doka (Ed.), *Living with grief: Loss in later life.* Washington, DC: Hospice Foundation of America, pp. 3–11.

Butler, R. N. (2002b). The life review. *Journal of Geriatric Psychiatry, 26*(1), 65–76.

Carr, D., & Khodyakov, D. (2007). End-of-life health care planning among young-old adults: an assessment of psychosocial influences. *The Journals of Gerontology Series B: Psychological Sciences and Social Sciences, 62*(2), S135–S141.

Carstensen, L. L. (1991). Selectivity theory: social activity in life-span context. *Annual Review of Gerontology and Geriatrics, Volume 11, 1991: Behavioral Science & Aging, 11*, 195.

Carstensen, L. L. (1993). Motivation for social contact across the life span: a theory of socioemotional selectivity. Paper presented at the Nebraska symposium on motivation, vol. 40, February, 1992, pp 209–254.

Cattell, H. (2000). Suicide in the elderly. *Advances in Psychiatric Treatment, 6*(2), 102–108.

Charmaz, K. (1999). Stories of suffering: subjective tales and research narratives. *Qualitative Health Research, 9*(3), 362–382.

Chatterjee, S. C., Patnaik, P., & Chariar, V. M. (2008). *Discourses on aging and dying*. New Delhi, India; Thousand Oaks, CA: SAGE Publications.

Cheryl Fischer Rn, M. S. (2000). Grief responses of senior and elderly widows: practice implications. *Journal of Gerontological Nursing, 26*(2), 35.

Cohen, G. D. (2009). Historical lessons to watch your assumptions about aging: relevance to the role of International Psychogeriatrics. *International Psychogeriatrics, 21*(03), 425–429.

Corr, C. A., Nabe, C. M., & Corr, D. M. (1997). *Death and dying, life and living*. Pacific Grove, CA: Brooks/Cole.

de Medeiros, K. (2009). Suffering and generativity: repairing threats to self in old age. *Journal of Aging Studies, 23*(2), 97–102. doi: 10.1016/j.jaging.2008.11.001.

de Medeiros, K., & Black, H. K. (2015). Suffering and pain in old age. In: J. Twigg & W. Martin (Eds.), *Routledge handbook of cultural gerontology*. London: Routledge, pp 181–188.

Erikson, E. H. (1950). *Childhood and society*. New York: W.W. Norton & Company.

Erikson, E. H., & Erikson, J. M. (1997). *The life cycle completed: Extended version with new chapters on the ninth state of development*. New York: W. W. Norton & Company.

Flor, H. (2001). Pain, health psychology of. In J. S. Neil & B. B. Paul (Eds.), *International encyclopedia of the social and behavioral sciences*. Oxford: Pergamon, pp 10990–10995.

Gagliese, L. (2009). Pain and aging: the emergence of a new subfield of pain research. *The Journal of Pain, 10*(4), 343–353.

Gagliese, L., & Melzack, R. (1997). Chronic pain in elderly people. *Pain, 70*(1), 3–14. doi: http://dx.doi.org/10.1016/S03043959(96)03266 6.

Glascock, A. P. (1990). By any other name, it is still killing: a comparison of the treatment of the elderly in America and other societies. In: J. Sokolovsky (Ed.), *The cultural context of aging. Worldwide perspectives* (1st edn). Boston: Bergin Publishing, pp 43–56.

Glascock, A. P., & Feinman, S. L. (1981). Social asset or social burden: treatment of the aged in non-industrial societies. In: C. Fry (Ed.), *Dimensions: Aging, culture, and health*, New York: Praeger, pp 13–32.

Hegge, M. and C. Fischer (2000). Grief responses of senior and elderly widows: practice implications. *Journal of Gerontological Nursing, 26*(2), 35-43.

Jacobs, C., Mazure, H., & Prigerson, S. (2000). Diagnostic criteria for traumatic grief. *Death Studies, 24*(3), 185–199.

Kaufman, S. R. (2000). Narrative, death, and the uses of anthropology. In: T. R. Cole, R. Kastenbaum & R. E. Ray (Eds.), *Handbook of the humanities and aging* (2nd edn). New York: Springer Publishing Company, pp 342–364.

Kaufman, S. R., & Morgan, L. M. (2005). The anthropology of the beginnings and ends of life. *Annual Review of Anthropology, 34*, 317–341.

Kenyon, G. M., Ruth, J. E., & Mader, W. (1999). Elements of a narrative gerontology. In: G. M. Kenyon, J. E. Ruth, W. Mader, V. L. Bengtson, & K. W. Schaie (Eds.), *Handbook of theories of aging* (1st edn). New York: Springer Publishing Company, pp 40–58.

Kjølseth, I., Ekeberg, Ø., & Steihaug, S. (2010). Why suicide? Elderly people who committed suicide and their experience of life in the period before their death. *International Psychogeriatrics, 22*(02), 209–218.

Lamb, S. (1997). The making and unmaking of persons: notes on aging and gender in North India. *Ethos, 25*(3), 279–302.

Lorenz, K. A., Lynn, J., Dy, S. M., Shugarman, L. R., Wilkinson, A., Mularski, R. A., ... Maglione, M. (2008). Evidence for improving palliative care at the end of life: a systematic review. *Annals of Internal Medicine, 148*(2), 147–159.

Luanaigh, C. Ó., & Lawlor, B. A. (2008). Loneliness and the health of older people. *International Journal of Geriatric Psychiatry, 23*(12), 1213–1221.

Lynn, J., & Adamson, D. M. (2003). Living well at the end of life. Adapting health care to serious chronic illness in old age, White Paper WP137. Santa Monica, CA: Rand Health.

Mao, J. (2009). Translational pain research: achievements and challenges. *The Journal of Pain, 10*(10), 1001–1011. doi: http://dx.doi.org/10.1016/j. jpain.2009.06.002.

Meagher, D. K., & Balk, D. E. (2013). *Handbook of thanatology: The essential body of knowledge for the study of death, dying, and bereavement*. London: Routledge.

Miguel, E. (2005). Poverty and witch killing. *The Review of Economic Studies, 72*(4), 1153–1172.

Newall, N. E., et al. (2009). Causal beliefs, social participation, and loneliness among older adults: a longitudinal study. *Journal of Social and Personal Relationships, 26*(2–3), 273–290.

Onion (1997). World death rate holding steady at 100 percent. *The Onion*. Retrieved from http://www.theonion.com/article/world-death-rate-holding-steady-at-100-percent-1670.

OED (1989). *Oxford English Dictionary*. Eds. J. Simpson and E. Weiner. Oxford: Clarendon Press.

Pearson, J. L., & Conwell, Y. E. (1996). *Suicide and aging: International perspectives*. New York: Springer Publishing Co.

Pinquart, M., & Sörensen, S. (2001). Influences on loneliness in older adults: a meta-analysis. *Basic & Applied Social Psychology, 23*(4), 245–266.

Platt, L. A., & Persico, V. R. (1992). *Grief in cross-cultural perspective: A casebook*. New York: Garland Publishing.

Rubinstein, R. L., Girling, L. M., de Medeiros, K., Brazda, M., & Hannum, S. (2014). Extending the framework of generativity theory through research: a qualitative study. *The Gerontologist, 55*(4), 548–558. doi: 10.1093/geront/gnu009

Sapp, S. (2010). Aging in world religions: an overview. In T. R. Cole, R. E. Ray & R. Kastenbaum (Eds.), *A guide to humanistic studies in aging: What does it mean to grow old?* Baltimore: Johns Hopins University Press.

Small, N., Katz, J., & Hockey, J. (2001). *Facing death*. Philadelphia: Open University Press.

Stroebe, M., & Schut, H. (1998). Culture and grief. *Bereavement Care, 17*(1), 7–11.

Tilak, S. (1989). *Religion and aging in the Indian tradition*. New York: SUNY Press.

Tomer, A., & Eliason, G. (2000). Attitudes about life and death: toward a comprehensvie model of death anxiety. In: A. Tomer (Ed.), *Death attitudes and the older adult: Theories, concepts and applications*. Philadelphia: Taylor & Francis, pp 3–24.

Van, C., & Lee, D. (2000). A political analysis of legal pluralism in Bolivia and Colombia. *Journal of Latin American Studies, 32*(1), 207–234.

Victor, C. R., Scambler, S. J., Bowling, A. N. N., & Bond, J. (2005). The prevalence of, and risk factors for, loneliness in later life: a survey of older people in Great Britain. *Ageing and Society, 25*(06), 357–375.

Vincent, J. A. (2003). *Old age*. New York: Psychology Press.

Waern, M., Rubenowitz, E., & Wilhelmson, K. (2003). Predictors of suicide in the old elderly. *Gerontology, 49*(5), 328–334.

Walter, T. (2008). The sociology of death. *Sociology Compass, 2*(1), 317–336.

West, K., & Glynos, J. (2014). 'Death talk', 'loss talk' and identification in the process of ageing. *Ageing & Society, FirstView*, 1–15. doi:10.1017/S0144686X14001184.

SEVEN

Social location and place

Each chapter in the *Short Guide* has pointed to ways in which older age has been marginalized or positioned as 'less than' other ages, especially middle age. This chapter will spend a bit more time exploring why. It considers how social location (for example, age, gender, socioeconomic status, race and ethnicity, geographical location) and place (for example, neighborhood, home, shared dwelling, formal institutional care) influence the experience of aging. As has been discussed in previous chapters, age is a well-recognized basis for social stratification and structured inequality. Chronological age is used as a formal marker to determine social location and place in many cultures and societies and subsequently can lead to either exclusion in certain areas (for example, age-based mandatory retirement) or inclusion to others (for example, availability of government benefits, access to certain types of housing). Functional ability and physical appearance are types of informal markers of age-based social location, as are other personal characteristics such as gender, sexual orientation, socioeconomic status, citizenship status and others. Such markers can affect one's access to place because of accessibility or even pressured exclusion (for example, withdrawing to age-segregated communities). The experiences associated with social location and place can have profound effects on individuals and groups, as has been seen in other chapters throughout the *Short Guide*.

In light of the roles that social location and place play in gerontology and the lives of older people, the chapter begins with an exploration of various ways in which social location affects aging, with ageism being a major consideration. The section that follows explores more of the ways that social location plays a role in aging, specifically by looking at age and ageism as an important framework, gender, sexual orientation, socioeconomic status, functional status and citizenship status.

The second part of the chapter looks at place, to include its meanings, the types of spaces available to older people (for example, multi-generation housing, single dwelling and institutional settings), neighborhoods, and concepts used to describe how people experience place, and others. This includes new efforts toward age-friendly cities and the recognition of the role that place can take in empowering and limiting people of all ages and abilities.

Another look at the problematization of later life

Social location historically involves questions about role, access, power and representation such as: what function is this group or individual expected to perform? Who has access to what resources? Who has the power to make decisions over an individual or group? How is the individual or group represented? Many of the issues surrounding social location and aging can be found in the objectification of older people and in the problem orientation of aging in which 'old age' is positioned as a problem that needs to be addressed, managed and controlled. Jason Powell (2006a) writes that the problem orientation is

> historically configured in the biomedical sciences and discourses that specialize in one terminology of gerontology. The medical science "problem" approach to aging can be related to how human subjectivity was structured as occidental modernity crystallized, when, beginning in the seventeenth and eighteenth centuries, the "social sciences", industrial capitalism, and bureaucratic politics

simultaneously developed novel ways of objectifying individuals and populations in Western societies. (p 19)

Powell reiterates others' observations, that the very development of gerontology as a 'science', as described in Chapter Two, coincides with later life being identified as a problem.

Prior to medical categorizations of old age, later life was certainly recognized as a stage of life, but not necessarily treated as a problem to be solved (Achenbaum, 1995; Achenbaum & Levin, 1989). As the scientific community began to view age as something that could potentially be 'cured', older people were also being increasingly recognized as a growing impoverished group and in need of social intervention (Katz, 1996). Poorhouses or alms-houses, in Europe and the United States, began to see a rise in older occupants, which then led to public welfare programs developed specifically for older adults (Thane, 2000, 2010) (see Chapter Eight).

Dale Dannefer (1999) also points to the problematization of age through its medicalization, citing the words 'adaption, selection, adjustment, and goodness-of-fit' (p 69) in the development of discourse about aging. These words, he argues, imply that the aging person is 'pre-wired' in many ways and understanding aging can take the same form as other scientific problems to be studied. This biomedical view ignores the role that context plays as one moves through the lifecourse into old age. He writes: 'The notion of an interaction in which the person is constituted and in which the social context is constituted, is absent' (p 69). Age is experienced in various contexts, in various environments. Differing social practices and cultural assumptions shape those contexts and environments (Dannefer, 1999). As Dannefer points out, age is not only biological, it is social. A person's position within the social hierarchy, attitudes towards various social positions and other conditions, including environment, all affect how one ages.

Another perspective about the problematization of aging comes from Catherine Silver (2003), who argues that in many social institutions and environments such norms based on chronological age are 'largely attempts to control the fears of ageing and death among the non-aged. These fears are redefined and rationalized as social problems. They are responded to in ways that allow the nonaged to control the lives of older men and women' (p 380). The ties between problematization and control link back to the connection between age, decline and death that has been mentioned throughout. What Silver suggests is that policies and programs that define old age and concerns of old age provide a means to separate old age (however it is defined) from the rest of the lifecourse and to label old age as different. This is not to say that old age is purely a social category and does not occur in a biological or functional sense. Rather, it speaks to the way that biological changes are socially interpreted and regulated. Reaching a chronological age (for example, 65), which itself says nothing about the abilities of a person, becomes a means through which to exclude people of that age or older from participating in certain social institutions (such as paid work), or of 'entitling' them to others (for example, specialized housing, income supplements).

Social location

This section will specifically explore social location and age and ageism, sex and gender, sexual orientation, socioeconomic and social class, functional status, and migration and citizenship status.

Age and ageism

The first aspect of social location to be addressed is ageism (Butler, 1969; Gullette, 2004). This includes how assumptions about midlife have shaped later life (Hazan & Raz, 1997) and how ageism is practiced. Ageism is the systematic discrimination of a person based on his or her age, including assumptions about abilities and function (Butler, 1980; Gendron, Welleford, Inker, & White, 2015). Words such as 'elderly', 'senior' and others to describe people with certain characteristics (for example, grey hair) carry with them certain negative connotations such as lack of competence, forgetfulness and others. Although ageist practices can be directed toward younger people (for example, making the assumption that a person who has just joined the workforce is unable to perform certain tasks because of lack of experience), it is most commonly associated with attitudes toward older people (Gullette, 2004; Cruikshank, 2013).

Stereotyping people based on older age (often as a result of appearance) has a long cultural history. Older women in fairy tales are often witches (Cruikshank, 1995; Robinson, Callister, Magoffin, & Moore, 2007). Older Disney characters (especially women) are portrayed as ugly and evil, albeit powerful (Robinson et al, 2007). In the mid-1970s, Edward Ansello (Ansello, 1977, 1978) reviewed over 650 pieces of early children's literature (in English) and found that older characters were under-represented, were often depicted as sad and poor and were overwhelmingly cast in minor, uninteresting roles. This, he concluded, laid a foundation for future ageism and stereotyping. More recent studies on ageism in sources ranging from college texts to television commercials continue to find that older people are not represented at all, are represented in terms of weakness or deficit (for example, memory loss) or are portrayed in comical ways (for example, oversexed, socially unaware) that reinforce ageist stereotypes (Bytheway, 1995; Laws, 1995; McHugh, 2003; Gullette, 2004; Davidovic, Djordjevic, Erceg, Despotovic, & Milosevic, 2007).

Part of the rationale for why ageist practices exist is based on the position of middle age in relation to older age. As Haim Hazan and Aviad Raz (1997) have pointed out, the view of older age is almost always from that of the middle age intellectualizing later life rather than from older age itself. This can be readily seen in Table 1.1, which provides a historical overview of the stages life. In the chronological stages, age 50 or so begins old age and is described in terms such as 'the sun may not go higher' (Cole, 1992), or the 'young-old' for people aged 55 to 75 (Neugarten, 1974; Riley, 1987). In the function-based models, later life is described in binaries of either stasis or decline (Cole, 1992), green old age or sad decrepitude (Thane, 2000), or the third or fourth age (Gilleard & Higgs, 2010; Higgs & Gilleard, 2015). Throughout all of these stages, there is a link between mid-life as the highest point and later life as somehow less than. As Cole (1992) points out in reference to the stages of life, mid-life is positioned on the top of the hill. After reaching that point, one is 'over the hill', a common phrase used to describe people past midlife.

Ageist practice also includes 'paternalistic' treatment toward older people under the guise of protection. As mentioned in earlier chapters, several scholars have argued that the creation of particular policies that define older adults as a group who need protecting through special services further stigmatizes aging itself. Instead, if a functional approach were taken – including economic status and functional status rather than chronological age – then perhaps old age would become less associated with need and decline. This is, of course, an oversimplification. Ageist attitudes are not just externally formed, but are internally formed as well. Individuals and societal attitudes of age norms regarding what it is possible for a person of a certain age to do – how to dress, how to behave and so on – also in turn affect what people desire from policies for themselves and others (Estes, Biggs, & Phillipson, 2003). Ageism, therefore, is just one of the many complicated layers in social location that affects later life.

Sex and gender

There are several important considerations with regard to sex, gender and aging. First, the gerontological literature often treats older people as a sexless and genderless group. Data are often not broken down by sex, a biological marker often inappropriately used synonymously with 'gender' (a social construction based on culturally accepted norms of behavior associated with one's sex). In addition, many research studies statistically control for gender rather than exploring gender differences.

Second, women, especially older women, have historically held lower status in most societies and cultures across time. Andrew Achenbaum (2010b) explains the evolution of the derogatory word 'hag' to describe older women. He writes, 'Although older women seldom predominated in secular affairs, contacts with the Sacred empowered them with wisdom. Aged women in ancient times were respectfully called "hags". Derived from the Greek term for "holy woman", *hagia* was related to the ancient Egyptian word *heq*' (p 24). He further explains that wisdom was associated 'with many goddess[es] across many ancient civilizations, such as Athena, who possessed Zeus' wisdom, Shakti, who was a goddess of wisdom in India and the 'Old Woman' who was worshipped by pre-Islamic Arabs. He describes how the role of wise older woman was later transformed into women 'who embodied the fearful potential for rejection, abandonment, death' (p 25), leading to images of women as witches, wicked stepmothers and other contemptuous characters. Third, women have a uniquely disadvantaged location in aging. They comprise the majority of older people throughout the world. Globally in 2013, there were 85 men per 100 women in the age group 60 and over and 61 men per 100 women for those aged 80 and over (United Nations, 2013). As mentioned, the devaluation of women across the lifecourse influences access to education, which can then in turn affect access to employment or other financial resources, which can then affect access to healthcare and so on (Alli & Maharaj, 2013). These differences will certainly have differing effects depending on the larger cultural framework (Alli & Maharaj, 2013).

Fourth, there has been surprisingly little research on men's gendered roles in later life. Edward Thompson (2007) and others have argued that older men remain invisible in contemporary society for several reasons (Davidson, Daly, & Arber, 1970; Bernard, Itzin, Phillipson, & Skucha, 1995; Arber & Cooper, 1999; Arber, 2004). One reason, as mentioned earlier, is the tendency for gerontological literature to treat older people as genderless. Consequently, masculinities in older age – a gendered phenomenon – are rarely explored (Calasanti, Pietilä, Ojala, & King, 2013; King & Calasanti, 2013). In addition, older men have been depicted in the research literature as an advantaged group, as compared to older women, which has in turn led to a focus in research on older women when gender is taken up as an area of study. In this sense, older men as a whole have been assumed to be at a quality-of-life advantage, given their tendency to have had better access to paid employment during their lifetime and subsequently to retirement income. Older men's views on later life, unique problems they may experience and other age-related issues that are specifically related to male gender have been under-explored (Calasanti, 2004; Bennett, 2007; Holwerda et al, 2012; King & Calasanti, 2013).

Fifth, newer categories of gender, such as transgender, transsexual, intersex or gender non-conforming persons have yet to be adequately addressed in the literature.[1] While there is a growing body of work on the experiences of individuals outside of the traditional categories of 'male' and 'female', such work is relatively new and has yet to focus on these gendered experiences in later life (Cook-Daniels, Kimmel, Rose, & David, 2006; Persson, 2009; Finkenauer, Sherratt, Marlow, & Brodey, 2012; Witten & Eyler, 2012). As Sabine Finkenauer and colleagues (2012) explain, in their systematic review of trans aging, 'research on trans and gender-nonconforming older adults is often conducted under the rubric of lesbian, gay, bisexual and transgender (LGBT) aging research' (p 315). As such, the experiences of transgendered persons become co-mingled with research on lesbian, gay and bisexual persons and the research does not therefore provide insight specifically into experiences of transgendered older adults (Cook-Daniels et al, 2006).

Sexual orientation

Sexual orientation differs from gender. As mentioned in the previous section, gender is a social construction. Sexual orientation is not. For example, a person may be biologically female, gender-identify as female and be heterosexual, bisexual or lesbian. Sexual orientation is therefore not a proxy for gender and should be considered as its own category. The overwhelming majority of research on sexual orientation and aging has focused on heterosexual older adults. The body of research on same-sex oriented or bisexual older adults is rather new but growing. Basic issues related to bisexual or homosexual elders include: fear of disclosing their sexual orientation because it might jeopardize access to government benefits (including housing and pensions) and to family and support systems; and fear of discrimination by the medical system and others (Orel, 2004). Research on social networks of same-sex older adults is relatively new and consequently lacking a substantial literature. One Dutch study found that gay men aged 75 and over tended to hold a negative view of their own sexuality, due to cohort-related stigmatization of homosexuality, and were consequently prone to social isolation (Kuyper & Fokkema, 2010). Other studies have found the opposite and suggest that gay, lesbian and bisexual elders often have more robust social networks than heterosexual elders and are therefore better able to cope with losses that might come with age (Orel & Fruhauf, 2013). Overall, this is a much-needed area of future research.

Socioeconomic status and social class

As Pat Thane (2000) explains, although there have always been a small group of older people who possessed substantial property with which to support themselves and employ others, 'most old people for most of recorded history have been more or less poor' (p 15). As has been mentioned throughout the *Short Guide*, women comprise the majority (around 75%) of the poor ages 65 and over (Kinsella, Wan, & US Bureau of the Census, 2009).

However, consideration of socioeconomic status should not be limited to looking at aging people as a group but, rather, how cumulative poverty over time affects the eventual experience of later life. Table 2.1 includes two perspectives directly related to this: cumulative advantage/disadvantage (Dannefer, 1999, 2003) and cumulative inequality (Ferraro & Shippee, 2009). Albeit in slightly different ways, both speak to the idea that the advantages (or disadvantages) that one has at the beginning of life, such as access to education, medical care, safe housing, clean environment, will build over time, leading to more opportunities such as access to finances. Lack of access to institutions and resources will also have their effect over time, creating health challenges, employment barriers and other disadvantages that ultimately can affect a person in later life. When thinking of the older individual, it is therefore important to consider earlier exposures and opportunities.

Functional status

Functional status can involve physical, cognitive and emotional levels (see Chapter Four for an in-depth discussion). Some aspects of functional status are obvious to the outsider (for example, use of assistive devices). Others are not (for example, depression.) Stephen Katz (1996), Jason Powell and Simon Biggs (2000), Chris Gilleard and

Paul Higgs (2010), Chris Phillipson (2007) and others have explored various forms of stigmatization and marginalization based on real or perceived functional limitations or changes in functional status.

Migration and citizenship status

Migration and citizenship status carry a variety of personal, social and economic realities. For example, depending on the reasons for migration (for example, personal choice, escaping oppression), change in place and familiarity can have profound meaning (Becker, 2003). Migration can also impact later-life health, wellbeing and economic situations. For example, as an immigrant, one's age at the time of immigration and the economic conditions surrounding the migration can greatly affect one's economic position in older age. The older the immigrant, the fewer years he or she has to participate in the labor market, contribute to pension savings and potentially earn benefits upon retirement if they are available (Lewin & Stier, 2010). In addition, the economic conditions at the time of migration affect what types of employment opportunities are available, which in turn will also affect retirement or later life savings. For some, especially people from higher socioeconomic or class levels who leave their home country, the experience of late-life migration can create an economic and social condition very different from what was experienced over the person's lifecourse. Challenges for immigrants include potential language barriers, accessibility of government pension and assistance, social networks that may be compromised and differing expectations of later life. As with many areas in gerontology, understanding the experiences of older immigrants across various geographical and economic dimensions is in need of further study.

Place

Place can describe the physical dwelling where one lives (for example, own house or apartment, congregate living, care facility), the geographical location (for example, country, urban versus rural), neighborhood or other aspects of location, all of which carry different meanings and historical and cultural underpinnings that link back to questions of access, power and representation. Gay Becker (2003) defines places as 'a situational context constructed by and for human action, while places are centers of "human significance and emotional attachment" (Tilley, 1994, p 15)' (p 130). It is the situational context that plays an important part in consideration of place and age, since context (for example, type of residence, decision to move to the residence) ultimately will affect one's experience with place. As Hans-Werner Wahl and Gerald Weisman write (2003), 'the physical, social, organizational and cultural environment are deeply interwoven' (Wahl & Weisman, 2003, p 615). Environments evolve over time, yet can hold deep cultural meanings still entrenched in the past. Place does not exist without the cultural meanings that are placed upon it. As Robert Rubinstein and Kate de Medeiros (2003) have suggested, 'Space has no meaning unless it is culturalized. We make constant inferences and interpretations about the nature of space based on who we are as cultural beings' (p 73).

Also important to 'space' is the degree to which a person perceives that his or her past aligns with the present and anticipated future. This section will specifically examine: historical perspectives of place and space; explanatory stances with regard to environments; and how changes (for example, family structure, migration) affect these. As noted in the previous chapter, although living arrangements overlap in some respects with housing, they speak to slightly different issues, such as socialization, rather than to housing alone. Living arrangements were addressed in the previous chapter on families. This section will focus on housing, home and geographical place.

Housing and home

Much of the literature suggests that older adults around the world spend the majority of their time where they are housed (Gitlin, 2003; Golant, 2003). There are several ways one can look at place. These include physical dwellings, housing types, the idea of home, living arrangements and neighborhoods. 'Physical dwellings' describes where, at a minimum, a person sleeps on a regular basis. This could be in one's own house or apartment, in a type of congregate living such a multigenerational house (either kin or non-kin), in an institutionalized care facility or others .

Housing

Housing describes 'the physical structures and services, governmental and economic influences, and the symbolic characteristics associated with where one lives. Minimally, housing is the setting in which a person sleeps and prepares meals' (Rubinstein & de Medeiros, 2006, p 546). Within the larger umbrella of housing, there are various types listed in Table 7.1.

Table 7.1: Description of selected housing types for older adults

Housing type	Description
Age-segregated housing	Housing for which one must meet a certain age criterion to live there. This includes private developments marketed to a particular age group (for example, 55 and over) or government-sponsored housing (Golant, 1985).
Assisted living	A type of housing where a person lives independently within a defined, structured community and generally age-segregated retirement community (as opposed to remaining at home in the larger community) but receives assistance with personal services such as meals, housekeeping, transportation and activities of daily living. In the U.S. this type of housing is regulated at the state level as it's generally paid for out-of-pocket (Roth & Eckert, 2011; Rubinstein & de Medeiros, 2006).
Hostel	'residences with limited assistance for individuals with deficits in the activities of daily living' (Ribbe et al, 1997, p 4).

Housing type	Description
Independent housing	Describes housing not specifically designed for an older person. This includes multi-generational homes, apartments and houses. The majority of older adults in the world live in a form of independent housing (Rubinstein & de Medeiros, 2006). People needing assistance or health services would receive them in their home (Savla, Davey, Sundström, Zarit, & Malmberg, 2008).
Nursing home	Miel Ribbe and colleagues (Ribbe et al, 1997) base their definition of 'nursing home' on a comparison of 10 countries, although they note that subtle differences can be found based on location. Nursing homes, according to them, describe 'an institution providing nursing care 24 hours a day, assistance with activities of daily living and mobility, psychosocial and personal care, paramedical care, such as physiotherapy and occupational therapy, as well as room and board' (p 4). They note that nursing homes mainly serve frail elders with chronic physical and/or cognitive disabilities.
Residential home for the aged	This describes 'an institution providing living conditions adjusted to the needs of residents usually requiring no more nursing care than can be given by a visiting nurse' (Ribbe et al, 1997, p 7). Ribbe and colleagues note that most of the care in this type of setting is provided by nursing aides or personnel with little or no training.
Skilled nursing facility	This is similar to the definition of nursing home. However, in the United States and other countries, skilled nursing facilities can be used for short-term stays primarily for rehabilitation for conditions such as hip replacement. Once rehabilitation has occurred (generally in less than 6 months), the person returns to his/her primary residence (Ribbe et al, 1997).
Unskilled nursing home	This is similar to the residential home for the aged described above.

Home

'Home' is a subjective collection of essential meanings and experiences that may be related to notions such as comfort, support, intimacy and privacy (Gitlin, 2003). A person can live in a place that he or she does not consider to be a home. It is a physical place for shelter, safety and privacy; a social space where social investments are made (for example, engagement with the surrounding community, interactions with neighbors) (Rubinstein & Kilbride, 1992; Nygren et al, 2007; de Medeiros, Rubinstein, & Doyle, 2013). 'Physical dwelling' and the notion of home do not necessitate one another (Rubinstein & de Medeiros, 2005). Robert Rubinstein and Janet Kilbride (1992) identified three classes of psychosocial processes that give meaning to the home environment, namely social-centered (ordering of the home environment based on a person's version of sociocultural rules for domestic order), person-centered (expression of one's lifecourse in features of the home and personal biography) and body-centered processes (the ongoing relationship of the body to the environmental features that surround it). Embodiment 'comprises a continuing negotiating and reinterpretation between the self, a myriad of externally placed identities relative to the physical body, and the relationship between the body (past, present and future) and the environment' (p 63). The experience of place isn't just one that is emotional or physical in the sense that one's body inhabits a certain environment. The experience is also embodied in that various aspects of one's physical sense of being come into play (for example, smell, feel, other senses).

Three functions of the home have been described. First, there is maintenance, or to feel at home or the meaning of home. This can be especially important when one moves from his or her traditional or community home to other types of living situations in older age (for example, moving in with a family member, moving to an institution). Second is stimulation or features that affect positive or negative behavioral and emotional functioning within the home. These might include one's history within the home (for example, living in a place for a long time). Third is support, to include the physical and spatial characteristics that help one socially, physically and emotionally (Wahl & Weisman, 2003). Supports can include assistive devices (for example, grab bars), proximity to transportation (for example, metro or bus stations, taxis), or closeness to neighbors or other social partners. Other practical aspects of homes include their location relative to needed amenities (for example, grocery stores), safety (for example, is the home located in a high-crime area?) and aesthetics (for example, what do I see when I look out of my window?) (Rowles & Chaudhury, 2005; Nygren et al, 2007).

Graham Rowles (Rowles, 1981, 1984, 1993) introduced several imporant concepts in relation to neighborhoods and home. The idea of the 'surveillance zone' recognized that the visual field – what a person sees when looking out of the window – holds special significance. It is the way in which people see life going on outside of their own homes. It is also how people notice neighborhood change, which may influence whether they still feel comfortable where they live.

Homes may be isolated from neighbors in rural or suburban settings, located in busy apartment complexes with many neighbors, or in age-defined communities. In addition, many current perspectives on home, particularly with regard to later-life functioning, are grounded in Powell Lawton and Lucille Nahemow's (1973) ecological theory of aging, which addresses person–environment (P-E) fit. In short, P-E fit describes a person's competence in relationship to the demands or press of the environment. Environmental demands such as the need to climb stairs may be stronger than the person's ability to engage in such physical action, therefore creating a situation that could compromise the person's wellbeing. When considering place, it is therefore important to consider the wide spectrum of what place entails.

Geographical place

Geographical place, in addition to housing, is another important consideration with regard to age. Although growth of the aging population is happening throughout the world, the largest growth in the percentage of older people can be seen in the less-developed regions of the world. The United Nations (United Nations, 2013) estimates that by 2050, nearly 80% of the people aged 60 and over will live in less-developed regions of the world. As has been highlighted through the *Short Guide*, access to healthcare services, finances, education and other institutions and services throughout one's life has a great impact on one's old age. Geographical place can affect access to clean water, sanitation and health resources.

Another important consideration regarding geographical place is urban versus rural location. In Africa, the majority of older people live in rural areas; many of these are older women (Debpuur, Welaga, Wak, & Hodgson, 2010; Fonchingong, 2013; Maharaj, 2013). In Vietnam, there are 3.5 times more older people living in rural areas than in urban ones (Van Minh, Byass, Chuc, & Wall, 2010). John Bongaarts and Zachary Zimmer (2002) write that 'compared with persons aged 18–65, older adults are more likely to live in rural areas and to have substantially less school' (p 150). In their study, which sampled from countries in Africa, Asia and Latin America, they found that more than half the males and three-quarters of the females over age 65 had had no schooling at all. In Yemen, for example, no older women were recorded as having received any formal schooling. In general, rural morbidity is much higher than urban morbidity for these reasons.

Around the world, urbanization is happening at a fast pace. More than half of the population in sub-Saharan Africa is projected to be living in urban areas by 2030 (Kyobutungi, Egondi, & Ezeh, 2010). In addition, the educational level of urban dwellers is overall higher, which can lead to better jobs and which in turn may also contribute to better health outcomes (Alli & Maharaj, 2013). It is important, though, to characterize the type of urban dwelling. Kyobutungi, Egondi and Ezeh (2010) have estimated that 70% of urban residents in sub-Saharan Africa live either in slums or in slum-like conditions. Residents in these slums have poorer health outcomes than residents in rural areas in these countries. Where one lives geographically is therefore an important aspect of place.

Age-friendly cities and communities

It is important to note the work being done on an international level regarding age-friendly cities communities (Buffel et al, 2012; Buffel &

Phillipson, 2012). Age-friendly cities and communities is an initiative supported by the World Health Organization (Buffel & Phillipson, 2012) to encourage the elimination of barriers such as lack of adequate crosswalks, accessible transportation, green spaces and others. It is a way of recognizing that people can be 'disabled' or 'enabled' by environments and that awareness of ways in which the physical environment can restrict participation can lead to solutions that can in turn make them accessible.

Summary

Social location and place are shaped by cultural values and expectations, social norms and personal biography. It can be argued that social location and place are the fundamental considerations of gerontology, since representations, past and present, frame aging. How one ages is influenced by the resources he or she has access to during earlier phases of life. Where one ages will greatly affect his or her current experience. Sex and gender, sexual orientation, socioeconomic status and functional status all play a role in not only how age is perceived but what is available (for example, housing) based on these characteristics. Although social location has been addressed in gerontology to some extent, much more work is needed. The same can be said of housing. Although there has been much written about the types of housing and even the meaning of home from a broad perspective, closer attention to social location and its relation to space is important.

Note
[1] Transgender is defined as 'a community of individuals whose biological sex is not entirely congruent with their gender identity' (Persson, 2009).

Further reading
Gullette, M. M. (2004). *Aged by culture*. Chicago, IL: University of Chicago Press.

Higgs, P., & Gilleard, C. (2015). *Rethinking old age: Theorising the fourth age*. London: Palgrave.

Kimmel, D. C., Rose, T., & David, S. (2006). *Lesbian, gay, bisexual, and transgender aging: Research and clinical perspectives*. New York: Columbia University Press.

Powell, J. L. (2006b). *Social theory and aging*. Landham, MD: Rowman & Littlefield.

Rowles, G. D. and H. Chaudhury (2005). *Home and identity in late life: International perspectives*. New York: Springer Publishing.

Wahl, H.-W., & Weisman, G. D. (2003). Environmental gerontology at the beginning of the new millennium: reflections on its historical, empirical, and theoretical development. *The Gerontologist, 43*(5), 616–627.

References

Achenbaum, W. A. (1995). *Crossing frontiers: Gerontology emerges as a science*. New York: Cambridge University Press.

Achenbaum, W. A. (2010a). 2008 Kent Award lecture: a historian interprets the future of gerontology. *The Gerontologist, 50*(2), 142–148.

Achenbaum, W. A. (2010b). Past as prologue: toward a global history of ageing. In: D. Dannefer & C. Phillipson (Eds.), *The SAGE handbook of social gerontology*. Thousand Oaks, CA: Sage Publications, pp 20–32.

Achenbaum, W. A., & Levin, J. S. (1989). What does gerontology mean? *The Gerontologist, 29*(3), 393–400.

Alli, F., & Maharaj, P. (2013). The health situation of older people in Africa. In: Pranitha Maharaj (Ed.), *Aging and health in Africa*. New York: Springer, pp 53–89.

Ansello, E. F. (1977). Age and ageism in children's first literature. *Educational Gerontology: An International Quarterly, 2*(3), 255–274.

Ansello, E. F. (1978). Ageism – the subtle stereotype. *Childhood Education, 54*(3), 118–122.

Arber, S. (2004). Gender, marital status, and ageing: linking material, health, and social resources. *Journal of Aging Studies, 18*(1), 91–108. doi: http://dx.doi.org/10.1016/j.jaging.2003.09.007.

Arber, S., & Cooper, H. (1999). Gender differences in health in later life: the new paradox? *Social Science & Medicine, 48*(1), 61–76. doi: http://dx.doi.org/10.1016/S0277-9536(98)00289-5.

Becker, G. (2003). Meanings of place and displacement in three groups of older immigrants. *Journal of Aging Studies, 17*(2), 129–149. doi: http://dx.doi.org/10.1016/S0890-4065(03)00007-0.

Bennett, K. M. (2007). 'No sissy stuff': towards a theory of masculinity and emotional expression in older widowed men. *Journal of Aging Studies, 21*(4), 347–356. doi: http://dx.doi.org/10.1016/j.jaging.2007.05.002.

Bernard, M., Itzin, C., Phillipson, C., & Skucha, J. (1995). Gendered work, gendered retirement. In S. Arber, & J. Ginn (Eds.), *Connecting gender and ageing: A sociological approach*. Philadelphia: Open University Press, pp 56–68.

Bongaarts, J., & Zimmer, Z. (2002). Living arrangements of older adults in the developing world: an analysis of demographic and health survey household surveys. *The Journals of Gerontology Series B: Psychological Sciences and Social Sciences, 57*(3), S145–S157.

Buffel, T., & Phillipson, C. (2012). Ageing in urban environments: developing 'age-friendly' cities. *Critical Social Policy, 32*(4), 597–617.

Buffel, T., Verté, D., De Donder, L., De Witte, N., Dury, S., Vanwing, T., & Bolsenbroek, A. (2012). Theorising the relationship between older people and their immediate social living environment. *International Journal of Lifelong Education, 31*(1), 13–32.

Butler, R. N. (1969). Age-ism: another form of bigotry. *The Gerontologist, 9*(4 Part 1), 243–246. doi: 10.1093/geront/9.4_Part_1.243.

Butler, R. N. (1980). Ageism: a foreword. *Journal of Social Issues, 36*(2), 8–11.

Bytheway, B. (1995). *Ageism*. Buckingham: Open University Press.

Calasanti, T. (2004). Feminist gerontology and old men. *The Journals of Gerontology Series B: Psychological Sciences and Social Sciences, 59*(6), S305–S314.

Calasanti, T., Pietilä, I., Ojala, H., & King, N. (2013). Men, bodily control, and health behaviors: the importance of age. *Health Psychology, 32*(1), 15.

Cole, T. R. (1992). *The journey of life: A cultural history of aging in America*. New York: Cambridge University Press.

Cook-Daniels, L., Kimmel, D., Rose, T., & David, S. (2006). Trans aging. In: D. Kimmel, T. Rose & S. David (Eds.), *Lesbian, gay, bisexual, and transgender aging*. New York: Columbia University Press, pp 20–35.

Cruikshank, M. (1995). *Fierce with reality: An anthology of literature on aging*. Clearwater, MN: North Star Press of St Cloud.

Cruikshank, M. (2013). *Learning to be old: Gender, culture, and aging*. Landham, MD: Rowman & Littlefield Publishers.

Dannefer, D. (1999). Neoteny, naturalization and other constituents of human development. In: C. Ryff & V. M. Marshall (Ed.), *The self and society in aging processes*. New York: Springer, pp 67–93.

Dannefer, D. (2003). Cumulative advantage/disadvantage and the life course: cross-fertilizing age and social science theory. *The Journals of Gerontology Series B: Psychological Sciences and Social Sciences, 58*(6), S327–S337.

Davidovic, M., Djordjevic, Z., Erceg, P., Despotovic, N., & Milosevic, D. P. (2007). Ageism: does it exist among children? *The Scientific World Journal, 7*, 1134–1139.

Davidson, K., Daly, T., & Arber, S. (1970). Exploring the social worlds of older men. *Gender and ageing: Changing roles and relationships*. Maidenhead: Open University Press, pp 168–185.

de Medeiros, K., Rubinstein, R. L., & Doyle, P. (2013). A place of one's own: reinterpreting the meaning of home among childless older women. In: G. Rowles & M. Bernard (Eds.), *Environmental gerontology: Making meaning places in old age*. New York: Springer, pp 79–104.

Debpuur, C., Welaga, P., Wak, G., & Hodgson, A. (2010). Self-reported health and functional limitations among older people in the Kassena-Nankana District, Ghana. *Global Health Action, 3*(Suppl. 2), 54–63.

Estes, C. L., Biggs, S., & Phillipson, C. (2003). *Social theory, social policy and ageing: A critical introduction*. Maidenhead: Open University Press.

Ferraro, K. F., & Shippee, T. P. (2009). Aging and cumulative inequality: how does inequality get under the skin? *The Gerontologist, 49*(3), 333–343.

Finkenauer, S., Sherratt, J., Marlow, J., & Brodey, A. (2012). When injustice gets old: a systematic review of trans aging. *Journal of Gay & Lesbian Social Services, 24*(4), 311–330.

Fonchingong, C. C. (2013). On the fringe of poverty: care arrangements for older people in rural Cameroon. In: Pranitha Maharaj (Ed.), *Aging and health in Africa*. New York: Springer, pp 157–170.

Gendron, T. L., Welleford, E. A., Inker, J., & White, J. T. (2015). The language of ageism: why we need to use words carefully. *The Gerontologist*, 1–10, doi: 10.1093/geront/gnv066.

Gilleard, C., & Higgs, P. (2010). Aging without agency: theorizing the fourth age. *Aging & Mental Health, 14*(2), 121–128.

Gitlin, L. N. (2003). Conducting research on home environments: lessons learned and new directions. *The Gerontologist, 43*(5), 628–637. doi: 10.1093/geront/43.5.628.

Golant, S. M. (1985). In defense of age-segregated housing. *Aging, 348*, 22–26.

Golant, S. M. (2003). Conceptualizing time and behavior in environmental gerontology: a pair of old issues deserving new thought. *The Gerontologist, 43*(5), 638–648.

Gullette, M. M. (2004). *Aged by culture*. Chicago, IL: University of Chicago Press.

Hazan, H., & Raz, A. E. (1997). The authorized self: how middle age defines old age in the postmodern. *Semiotica, 113*(3–4), 257–276.

Higgs, P., & Gilleard, C. (2015). *Rethinking old age: Theorising the fourth age*. London: Palgrave.

Holmerova, I., Vankova, H., Juraskova, B., & Hrneiarikova, D. (2011). Population ageing in the Czech Republic. In A. Hoff (Ed.), *Population ageing in Central and Eastern Europe: Societal and policy implications*. Aldershot: Ashgate Publishing, Ltd, pp 79–94.

Holwerda, T. J., Beekman, A. T. F., Deeg, D. J. H., Stek, M. L., van Tilburg, T. G., Visser, P. J., ... Schoevers, R. A. (2012). Increased risk of mortality associated with social isolation in older men: only when feeling lonely? Results from the Amsterdam Study of the Elderly (AMSTEL). *Psychological Medicine: A Journal of Research in Psychiatry and the Allied Sciences, 42*(4), 843–853. doi: 10.1017/S0033291711001772.

Katz, S. (1996). *Disciplining old age: The formation of gerontological knowledge*. Charlottesville, VA: University of Virginia Press.

Kimmel, D. C., Rose, T., & David, S. (2006). *Lesbian, gay, bisexual, and transgender aging: Research and clinical perspectives*. New York: Columbia University Press.

King, N., & Calasanti, T. (2013). Men's aging amidst intersecting relations of inequality. *Sociology Compass, 7*(9), 699–710.

Kinsella, K. G., Wan, H., & US Bureau of the Census (2009). *An aging world: 2008*. Washington, DC: US Department of Commerce, Economics and Statistics Administration, US Census Bureau.

Kuyper, L., & Fokkema, T. (2010). Loneliness among older lesbian, gay, and bisexual adults: the role of minority stress. *Archives of Sexual Behavior, 39*(5), 1171–1180.

Kyobutungi, C., Egondi, T., & Ezeh, A. (2010). The health and well-being of older people in Nairobi's slums. *Global Health Action, 3*(Suppl. 2), 45–53.

Laws, G. (1995). Understanding ageism: lessons from feminism and postmodernism. *The Gerontologist, 35*(1), 112–118. doi: 10.1093/geront/35.1.112.

Lawton, M. P., & Nahemow, L. (1973). *Ecology and the aging process.* Washington, DC: American Psychological Association.

Lewin, A. C., & Stier, H. (2010). Immigration, state support and the economic well-being of the elderly in Israel. In: S. Carmel (Ed.), *Aging in Israel: Research, policy and practice.* New Brunswick, NJ: Transaction Publishers, pp 277–300.

Maharaj, P. (2013). *Aging and health in Africa.* New York: Springer.

McHugh, K. E. (2003). Three faces of ageism: society, image and place. *Ageing and Society, 23*(02), 165–185.

Neugarten, B. L. (1974). Age groups in American society and the rise of the young-old. *The Annals of the American Academy of Political and Social Science, 415*(1), 187–198. doi: 10.1177/000271627441500114.

Nygren, C., Oswald, F., Iwarsson, S., Fänge, A., Sixsmith, J., Schilling, O., ... Wahl, H.-W. (2007). Relationships between objective and perceived housing in very old age. *The Gerontologist, 47*(1), 85–95.

Orel, N. A. (2004). Gay, lesbian, and bisexual elders: expressed needs and concerns across focus groups. *Journal of Gerontological Social Work, 43*(2–3), 57–77.

Orel, N. A., & Fruhauf, C. A. (2013). Lesbian, gay, bisexual, and transgender grandparents. In: A.E. Golberg & K.R. Allen (Eds.), *LGBT-parent families.* New York: Springer, pp 177–192.

Persson, D. I. (2009). Unique challenges of transgender aging: implications from the literature. *Journal of Gerontological Social Work, 52*(6), 633–646.

Phillipson, C. (2007). The 'elected' and the 'excluded': sociological perspectives on the experience of place and community in old age. *Ageing and Society, 27*(03), 321–342.

Powell, J., & Biggs, S. (2000). Managing old age: the disciplinary web of power, surveillance and normalization. *Journal of Aging and Identity, 5*(1), 3–13.

Powell, J. L. (2006a). *Rethinking social theory and later life*. New York: Nova Science Publishing Incorporated.

Powell, J. L. (2006b). *Social theory and aging*. Lanham, MD: Rowman & Littlefield.

Ribbe, M. W., Ljunggren, G., Steel, K., Topinkova, E. V. A., Hawes, C., Ikegami, N., ... Jónnson, P. V. (1997). Nursing homes in 10 nations: a comparison between countries and settings. *Age and Ageing, 26*(Suppl. 2), 3–12.

Riley, M. W. (1987). On the significance of age in sociology. *American Sociological Review, 52*(1), 1–14. doi: 10.2307/2095388.

Robinson, T., Callister, M., Magoffin, D., & Moore, J. (2007). The portrayal of older characters in Disney animated films. *Journal of Aging Studies, 21*(3), 203–213.

Roth, E., & Eckert, J. K. (2011). The vernacular landscape of assisted living. *Journal of Aging Studies, 25*(3), 215–224. doi:10.1016/j.jaging.2011.03.005.

Rowles, G. D. (1981). The surveillance zone as meaningful space for the aged. *The Gerontologist, 21*(3), 304–311.

Rowles, G. D. (1984). Aging in rural environments. In: I. Altman, P.M. Lawton, & J.F. Wohlwill (Eds.), *Elderly people and the environment*. New York: Springer, pp 129–157.

Rowles, G. D. (1993). Evolving images of place in aging and 'aging in place'. *Generations, 17*(2), 65–70.

Rowles, G. D., & Chaudhury, H. (2005). *Home and identity in late life: International perspectives*. New York: Springer Publishing.

Rubinstein, R. L., & de Medeiros, K. (2003). Ecology and the aging self. In: H.-W. Wahl, R. J. Schiedt, & P. G. Windely (Eds.), *Annual review of gerontology and geriatrics* (Vol. 23). New York: Springer, pp 59–82.

Rubinstein, R. L., & de Medeiros, K. (2005). Home, self, and identity. In: G.D. Rowles & H. Chaudhury (Eds.), *Home and identity in late life international perspectives*, New York: Springer, pp 47–62.

Rubinstein, R., & de Medeiros, K. (2006). Housing. In R. Schulz (Ed.), *Encyclopedia of aging* (4th edn). New York: Springer, pp 546–548.

Rubinstein, R. L., & Kilbride, J. C. (1992). *Elders living alone: Fraility and the perception of choice*. New Brunswick, NJ: Transaction Publishers.

Savla, J., Davey, A., Sundström, G., Zarit, S. H., & Malmberg, B. (2008). Home help services in Sweden: responsiveness to changing demographics and needs. *European Journal of Ageing, 5*(1), 47–55.

Silver, C. B. (2003). Gendered identities in old age: toward (de)gendering? *Journal of Aging Studies, 17*(4), 379–397.

Thane, P. (2000). *Old age in English history: Past experiences, present issues.* Oxford: Oxford University Press.

Thane, P. (2010). The history of aging and old age in 'Western'cultures. *A guide to humanistic studies in aging: What does it mean to grow old.* Baltimore, MD: Johns Hopkins University Press, pp 33–56.

Thompson, E. H. (2007). Older men as invisible men in contemporary society. *Understanding inequality: The intersection of race/ethnicity, class, and gender.* London: Rowman & Littlefield Publishers, Inc., pp 289–298.

Tilley, C. Y. (1994). *A phenomenology of landscape: Places, paths, and monuments.* Oxford: Berg.

United Nations (2013). *World population ageing 2013.* New York: United Nations.

Van Minh, H., Byass, P., Chuc, N. T. K., & Wall, S. (2010). Patterns of health status and quality of life among older people in rural Vietnam. *Global Health Action, 3*(Suppl. 2), 64–69.

Wahl, H.-W., & Weisman, G. D. (2003). Environmental gerontology at the beginning of the new millennium: reflections on its historical, empirical, and theoretical development. *The Gerontologist, 43*(5), 616–627.

Witten, T. M., & Eyler, A. E. (2012). *Gay, lesbian, bisexual, and transgender aging: Challenges in research, practice, and policy.* Baltimore, MD: Johns Hopkins University Press.

WHO (World Health Organization) (2015). *World health statistics 2015.* Geneva, Switzerland: WHO.

EIGHT

Financing old age

This chapter addresses some of the issues surrounding financing old age, starting first with the worldwide demographic transition. In light of population changes, specific issues are addressed in this chapter such as pension systems, work, unemployment and aging, and other ways in which older age is supported, both externally (for example, government, charities) and internally (for example, family, villages). The chapter starts with an overview of recent demographic trends to provide a context for understanding changes in policies and programs. It then briefly examines retirement as a relatively new concept and life phase. Next, pension systems, including economic change and reform strategies, are explored. Although changes in family structure were addressed in the previous chapter, issues around family and intergenerational support and transfer of wealth are briefly addressed in this chapter.

Although it is common for books or journal articles to begin with the latest demographic predictions that point to a drastically aging society, the demographic transition has purposely been left toward the end of this book for several reasons. First, the increasing percentage of older adults has often been positioned negatively. Words and phrases like 'grey tsunami', 'the coming age storm', 'burdens of an aging society' and others are very common and reinforce the idea of generational conflict and older people as a drain on society. What often is not highlighted is that in many respects, the increase in the percentage of older people is a success story and offers new opportunities to rethink possibilities throughout the lifecourse, as well as challenges associated with these changes, both of which will be addressed in this chapter with regard to demographic dividends (Kinsella & Phillips, 2005; Kinsella, Wan, & US Bureau of the Census, 2009).

Although health is an important indicator of wellbeing in later life (with better health associated with higher ratings of wellbeing), wealth is also an important predictor (Larson, 1978; Diener & Chan, 2011). People with more resources tend to have higher levels of life satisfaction (and health), although not necessarily wellbeing, in later years (Lewin & Stier, 2010). Here, life satisfaction refers to how people view their lives overall; wellbeing refers to the emotional quality attributed to their everyday experiences (Kahneman & Deaton, 2010). It is beyond the scope of the chapter to address wealth (valuable assets, including savings, homes or other material goods or resources) in depth. However, the chapter will address issues of access to financial resources through pension systems and to housing as indirect indicators of wealth.

Three perspectives from Table 2.1 will be important in the current chapter. The first two, cumulative advantage/disadvantage (Dannefer, 1999, 2003) and cumulative inequality (Ferraro & Shippee, 2009), which were also brought up in Chapter Seven on social location and place, refer to the ways in which social systems generate inequalities (or advantages) that accumulate over one's lifetime and directly impact on older age. Access to paid work, healthcare, education and others will affect how one ages. The third perspective, the political-economy perspective (Estes, Swan, & Gerard, 1982; Estes, Biggs, & Phillipson, 2003), is described as a framework that 'recognizes old age as socially constructed, a product of struggles that result in the unequal distribution of societal resources' (Quadagno & Reid, 1999, p 344). This perspective also examines the social structures that shape how age is experienced. These underlying perspectives are important to consider with regard to financing later life and the establishment of social policy, and the impact of access throughout one's lifecourse.

The demographic transition

The demographic transition describes the interrelated changes in fertility, mortality and migration that result in the rapid growth and aging of a population (Harper, 2004; Kunkel, Brown, & Whittington, 2014). In 2008, there was a monthly average increase in the world of 870,000 people aged 65 (Kinsella et al., 2009). Table 8.1 shows fertility rates, median age, life expectancy at birth and percentage of the total population aged 65 and over for selected countries at three time periods: 1973, 1993, and 2013. As the data indicate, fertility rates are declining, average life expectancy at birth is increasing and the percentage of people aged 65 and over is increasing for nearly all countries in the world. All of these changes have a direct impact on a country's economy, including production and consumption of goods and services (for example, health insurance or old-age pensions.)

With regard to fertility and global aging, reductions in fertility rates around the world have been attributed to economics and industrialization as well as access to birth control. The idea that industrialization is linked to lower fertility points to less need for children to perform labor-intensive work such as farming. Economic links to lower fertility suggest that fertility patterns often follow economic cycles, with good economic cycles linked to higher fertility rates, as compared to bad economic times, which are linked to declines in fertility (Kunkel et al, 2014). Although fertility rates have been steadily declining in most places in the world, there can be a slight variation of increases and decreases based on current economic circumstances. In other words, economics doesn't always do a good job of predicting or explaining fertility patterns.

Table 8.1: Fertility rates, median age, and life expectancy at birth for selected countries at three time periods: 1973, 1993, and 2013

Region and country	Fertility rate*			Life expectancy at birth*			% total age ≤65		
	1973	1993	2013	1973	1993	2013	1973	1993	2013
East Asia and Pacific									
Australia[b]	2.49	1.86	1.92	71.85	77.88	82.20	8.52	11.6	14.4
China[c]	4.54	2.01	1.67	65.00	69.99	75.35	3.86	5.61	8.89
Japan[b]	2.14	1.46	1.43	73.76	79.29	83.33	7.52	13.4	25.00
Korea, Rep.[b]	4.07	1.65	1.12	63.23	72.68	81.46	3.42	5.50	12.20
Philippines[d]	5.93	4.11	3.04	61.37	65.71	68.71	3.08	3.10	4.40
Singapore[a]	2.80	1.78	1.19	69.44	76.05	82.35	3.77	6.00	10.50
Thailand[c]	4.95	1.96	1.40	60.93	70.53	74.37	3.55	5.07	9.74
Europe and Central Asia									
Austria[b]	1.94	1.5	1.44	71.0	76.07	80.89	14.50	15.10	18.40
Belgium[b]	1.95	1.61	1.79	71.64	76.35	80.39	13.90	15.70	17.80
Croatia[a]	1.97	1.52	1.51	69.03	71.52	77.13	10.40	12.80	18.30
Czech Republic[b]	2.31	1.67	1.45	70.02	72.77	78.28	12.80	13.10	17.00
Denmark[b]	1.92	1.75	1.73	73.68	75.12	80.30	13.00	15.50	18.00

Region and country	Fertility rate*			Life expectancy at birth*			% total age ≤65		
	1973	1993	2013	1973	1993	2013	1973	1993	2013
France[b]	2.28	1.73	2.01	72.36	77.30	81.97	13.20	14.70	18.20
Germany[b]	1.54	1.28	1.38	71.02	75.87	81.04	14.50	15.30	21.00
Ireland[b]	3.71	1.90	2.01	71.28	75.30	81.04	10.70	10.90	12.30
Italy[b]	2.30	1.25	1.43	72.03	77.72	82.29	11.70	15.90	21.60
Netherlands[b]	1.90	1.57	1.72	74.14	76.92	81.10	10.50	13.00	17.10
Norway[b]	2.23	1.86	1.85	77.44	77.15	81.45	13.30	16.20	15.70
Russian Federation[a]	2.01	1.39	1.7	68.44	76.05	82.35	8.48	11.50	13.20
Slovenia[b]	2.23	1.33	1.58	69.40	73.25	80.28	10.60	11.60	17.30
Spain[b]	2.84	1.27	1.32	72.61	77.55	82.43	10.00	14.30	18.10
Sweden[b]	1.87	1.99	1.91	74.87	78.06	81.70	14.50	17.70	19.30
Turkey[c]	5.26	2.84	2.01	54.10	65.84	75.18	4.24	4.85	7.27
Turkmenistan[c]	6.07	3.90	2.33	59.14	62.77	65.46	4.59	4.00	4.08
United Kingdom[b]	2.04	1.76	1.92	72.32	76.39	80.96	13.70	15.90	17.20

Region and country	Fertility rate*			Life expectancy at birth*			% total age ≤65		
	1973	1993	2013	1973	1993	2013	1973	1993	2013
Latin America and Caribbean									
Argentina[a]	3.20	2.88	2.12	67.47	72.22	76.19	7.43	9.38	10.70
Bolivia[d]	6.42	4.74	3.22	47.05	60.25	67.22	3.77	4.64	6.23
Brazil[c]	4.68	2.58	1.80	60.04	67.70	73.89	3.53	4.31	7.33
Chile[b]	3.50	2.51	1.82	63.91	74.44	79.84	5.62	6.81	10.40
Mexico[c]	6.36	3.12	2.19	62.84	71.98	77.35	3.73	4.48	6.18
Peru[c]	5.95	3.51	2.42	55.76	67.01	74.81	3.54	4.19	6.54
Middle East and North Africa									
Israel[b]	3.70	2.80	3.03	71.69	77.15	82.06	7.17	9.32	10.80
Jordan[c]	7.75	5.00	3.24	62.23	70.57	73.90	3.14	3.06	3.77
Morroco[d]	6.38	3.61	2.74	53.64	66.14	70.87	3.49	4.38	6.04
Saudi Arabia[a]	7.31	5.35	2.64	56.04	70.33	75.70	3.33	2.87	2.76
North America									
Canada[b]	1.89	1.70	1.61	73.16	77.69	81.40	8.24	11.70	15.2
United States[b]	1.88	2.02	1.87	71.36	75.42	78.84	10.20	12.60	14.00

Region and country	Fertility rate*			Life expectancy at birth*			% total age ≤65		
	1973	1993	2013	1973	1993	2013	1973	1993	2013
South Asia									
India[d]	5.24	3.63	2.48	51.02	59.47	66.46	3.45	3.99	5.38
Nepal[e]	5.93	4.91	2.3	43.72	57.36	68.40	3.09	3.61	5.26
Pakistan[d]	6.61	5.63	3.19	55.04	62.03	66.59	3.80	3.96	4.48
Sub-Saharan Africa									
Equatorial Guinea[a]	6.68	5.90	4.85	40.63	47.33	53.11	5.09	4.27	2.87
Ethiopia[e]	7.09	7.09	4.52	43.69	48.22	63.63	2.77	3.10	3.42
Ghana[d]	6.89	5.28	3.86	50.21	57.58	61.10	2.53	2.90	3.46
Kenya[d]	7.96	5.51	4.38	53.94	57.53	61.68	3.35	2.70	2.72
Nigeria[d]	6.63	6.35	5.98	42.49	46.07	52.50	2.84	2.89	2.76
South Africa[c]	5.42	3.30	2.39	53.87	62.19	56.74	3.35	3.31	5.03
Zimbabwe[e]	7.42	4.69	3.49	55.92	54.92	59.77	3.13	3.07	3.05

Notes: [a] High income: non-OECD; [b] High income: OECD; [c] Upper middle income; [d] Lower middle income; [e] Low income.

* Data from world bank, http://data.worldbank.org/indicator/SP.DYN.TFRT.IN?order=wbapi_data_value_2013%20wbapi_data_value%20 wbapi_data_value-last&sort=asc

Changes in mortality patterns from high infant mortality to mortality occurring much later in life also contribute to an aging society, as does migration. As mentioned earlier, improvements in public health, such as sanitation, clean water and childhood immunizations, have meant declines in childhood deaths in many countries (Alley & Crimmins, 2010). The ability to treat acute disease and help people better manage chronic disease that may otherwise be immediately fatal has also led to mortality at greater ages, therefore increasing average life-expectancy rates at birth.

Finally, migration, can affect the availability of jobs and food, security and economic opportunity. Migration also affects a population's age composition, leading some countries to age more rapidly if working-age citizens relocate, leaving behind older residents. The combination of fertility, mortality and migration rates has meant rapid aging for countries such as Thailand, shrinking (and aging) populations for countries such as Germany and Italy (United Nations, 2013).

Overall, this worldwide demographic transition will have a profound effect on how later life is financed and by whom, and which smaller groups within the larger category of 'old' receive what supports. For some countries, especially in Europe, the demographic transition may mean shrinking populations. For example, the European Union is expected to experience a 10% reduction in its population between 2000 and 2050 (Bonoli & Shinkawa, 2006). For others, especially in Asia, the transition will mean that there will be more older people needing care and support than there are younger people to provide for them (Naidoo et al, 2010). Africa, which still has a very small percentage of older people, is facing challenges with regard to supporting grandmothers who are the primary caregivers for grandchildren. This is due to absent parents who move to urban areas for work or who have been lost to disease such as HIV/AIDS. As in many issues with aging, older women have it particularly hard in most countries, given the lack of or reduced access to paid employment, the expectations that they will provide care for family members and their overall longevity (Burton, 1996; Koropeckyj-Cox, Pienta, & Brown, 2007; Maharaj, 2013).

Work, unemployment and aging

Social location was discussed in the previous chapter. As mentioned, access to paid labor and economic resources throughout one's lifecourse will directly influence the experience of aging. The United Nations (United Nations, 2013) estimated that the labor-force participation of people aged 65 and over in less-developed regions of the world was around 31%, as compared to 8% in more developed regions. Men comprise the majority of the total labor force among older adults. Table 8.2 lists World Bank data for the percentage of unemployment for the total workforce for selected countries as well as the labor-force participation of men and women aged 15 years and older for 1993, 2003 and 2013. The World Bank defines labor-force participation rate as 'the proportion of the population ages 15 and older that is economically active; all people who supply labor for the production of goods and services during a specified period' (World Bank, 2015). As is demonstrated by the data, there is great variability, especially in the percentage of women's participation. In addition, many countries show a decline in men's participation, although the declines are small, for the most part. This doesn't include specific information with regard to older workers but does provide some insight into changes in the workforce, which in turn can affect changes in retirement funding, opportunities for personal savings and other pathways to acquisition of wealth. For example, the life-cycle hypothesis of savings (Ando & Modigliani, 1963) suggests that people keep their consumption levels relatively the same over various periods of earning or retirement. Their greatest opportunity to save is during their working years. Knowing who is working and who is not due to unemployment, cultural attitudes toward women in the workforce, retirement policies and other issues are important to consider with regard to aging populations.

Certainly unemployment and employment rates alone do not tell a complete picture. For example, unemployment rates include only those who are currently not working but are available for and are seeking work in the formal sector. Countries like Thailand, which has a formal and an informal employment sector, would not count informal workers in official unemployment figures (Fox, 2005).

Looking at women's employment specifically is important, since women are often dependent on their spouses for economic support. When women are in the paid workforce, they are likely to be in jobs that pay substantially less than men's professions, offer fewer benefits and may even have earlier retirement ages than men's because of cultural attitudes towards women in the workforce. This puts older women at greater risk for poverty in later life (Alli & Maharaj, 2013). Given that many older women also serve as caregivers for sick children, grandchildren and spouses, lack of access to funds creates an even greater burden (Gomez-Olive, Thorogood, Clark, Kahn, & Tollman, 2010).

Another important consideration is the demographic dependency ratio, which is the number of working-age adults (age 16–64) relative to the number of people assumed to be non-working (age 15 and under, and age 65 and older) (Alley & Crimmins, 2010; Phillipson, 2013; Kunkel et al, 2014). The old-age dependency ratio specifically looks at people aged 65 and over compared to the 'working age' group. Figure 8.1 shows the old-age dependency ratios for 12 countries at two time points, 2008 and 2013.

With the exception of India and Ethiopia, the other countries depicted show an increase in the old-age dependency ratio, meaning that there are fewer working-age people to support the growing older population. Old-age dependency ratios are important to pay attention to, since they can identify potential upcoming economic issues that need to be addressed, such as how to maintain production and consumption levels to increase economic growth at a time when there are more 'non-producers' or people outside of the paid workforce who are consuming goods, as compared to people in the workforce. As many caution with regard to dependency ratios, however, there is an assumption in the calculation that people aged 65 and over are not working. This may or may not be true for a given area. Also, it assumes lack of productivity and does not take into account ways in which older people (especially older women) participate in production through non-paid work such as providing care, which may, in turn, free up others (for example, parents of children) to work.

Table 8.2: Percentage total unemployed and labor force participation for men and women aged 15 years and older for selected countries at three time periods

Region and country	Unemployment (% total workforce)*			Men 15+ years old labor force participation			Women 15+ years old labor force participation		
	1993	2003	2013	1973	1993	2013	1973	1993	2013
East Asia and Pacific									
Australia[b]	10.9	5.9	5.7	73.8	71.6	71.8	51.8	55.9	58.8
China[c]	4.3	4.3	4.6	84.8	80.9	78.3	72.4	68.2	63.9
Japan[b]	2.5	5.2	4.0	78.2	74.3	70.4	50.4	48.5	48.8
Thailand[c]	1.5	1.5	0.7	84.3	80.9	80.7	67.6	65.5	64.3
Europe and Central Asia									
Austria[b]	4.3	4.3	4.9	69.9	68.3	67.7	45.5	50.5	54.6
Denmark[b]	10.7	5.4	7.0	73.2	71.7	6.4	61.5	59.8	58.7
Netherlands[b]	6.3	3.6	6.7	69.7	73.1	70.6	45.6	55.8	58.5
Sweden[b]	9.5	5.9	8.1	67.9	67.4	67.9	59.9	58.6	60.3
United Kingdom	10.5	4.9	7.5	71.8	69.9	68.7	52.2	54.5	55.7
Latin America and Caribbean									
Argentina[a]	10.1	16.1	7.1	76.4	73.2	75.0	40.3	44.6	47.5
Bolivia[d]	4.9	5.4	2.6	82.4	81.6	80.9	53.2	60.5	54.2
Brazil[c]	6.0	9.7	6.5	85.6	81.4	80.8	53.0	56.6	59.4

Region and country	Unemployment (% total workforce)*			Men 15+ years old labor force participation			Women 15+ years old labor force participation		
	1993	2003	2013	1973	1993	2013	1973	1993	2013
Chile[b]	8.5	8.5	6.0	78.5	73.1	74.8	35.7	35.9	49.2
Middle East and North Africa									
Israel[b]	10.0	10.7	6.3	62.8	60.0	69.1	43.5	49.2	57.9
Jordan[c]	19.7	15.4	12.6	8.0	67.3	66.6	10.8	11.9	15.6
Morroco[d]	1.5	11.9	9.2	80.9	78.5	75.8	26.9	27.1	26.5
North America									
Canada[b]	11.4	7.6	7.1	73.2	73.2	71.0	57.1	61.1	61.6
United States[b]	7.0	6.1	7.4	74.3	72.3	68.9	56.6	58.5	56.3
South Asia									
India[d]	4.3	3.9	3.6	84.5	83.1	79.9	35.5	35.7	27.0
Nepal[e]	2.2	2.0	2.7	90.5	89.6	87.1	79.8	80.9	79.9
Pakistan[d]	4.3	7.7	5.1	83.0	83.4	82.9	14.2	17.0	24.6
Sub-Saharan Africa									
Ethiopia[e]	5.5	5.8	5.0	90.1	90.8	89.3	72.3	76.3	78.2
Kenya[d]	10.1	9.6	9.1	78.4	71.2	72.4	68.0	61.2	62.2
Nigeria[d]	7.4	7.6	7.5	73.0	63.3	63.7	40.6	46.8	48.2
South Africa[c]	25.3	27.1	24.6	66.8	62.8	60.5	42.5	47.5	44.5

Notes: [a] High income: non-OECD; [b] High income: OECD; [c] Upper middle income; [d] Lower middle income; [e] Low income.
* Data from World Bank, http://data.worldbank.org/indicator.

Figure 8.1: Old-age dependency ratios for selected countries, 2008 and 2013*

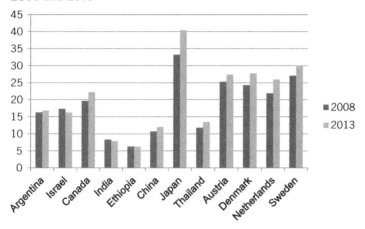

Note: *Data from World Bank (Holzmann, 2005; www.worldbank.org).

Retirement and pension systems

While the previous section looked at some aspects of labor, this section provides a brief overview of retirement. Retirement is a relatively new concept, although some types of retirement options have existed throughout the world for years. For example, men in ancient Rome were required to withdraw from military service at age 60 and were provided with a pension (Zickar, 2013). In medieval Europe, pensions were sometimes provided by wealthy individuals to their older servants, often through provisions in wills (Thane, 2010; Zickar, 2013). Changes in work practice from agriculture-based to new industrialization are credited as part of the reason for the development of pension programs. With changes in support structures (for example, charitable organizations such as churches and families), the modern welfare state emerged (Biggs, Estes, & Phillipson, 2003). Pat Thane (2010) notes that until the 20th century, poor men and women were expected to work into old age because of the existence of poor-relief systems that supplemented the incomes of poor older people if they completed tasks such as mending, caring for horses, caring for children, cleaning or other menial jobs.

Based somewhat on the stigmas of poverty-relief systems, retirement was not a concept that was met initially with enthusiasm and was driven by the need to encourage older workers to leave work for a couple of reasons. One reason to 'retire' older workers was based on assumptions that older workers would be unable to master new technologies that were being introduced through the development of factories. Another was to make room for younger workers who were currently unemployed (Thane, 2010).

Germany was the first country to establish a national old-age retirement system (von Herbay, 2014). Although the retirement age was initially set at 70 years, it was changed to 65 in 1916 (von Herbay, 2014). In the United States, prior to the enactment of the Social Security Act in 1935, there were pension programs for veterans and government workers and some optional pension programs in eight states. High unemployment caused by the Great Depression (Zickar, 2013) led to the passage of a national social security program in the United States. As Paul Higgs and Chris Gilleard (2015) explain with regards to pension systems in general:

> The rise and decline of earning power over the course of a man's working life came to reflect the rise and fall in his capacity to provide for his family leading to a corresponding decline in status. Concerns about the pauperisation of old age rose markedly in the urbanised industrial society of the nineteenth century. These concerns led eventually to the introduction of the state old age pension as a means of financially securing old age. (p 7)

Leaving the paid workforce was not a cultural norm, nor was it an expectation (or desire) of workers. Pat Thane (2000) explains, 'The first generation of men who were unexpectedly retired from manual work in the 1940s and 1950s had it thrust upon them, bewildered, after adult lifetimes dominated by work, unemployment, and war. They felt the shock of sudden exclusion the more acutely because it was often retirement into poverty without a cushion of accumulated savings' (p 7–8). The United States had a similar experience. Retirement as the 'golden years' became part of a marketing initiative driven by Florida real estate developers who offered affordable 'age restricted' communities for people aged 55 and over, ranging from mobile home parks to condominiums (Trolander, 2011). In this way, retirement was presented as a time of life to relax and enjoy, a time that a person deserved after a lifetime of work. The Western notion of retirement as a necessary and normative lifecourse phase subsequently became engrained in many countries.

In contrast, many regions have established pension systems only within the last 40 or so years. For example, the Republic of Korea established its system in 1973. Thailand's system was established in 1990 and Botswana's in 1996. There are two important reasons for this. In these and other countries, family support is still the cultural norm. Therefore, the expectation that government rather than family should care for older adults was simply not part of policy discussion, especially given competing resources for other services (for example, child healthcare). Second, the coming demographic transition was happening quickly and went somewhat unnoticed, due to its speed. For example, Thailand is experiencing the transition from being a relatively young country to having a high proportion of older people in a span of about 30 years. This is in contrast to France, whose demographic transition took around 120 years, giving France time to establish old-age pension policies (Kunkel et al, 2014). Given that Asia is expected to see the most dramatic change in population aging, Asian countries will need to be particularly mindful of sustainability in the future.

Table 8.3 lists the year that a formal old-age pension system was established, the current type of program and the pensionable ages of men and women for selected countries. The Organisation for Economic Cooperation and Development (OECD, 2011) defines 'pensionable age' as the 'age at which people can first draw full benefits' (p 20). It notes that pension ages are defined via legislation in most countries, although some countries consider years of contribution or participation in the system as the defining point for eligibility. Social insurance programs, such as those in nearly all of the countries included on the table (with the exception of Nigeria, Kenya and Botswana) refer to contributory programs in which people receive some type of benefit or services in return for their contribution. These can vary widely in coverage and scope. Social assistance programs 'are non-contributory transfers in cash or in-kind and are usually targeted at the poor and vulnerable' (World Bank, 2015). Eight of the countries listed (South Africa, Australia, Republic of Korea, Thailand, Argentina, Brazil, Canada and the United Kingdom) have social assistance programs in conjunction with social insurance. Mandatory individual account systems, like those in Nigeria and Kenya, can be private or public. Universal programs cover people

Table 8.3: Establishment by year of old-age programs in selected countries and regions

Country	Year established*	Current type of program*	Current pensionable age in years*	% 65 and over
Africa				
South Africa	1928	Social insurance (survivors) and social assistance	60 men and women	5.6%
Nigeria	1961	Mandatory individual account system	50 men and women	2.7%
Kenya	1965	Mandatory individual account (pension fund) and voluntary provident fund system	60 men and women	2.7%
Botswana	1996	Universal (residents of Botswana)	65 men and women	2.7%

Country	Year established*	Current type of program*	Current pensionable age in years*	% 65 and over
Asia and the Pacific				
Australia	1908	Social assistance and mandatory occupational pension system	65 men, 64 women	14.0%
Japan	1941	Social insurance system	65 men and women	24.1%
Korea, Rep. of	1973	Social insurance and social assistance	60 men and women	11.9%
Thailand	1990	Social insurance and social assistance	55 men and women	9.3%
Americas				
Argentina	1904–1958	Social insurance and social assistance	65 men, 60 women	10.8%
Brazil	1923–1936	Social insurance and social assistance	65 men, 60 women	7.4%
Canada	1927	Universal pension and social insurance	65 men and women	14.8%
United States	1935	Social insurance system	66 men and women	13.6%
Peru	1936 and 1962	Social insurance and individual account	65 men and women	6.3%

Country	Year established*	Current type of program*	Current pensionable age in years*	% 65 and over
Europe				
Germany	1889	Social insurance	65 men and women	20.8%
Denmark	1891	Universal and social insurance	65 men and women	17.3%
Belgium	1900	Social insurance	65 men and women	17.8%
Austria	1907	Social insurance	65 men, 60 women	18.1%
Ireland	1908	Social insurance and social assistance	65 men and women	12.1%
United Kingdom	1908	Social insurance, social assistance and occupational pension	65 men, 61 women	17.1%
France	1910	Social insurance, mandatory complementary pension, and social assistance program	60 men and women	17.4%
Luxembourg	1911	Social insurance	65 men and women	14.0%
Sweden	1913	Notional defined contribution (NDC), social insurance, mandatory individual account system	65 men and women	19.0%

Country	Year established*	Current type of program*	Current pensionable age in years*	% 65 and over
Spain	1919	Social insurance and social assistance	65 men and women	17.3%

Note: *Data from International Social Security Association (www. issa.int).

meeting citizenship requirements. As noted, many countries have more than one type of system in place.

Depending on whether work into later life is encouraged or discouraged based on economic conditions and factors such as unemployment rates, countries may use defined benefit plans or defined contribution plans. Defined benefit plans are those that provide a monthly benefit based on age, job tenure and earnings (Wheaton & Crimmins, 2012). In defined benefit plans, employees do not have incentives to work past their eligibility years. Defined contribution pensions 'specify the annual contribution of the employer, which may be matched by the employee' (p 29) (Frank, 1991). Defined contribution pensions do not typically have an age requirement and therefore can encourage labor-force participation past typical retirement ages.

As Chris Phillipson (2013) has pointed out, there have been substantial changes in retirement and welfare systems since the 1990s. Retirement ages are being raised in many places, therefore extending working lives. Also, mechanisms for funding programs such as healthcare and others have undergone change. This is true for both more-developed and less-developed countries, although for slightly different reasons. For people in less-developed countries, old-age income is a relatively new concept for relatively few in the country. People in less-developed countries neither expect income in their old age nor have a means of securing sustainable income in later life (Harper, 2006). Harper (2006) writes that most 'have no prospect of a secure and sustainable income in their old age. Few, even among workers, receive any public benefits. In contrast to the 84 percent of those over age 60 in OECD countries who receive a pension, under 20 percent in many Latin American countries, under 10 percent in Southeast Asia, and under 5 percent in some parts of sub-Saharan Africa do' (p 26). An additional challenge for older people in African countries is the focus on healthcare spending for treatment of catastrophic diseases such as HIV/AIDS, leaving very little funding to be allocated to older people (Mwanyangala et al, 2010).

Retirement preferences

Retirement decisions are based solely on retirement policy, but occur on the institutional and individual level (Hofäcker, 2015). At the nation-specific institution level, there are 'push', 'pull' and 'stay' factors. Push factors are ways in which older workers are pressured through policies such as mandatory retirement or other forms of age discrimination to leave the paid work-force. 'Pull' factors are incentives such as pensions or early retirement benefits that entice or pull the older worker away from employment. Unlike push and pull, 'stay' factors are aimed at keeping workers in paid employment longer by better integrating them into the workforce through strategies such as additional education and training. On the individual level, health, employment insecurity, financial difficulties and the household context (for example, coordination of retirement with a spouse or partner) influence individual decisions about retirement. In his study, Dirk Hofäcker (2015) found that many workers approaching retirement age intended to retire before the national retirement age. He concludes, 'Thus, even though compared to the millennium turn, desired retirement ages have risen, individual retirement plans still continue to be oriented at the idea of withdrawing from employment before mandatory eligibility ages' (p 1552).

Reform approaches

To better align personal preferences with sustainability questions, due to the increased number of older people eligible to leave the workforce, many countries have adopted reforms for their pension programs. The OECD (2011) describes pension policies as involving the balance of the adequacy of benefits with affordability and sustainability. It suggests three routes to pension reform: (1) longer working lives, (2) a focus on the most vulnerable in the population for public retirement, and (3) encouraging personal saving. The World Bank describes a five-pillar model composed of the following: a non-contributory zero pillar funded by the government to alleviate poverty; a mandatory first pillar composed of employee contributions through a pay-as-you-go system; a mandatory second pillar that is a defined contribution plan; a voluntary third-pillar that includes discretionary funds such as personal savings accounts; and a non-financial fourth pillar that includes informal support (for example, family), formal social programs (for example, health insurance) and non-financial assets (Holzmann, 2005). The five pillars differ from the 'three-legged stool' approach (composed of a public pension, a private pension and personal savings) in that they provide a flexible framework for countries to use based on their population's needs and economic strength.

According to Robert Holzmann (2005), pension reform is often not motivated by changes in demographics, including dependency ratios due to aging societies, but instead is 'initially driven by short-term budgetary pressures resulting from fiscally unsustainable public systems' (p 23). Sustainability, he argues, often does not figure prominently into initial talks about pension reform. He does report that 29 countries reformed their pension programs between 1988 and 2009 (Holzmann, 2013). The reforms include establishment of a main funded 'pillar'.

Internal and external supports

As stated, retirement is a relatively new concept and one that is not the primary source of income in later life in many countries. Other ways in which older age is supported, therefore, are externally (for example, government cash transfer programs, charities) and internally (for example, family). Cash transfer programs describe programs whereby cash is provided to individuals. Conditional cash transfers are contingent upon performing particular actions (for example, enrolling children in school) or unconditional (Duflo, 2003). Although there are no comprehensive data sources to estimate how much money is given to support older adults (many poor-relief organizations do not keep data on age), charitable organizations are still an important source of support.

Internal supports

Internal supports include family support, both direct and through the intergenerational transfer of wealth and property. In societies where private ownership of property and assets is a norm, inheritance is the mechanism for passing these assets to the next generation (Finch, 2013). Janet Finch (2013) points out that in 'ordinary families' wealth is generally inherited in middle age and therefore not likely to be reinvested or even passed to the next generation for their use. In other words, it seems to have little financial impact. Martin Kohli and Harald Künemund (2003) note that 'in the conventional story of modernization, the emergence of the nuclear family and of the public old-age security system were seen as parallel and mutually reinforcing processes. The basic assumption was that the development of the welfare state would crowd out the private support within families' (p 123). They add that 'recent evidence, however, points to the opposite conclusion: Welfare state provisions, far from crowding out family support, enable the family in turn to provide new intergenerational support and transfers' (p 124). The basic premise of their argument is that pensions provide resources to older people that they will eventually distribute to younger family members either directly by paying for things like food, housing or education; accidentally by dying before using all of their savings, therefore transferring 'left over' funds to next of kin; and strategically, by purposely setting up documents such as wills with the intention of transferring assets.

The demographic dividend

The demographic dividend describes the positive impact and benefits that a country might experience while transitioning from a 'young' population to an older one (Mason, 2005). There are two phases. Initially, as fertility rates decline, there can be an increase in workers per consumer, which in turn leads to an increase in production that is, hopefully, matched by an in increase in consumption. As Andrew Mason (2005) notes, this is based on the assumption that 'working age' people consume more than they produce.

A second demographic dividend can occur when governments or individuals plan for their aging populations and retirement years through investing and saving. On the country level, this can help to grow per capita income, despite a shrinking workforce. On the individual level, people can continue spending and/or investing in later life, which in turn will benefit the economy (Mason & Lee, 2006).

Despite the seemingly negative impact of a growing aging population on economies and welfare systems, there are potential gains to be had. Key to success appears to be thoughtful and purposeful planning so that adjustments can be made to the labor force and mechanisms for saving and investing.

Summary

This chapter has provided a very basic overview of a very complex topic. The purpose was not to provide a detailed description of all of the potential issues related to financing older age – the scope is simply too large and too specialized, depending on the issue being explored – but to provide a broad overview as a starting point for further readings on the many topics included. For example, the demographic transition, which describes the shift in a population from one composed of predominantly younger members to one with a greater population of older people, leads to issues concerning work, unemployment and retirement. Shifting supplies of workers and demand have led to the development of modern-day retirement systems as a way to, in times of high unemployment, encourage older workers to leave the workforce or, in times of short supply of workers, encourage them to remain. Changes in demographics and in understanding of supply and consumption patterns have in turn led to reforms in many pension systems. While pensions are not available to many people in the world, support through charitable organizations and family remains an important way for older people to have access to resources. Overall, the growing aging population should not be viewed as a 'problem', but as an opportunity for new growth and development across sectors.

Further reading

Biggs, S., Estes, C., & Phillipson, C. (2003). *Social theory, social policy and ageing: Critical perspectives*. Maidenhead: Open University Press..

Higgs, P., & Gilleard, C. (2015). *Rethinking old age: Theorising the fourth age*. London: Palgrave.

Scharf, T. (2010). Social policies for ageing societies: perspectives from Europe. In: D. Dannefer & C. Phillipson (Eds.), *The SAGE handbook of social gerontology*. Thousand Oaks, CA: Sage Publishing, pp 497–512.

Taylor, P. (2010). Cross-national trends in work and retirement. In: D. Dannefer & C. Phillipson (Eds.), *The SAGE handbook of social gerontology,* Thousand Oaks, CA: Sage Publishing, pp. 540–550.

References

Alley, D., & Crimmins, E. (2010). Epidemiology of ageing. In: D. Dannefer & C. Phillipson (Eds.), *The SAGE handbook of social gerontology*. Thousand Oaks, CA: Sage Publishing, pp 75–95.

Alli, F., & Maharaj, P. (2013). The health situation of older people in Africa. In: P. Maharaj (Ed.), *Aging and health in Africa*. New York: Springer, pp 53–89.

Ando, A., & Modigliani, F. (1963). The 'life cycle' hypothesis of saving: aggregate implications and tests. *The American Economic Review*, 53(1): 55–84.

Biggs, S., Estes, C., & Phillipson, C. (2003). *Social theory, social policy and ageing: Critical perspectives*. Maidenhead: Open University Press.

Bonoli, G., & Shinkawa, T. (2006). Population aging and the logics of pension reform in Western Europe, East Asia and North America. In: G. Bonoli & T. Shinkawa (Eds.), *Aging and pension reform around the world: Evidence from eleven countries*. Cheltenham, UK: Edward Elgar Publishing, pp 1–23.

Burton, L. M. (1996). Age norms, the timing of family role transitions, and intergenerational caregiving among aging African American women. *The Gerontologist, 36*(2), 199–208. doi: 10.1093/geront/36.2.199.

Dannefer, D. (1999). Neoteny, naturalization and other constituents of human development. In: C. Ryff & V.W. Marshall (Eds.), *The self and society in aging processes*. New York: Springer, pp 67–93.

Dannefer, D. (2003). Cumulative advantage/disadvantage and the life course: cross-fertilizing age and social science theory. *The Journals of Gerontology Series B: Psychological Sciences and Social Sciences, 58*(6), S327–S337.

Diener, E., & Chan, M. Y. (2011). Happy people live longer: subjective well-being contributes to health and longevity. *Applied Psychology: Health and Well-Being, 3*(1), 1–43.

Duflo, E. (2003). Grandmothers and granddaughters: old-age pensions and intrahousehold allocation in South Africa. *The World Bank Economic Review, 17*(1), 1–25.

Estes, C. L., Biggs, S., & Phillipson, C. (2003). *Social theory, social policy and ageing: Critical perspectives*. Maidenhead: Open University Press.

Estes, C. L., Swan, J. H., & Gerard, L. E. (1982). Dominant and competing paradigms in gerontology: towards a political economy of ageing. *Ageing and Society, 2*(02), 151–164.

Ferraro, K. F., & Shippee, T. P. (2009). Aging and cumulative inequality: how does inequality get under the skin? *The Gerontologist, 49*(3), 333–343.

Finch, J. (2013). Inheritance and financial transfer in families. In: A. Walker (Ed.), *The new generational contract: Intergenerational relations and the welfare state*. London: UCL Press, pp. 120–134.

Fox, N. J. (2005). Cultures of ageing in Thailand and Australia. (What can an ageing body do?). *Sociology, 39*(3), 481–498.

Frank, A. W. (1991). *At the will of the body: Reflections on illness*. Boston, MA: Houghton Mifflin.

Gomez-Olive, F. X., Thorogood, M., Clark, B. D., Kahn, K., & Tollman, S. M. (2010). Assessing health and well-being among older people in rural South Africa. *Global Health Action, 3* (Suppl. 2), 23–35.

Harper, S. (2004). *Families in ageing societies: A multi-disciplinary approach*. New York: Oxford University Press.

Harper, S. (2006). Mature societies: planning for our future selves. *Daedalus, 135*(1), 20–31.

Higgs, P., & Gilleard, C. (2015). *Rethinking old age: Theorising the fourth age*. London: Palgrave.

Hofäcker, D. (2015). In line or at odds with active ageing policies? Exploring patterns of retirement preferences in Europe. *Ageing and Society, 35*(7), 1529–1556. doi: 10.1017/S0144686X1400035X.

Holzmann, R. (2005). *Old-age income support in the 21st century: An international perspective on pension systems and reform.* Washington, DC: World Bank Publications.

Holzmann, R. (2013). Global pension systems and their reform: worldwide drivers, trends and challenges. *International Social Security Review, 66*(2), 1–29.

Kahneman, D., & Deaton, A. (2010). High income improves evaluation of life but not emotional well-being. *Proceedings of the National Academy of Sciences, 107*(38), 16489–16493.

Kinsella, K. G., & Phillips, D. R. (2005). *Global aging: The challenge of success* (Vol. 60). Population Reference Bureau Washington, DC.

Kinsella, K. G., Wan, H., & US Bureau of the Census (2009). *An aging world: 2008.* Washington, DC: US Department of Commerce, Economics and Statistics Administration, US Census Bureau.

Kohli, M., & Künemund, H. (2003). Intergenerational transfers in the family: what motivates giving. In: V.L. Bengston & A. Lowenstein (Eds.), *Global aging and challenges to families.* New York: Aldine de Gruyter, pp 123–142.

Koropeckyj-Cox, T., Pienta, A., & Brown, T. (2007). Women of the 1950s and the 'normative' life course: the implications of childlessness, fertility timing, and marital status for psychological well-being in late midlife. *International Journal of Aging & Human Development, 64*(4), 299–330. doi: 10.2190/8PTL-P745-58U1-3330.

Kunkel, S. R., Brown, J. S., & Whittington, F. J. (2014). *Global aging: Comparative perspectives on aging and the life course.* New York: Springer Publishing Company.

Larson, R. (1978). Thirty years of research on the subjective well-being of older Americans. *Journal of Gerontology, 33*(1), 109–125.

Lewin, A. C., & Stier, H. (2010). Immigration, state support and the economic well-being of the elderly in Israel. In: S. Carmel (Ed.), *Aging in Israel: Research, policy and practice.* New Brunswick, NJ: Transaction Publishers, pp 277–300.

Maharaj, P. (2013). *Aging and health in Africa.* New York: Springer.

Mason, A. (2005). Demographic transition and demographic dividends in developed and developing countries. Paper presented at the United Nations expert group meeting on social and economic implications of changing population age structures, 31 August–2 September.

Mason, A., & Lee, R. (2006). Reform and support systems for the elderly in developing countries: capturing the second demographic dividend. *Genus*, LXII, 11–35.

Mwanyangala, M. A., Mayombana, C., Urassa, H., Charles, J., Mahutanga, C., Abdullah, S., & Nathan, R. (2010). Health status and quality of life among older adults in rural Tanzania. *Global Health Action, 3* (Suppl. 2), 36–44.

Naidoo, N., Abdullah, S., Bawah, A., Binka, F., Chuc, N. T., Debpuur, C., ... Van Minh, H. (2010). Ageing and adult health status in eight lower-income countries: the indepth WHO-SAGE collaboration. *Global Health Action,* 11–22.

OECD (2011). *Pensions at a glance 2011*. Paris: OECD Publishing.

Phillipson, C. (2013). *Ageing*. Cambridge: Polity.

Quadagno, J., & Reid, J. (1999). The political economy perspective in aging. In: V.L. Bengston & K. Warner (Eds.), *Handbook of theories of aging* (1st edn). New York: Springer, pp 344–358.

Scharf, T. (2010). Social policies for ageing societies: perspectives from Europe. In: D. Dannefer & C. Phillipson (Eds.), *The SAGE handbook of social gerontology*. Thousand Oaks, CA: Sage Publishing, pp 497–512.

Taylor, P. (2010). Cross-national trends in work and retirement. In: D. Dannefer & C. Phillipson (Eds.), *The SAGE handbook of social gerontology*. Thousand Oaks, CA: Sage Publishing, pp. 540–550.

Thane, P. (2000). *Old age in English history: Past experiences, present issues*. Oxford: Oxford University Press.

Thane, P. (2010). The history of aging and old age in 'Western' cultures. In: T. Cole, R.R. Ray, & R. Kastenbaum (Eds.), *A guide to humanistic studies in aging: What does it mean to grow old*. Baltimore, MD: Johns Hopkins University Press, pp 33–56.

Trolander, J. A. (2011). Age 55 or better active adult communities and city planning. *Journal of Urban History, 37*(6), 952–974.

United Nations, Population Division (2013). *World Population Ageing 2013*. New York: United Nations.

von Herbay, A. (2014). Otto von Bismarck is not the origin of old age at 65. *The Gerontologist, 54*(1), 5. doi: 10.1093/geront/gnt111.

Wheaton, F., & Crimmins, E. M. (2012). The demography of aging and retirement. In: M. Wang (Ed.), *The Oxford handbook of retirement*. Oxford: Oxford University Press, pp 22–41.

World Bank, The (2015). Indicators. Retrieved 19 December 2015, from http://data.worldbank.org/indicator/.

Zickar, M. J. (2013). The evolving history of retirement within the United States. In: M. Wang (Ed.), *The Oxford handbook of retirement*. Oxford: Oxford University Press, pp 10–21.

NINE

Narrative and creativity

Much in gerontology and in this book has pointed to ways in which aging has been portrayed negatively (Gullette, 2004; Powell, 2009), mostly in terms of measurable change in function with age and fears of death and loss. Most gerontologists recognize and work to resist the pervasive 'aging as decline' message. Yet, as Robert Butler (1974) noted more than forty years ago, 'In our culture few people think of old age as a time of potential health and growth' (p 530). Despite this, examples of age as a type of liberation (De Beauvoir, 1972; Sohm, 2007) and time of deep personal introspection can be found (Savishinsky, 2001). This chapter will profile narrative gerontology, creativity and creative expression in later life. As the concluding chapter to the *Short Guide*, it will highlight the many positive ways in which age can be viewed and experienced. Overall, it will explore the 'growth' aspect of growing old through narrative studies, creativity, wisdom and the arts.

Narrative and narrative gerontology

Narratives – written, verbal, visual and others – give voice to the experience of aging in ways that surveys and assessments cannot. Depending on the type of narrative and how it is used, narrative expression can provide voice to people who themselves are aging. It can provide scholars in aging with a perspective that is not limited to a pre-established measurement or paradigm. Narratives can also give people like novelists and other artists the opportunity to imagine age and create a space where age can be vicariously experienced by a reader, viewer or listener, and create new pathways of knowing.

Thomas Cole, Ruth Ray and Robert Kastenbaum (2010) write that 'rediscovery of narrative as an essential form of seeking and representing knowledge has profoundly shaped gerontology's understanding of the search for meaning and identity' (p 10). Within the purview of narrative, they cite Robert Butler's (1963) original formulation of the life review (Burnside, 1996; Butler, 2002), reminiscence in a variety of arenas including clinical practice and group work with older adults (Kaminsky, 1984; Burnside, 1996; Bohlmeijer & Westerhof, 2011), the evolution of narrative gerontology (Kenyon, Bohlmeijer, & Randall, 2010; de Medeiros, 2013), life-story writing among elders (Ray, 2000; de Medeiros, 2007, 2011b) and others. This chapter will start with an overview of narrative gerontology. It should be noted that although Thomas Cole and colleagues do focus on narratives in language (for example, writing, speaking), there are many non-language forms of narratives (for example, gestures, music, painting).

Narratives are an important part of gerontology. Stories of people's lives and experience can provide insight into what it is like to age, not just about how we age. A simple definition of narrative is 'a telling of some aspect of self through ordered symbols' (de Medeiros, 2013, p 2). Other definitions include 'the process of making a story' (Polkinghorne, 1988, p 13) and 'the stories people tell about themselves' (Becker, 1997, p 25). Gary Kenyon and colleagues (2001) use the term 'narrative gerontology' to describe aging 'as it is experienced and expressed in the stories of older persons' (p xi). Narrative gerontology is therefore focused on a variety of stories told from later life.

Narratives can refer to either oral or written stories (Riessman, 1993, 2007). They can be purposefully structured, as in a written autobiographical account, or spontaneously solicited, as in a personal interview. Personal narratives refer to the stories told by an individual and can be broadly thought of as frameworks through which that individual selects, sequences and 'tells' events to some listener (for example, an interviewer, a reader, one's self) (Cohler & Cole, 1996; Gubrium & Holstein, 1998; de Medeiros, 2013), as opposed to other types of narratives (for example, political) that may be used to tell the story of a larger group or organization. The points about 'selection' and 'sequence' are important because these point to the malleability and adaptability of narratives. One doesn't just have a life narrative. Instead, different situations, people, objectives and so on will lead to different types of narratives.

Research narratives

In gerontology, narratives first fell predominantly within the purview of cultural anthropology through ethnography, whereby a researcher would spend months observing the environment, interviewing members of the community of interest and working toward understanding the cultural rules and how the players interact. An excellent example of an ethnography of aging is Barbara Myerhoff's (1980) *Number our days*, an ethnography of a senior day center in Venice, California. The people she observed and came to know were Jewish elders from Europe who resettled after World War Two. What she describes are people who are closely bonded through not only their past but their present as they cope with change and maintaining tradition in the United States The ethnography became a documentary that received numerous awards and brought attention to an otherwise invisible group. Myerhoff also, notably, became a participant-observer as her own illness progressed and the community embraced her.

Also important was Sharon Kaufman's (1986) well-known work on the 'ageless self', a book composed of interviews with people about their views on growing old. What she reports is a sense of not continuity per se, but views of a self that continues to evolve with every experience and interaction, thereby creating a sense of an ageless self that remains unchanged over time. Robert Rubinstein, a cultural anthropologist, also used in-depth, ethnographic interviews to explore a variety of experiences including elders living alone (Rubinstein & Kilbride,

1992; Yetter, 2010), the meaning of suffering in later life (Black & Rubinstein, 2004), the experiences of women aged over 65 who did not have children (Rubinstein, 1987a), home and the significance of personal objects (Rubinstein, 1987b; Rubinstein & de Medeiros, 2005) and others. The type of in-depth, ethnographic interviewing that Rubinstein and others used would later become a more common way of understanding elders' perspectives within gerontology than through traditional ethnographies that involve embedding oneself in a community and conducting observation and artifact review in addition to key informant interviews.

Life stories

Another direction that narratives have taken in gerontology is through the life story. Charlotte Linde (1993) describes life stories as the stories people tell about themselves. Structured life-story work has taken many forms, from the broad field of reminiscence in aging (Haight & Webster, 1995; Webster & Haight, 2002), to structured life review (Haight & Haight, 2007), to guided autobiography (De Vries, Birren, & Deutchman, 1990; Birren & Cochran, 2001), to writing groups for older adults (Ray, 2000; de Medeiros, 2007, 2011a). In reminiscence, the focus is on the act of remembering and reliving an experience (Kaminsky, 1984). The purpose is not to verify the accuracy of one's memory or recall of events, but is more concerned with the emotional act of actively thinking about the past and either telling a personal story or participating in a group remembrance of some shared event. The overall purpose of the structured life review is based on Robert Butler's (1963) concept of life review as discussed in earlier chapters, where the overarching goal is to resolve past conflicts if possible in order to make sense of one's life in the present.

The guided autobiography overlaps somewhat with the life review in that particular stages of development (for example, childhood, adolescence) are suggested as the focus of writing. Finally, the broader category of writing groups can involve any type of writing. Some, like Ruth Ray (2000), use a group structure to co-create stories. Others, like Kate de Medeiros (de Medeiros, 2007, 2011b, 2013), move away from developmental models of writing (for example, life stages) and instead use literary genres (such as letter writing, poetry) as frames to help participants tell new stories about themselves, stories that typically would not be told through a traditional autobiographical format.

Narrative interventions in research

There has been some research literature on the effects of narrative interventions, especially in later life. James Pennebaker and Janel Seagal (1999) found health benefits to writing, specifically with regard to pain. People in their research study who wrote about their pain scored better on self-assessments than those who did not. For a time, Susan Kemper and colleagues' (2001) findings from 'The Nun Study' suggested that idea density and grammatical complexity expressed in the autobiographical writings of novice nuns predicted who would exhibit signs of dementia in later life. Although this work created strong interest in the link between education and later cognitive health, subsequent research has produced inconclusive results.

Other narrative research in later life has examined memory performance and self-concept. Kate de Medeiros and colleagues' (de Medeiros, Kennedy, Cole, Lindley, & O'Hara, 2007) randomized control trial of a structured writing intervention sought to examine the role of active recall through writing and its potential effect on autobiographical memory. Although they did not find a significant difference in memory performance across the three study groups (participants in the writing workshop, an active control group who participated in a reminiscence group, and a no-intervention control group), they did see potential evidence of a positive effect on self-concept. Overall, there is great potential in narrative research in gerontology. The link between narratives and personal meaning may offer opportunities missing from traditional interventions.

Narratives and fiction

Perhaps newest to the field of gerontology are fictional narratives of aging. Although this work has existed in the humanities for many years, it has been relatively absent within gerontology itself. Anne Wyatt-Brown (2000), in describing 'literary gerontology,' identifies five categories:

> 1) literary attitudes toward aging, largely examined from a postmodern sociological perspectives, 2) late style creativity across the life course, using psychoanalytic and biological perspectives, 3) cultural studies of aging, in particular those that analyse the politics of decline and progress discourses, 4) narrative studies of the life review and guided autobiography, and 5) explorations of emotions. (p 42)

Examples of the first include Hannah Zeilig and colleagues' (1997) work on *King Lear*. Wyatt-Brown cites de Beauvoir's (1972) *Coming of age*, among several others, as an important work in late-life creativity.

More recently, scholars have also been publishing on various aspects of aging portrayed in literature and in cultural studies. Examples include Lauren Marshall Bowen's (2014) 'The literacy narrative of Chadwick's The First Grader', Amelia DeFalco's (2010) work that uses methods from humanities to explore representations of aging in fiction and film, and many others (Swinnen & Stotesbury, 2012).

The structure of narrative

In reference to the use of narrative approaches to understanding the experience of older adults, it is important to consider the structure of a narrative and what it can and cannot do, a point that was alluded to earlier in the chapter. Narratives are influenced by the orienting construct, genre or form, such as autobiography, that guides the structure and content of a narrative and that requires the narrator to select and place events in an orderly sequence that mirrors the linear progression of the story form (Polkinghorne, 1988; de Medeiros, 2005, 2007). The role and influence of an orienting image (for example, telling about your life as if it were a chapter in a book) in framing interviews has been described in literature on interviewing techniques (Mishler, 1986; Rubinstein, 2001), but often not explicitly within gerontology. The orienting frame is important since, in research activities such as interviewing, informants' responses to interview questions are very much shaped by the frame through which the informants are asked to narrate their experiences (Rubinstein, 2001; Chase, 2003; Gubrium & Holstein, 2012). Asking people to describe their life as chapters in a book will require them to order their life events to meet the inquiry frame (for example, to mimic the orderly succession of book chapters). Asking people to describe their life as a collage is likely to yield a very different response, since the collage as a frame is disorderly in structure. One must be careful, then, when soliciting or interpreting narratives that the limits of the orienting framework are understood. In other words, is the person's narrative more about their experience or more about the way the question was asked?

Linked to the idea of orienting image or form of the narrative is the way in which narrative is composed and delivered – again, either orally or in writing. Van Langenhove and Harré (1994) describe oral narratives as 'the result of an interaction between the narrator, the audience, and the narrator's memory. A storyteller has to speak in accordance with the demands of his or her audience' (p 87). The speaker in an oral narrative reacts to the responses of the listener and can consequently alter the narrative, based on perceived response. If a listener looks uninterested, bored, shocked or a variety of emotions, the teller is likely to change his or her story. Oral narratives are therefore very much shaped by the listener (Kaminsky, 1984; Mishler, 1986; Myerhoff & Kaminsky, 1992; Cohler & Cole, 1996). This can result in a narrative that better matches what the listener wants to hear rather than what the speaker wants to tell or feels is permissible to tell. Stories about trauma, discrimination, loss or others may be silenced through the actions, intentional or unintentional, of the listener.

In contrast to the speaker in an oral narrative, the 'speaker' or writer in a written narrative does not change narrative techniques mid-stream based on a direct audience response, but instead anticipates response and attempts to produce an effect through the structuring of words and phrases (Polkinghorne & Birren, 1996). In short, the story a person tells during an interview may differ from the story he or she writes down (van Langenhove & Harré, 1994; Ray, 2000; de Medeiros, 2011b).

Whereas events in an oral narrative may be changed to accommodate the perceived reaction of the listener, events in a written narrative may be included precisely because the reader is unknown or, in the case of a letter for example, directly and more intimately known. Written narratives use literary forms that are influenced by culture and have evolved and been shaped over time to serve certain communicative needs. Therefore, different written literary forms, through their development over time, have come to carry with them different rules and expectations about appropriate content, structure and aesthetics (de Medeiros, 2013).

In addition, narratives and narrative frames exist within cultural norms of power and authority (Bruner, 1991), just like other aspects of aging discussed. More specifically, the 'I' or the speaking voice in narratives is in many ways a public voice (de Medeiros, 2013). Consequently the inherent power structure of some narrative approaches may therefore limit the ways in which non-dominant people (for example, older adults, women) who have not traditionally held cultural positions of power express themselves (Maines, 1999). It is therefore important to think beyond the narratives themselves and to take into consideration the conditions under which the narrative was obtained (for example, an interview) and the power differences that might exist between teller and listener. Otherwise, narrative work runs the risk of being a vehicle for repeating master cultural narratives about experiences, such as the experience of aging. Overall, while narratives offer great opportunities for understanding later life, their potential limits must also be recognized so that a skewed version of later life, more geared to the expectations of the listener than to the experience of the speaker, is not produced.

Creativity and later life

Another important topic considered in this chapter is creativity in later life. Creativity offers liberation from the framework of decline. Gene Cohen (2001, 2009), who challenged established notions of what is possible in later life through his investigation into creativity, was a major figure in changing how creative potential is viewed. His work is important because the idea of creative possibilities throughout the lifecourse counters the biomedicalization of aging and the focus on decline as an overarching explanatory framework that does not consider growth as a possibility in later life (Powell, 2009).

Martin Lindauer (2003) points to many parallels between attitudes toward aging and creativity. Both terms are ambiguous. Just as it is difficult to determine when a person is 'old', the same can be said for what it means to be 'creative'. There area numerous definitions. Lindauer (2003) writes: 'According to the negative view of old age, losses take precedence over gains, bad things are more likely to happen than good ones, and despair triumphs over hope' (p 4). In contrast, 'A positive view of aging points out that training and practice can offset some mental losses' (Lindauer, 2003, p. 6). With regard to late-life creativity, Lindauer (2003) writes: 'Are creative people made? Is everyone creative? Is creativity innate or learned? How are creativity and intelligence related? Is creativity a personal or cognitive trait? A process? A behaviour? Is creativity the same as new, original, unique and valuable?' (p 10). According to him, 'Elderly artists reported that four aspects of creativity – quality (originality), quantity (productivity), sources of creative ideas (the process), and approach (style) – improved with age' (Lindauer, 2003, p 140).

With regard to the study of creativity, a great deal of literature from the 1970s through the 1990s focused on the creative output of artists rather than on examining creative potential in old age. Dean Keith Simonton (1990), for example, cites work on output curves that suggests that artists are generally most productive from their late 30s through their 40s, with drops in productivity from ages 50 and beyond. The problem with examining creativity in this way, however, is that it assumes that productivity and creativity are the same, and that quality is also linked with quantity. When interviewing older artists about their views of their creativity and quality of work with age, Martin Lindauer, Lucinda Orwoll and Catherine Kelly (1997) found that the artists felt their creativity and quality of work improved steadily with age and that later-life work had a reflective and contemplative quality not found in the work during their 'productive' periods.

With regards to brain, mind and behavior with aging, Gene Cohen (2009) writes that there has been 'a long series of false assumptions and conclusions lacking evidence-based research to support them' (p. 426). For example, Cohen notes, 'In 1905, Sigmund Freud (1856–1939) asserted that "about the age of 50, the elasticity of the mental processes on which treatment depends, is, as a rule, lacking. Old people are no longer educable" (Freud & Strachey, 1905, p 426).' As Cohen notes, this assumption was present in much of the discourse on the aging brain until fairly recently, when studies began to show that new learning is possible (Baltes, 1997). Paul Baltes' (1997) and Margret Baltes' (1988) concept of 'selective optimization with compensation' describes how older people are able to implement new resources through a creative thinking process in order to achieve a goal. This perspective is generally applied to solutions in everyday living, not with regard to creativity specifically. However, one can argue that such problem-solving abilities do point to a form of later-life creativity.

Gene Cohen also points to Ramón y Cajal, who, in his 1913 work *Degeneration and regeneration*, described the adult brain as having fixed nerve pathways that were not able to be regenerated once dead. As Cohen notes, Gerd Kempermann and colleagues (2004) demonstrated that new cells could, in fact, be produced, opening a new avenue to explore previously overlooked potential in later life (Cohen, 2006). Cohen (2009), a pioneer in the study of creativity and aging, later concluded that 'With the new focus on potential, many researchers have, for example, described the concept of "pragmatic creativity" or "practical intelligence", finding that it actually increases with aging' (p 427).

Wisdom

An important link with creativity and the view of aging as liberation is the idea of wisdom. Wisdom is one of the few positive aspects of aging that has been clearly recognized over time. Despite its prominence, however, it still has not been widely researched (Ardelt, 2003; Edmondson, 2005, 2009; Jeste et al, 2010), as compared to other concepts. Dean Keith Simonton (1990) writes that 'our species [humans] can boast two abilities that fail to have proper counterparts elsewhere ... The first capacity is wisdom. Rather than live from moment to moment with minimal reflection and even less foresight, human beings can acquire a broad perspective on life, discerning a larger view of life's meaning than permitted by a hand-to-mouth subsistence' (p 320). The second capacity he cites is creativity, which he defines as 'the ability to innovate, to change the environment rather than merely adjust to it in a more passive sense' (p 320). Again, this can be linked back to Paul Baltes (1997) and Margret Baltes' (1998) work and the creative process.

Ricca Edmondson (2005) defines wisdom as 'an accretion of knowledge, tacit or explicit, about how to respond to another person, to oneself and to profound problems of human existence that lack predetermined answers' (p 339). She adds that it has often been considered as the highest aim of life and that it has a practical quality deriving from experience. Despite the fact that the idea of wisdom has existed for thousands of years, there has been little empirical research on wisdom (Simonton, 1990; Jeste et al, 2010). Using a Delphi panel, Dilip Jeste and colleagues (Jeste et al, 2010) tried to identify unique attributes of wisdom that differed from other potentially similar constructs such as spirituality. They found a strong consensus that wisdom was a distinct concept that differed from intelligence and spirituality. Their conclusion was that 'wisdom is a uniquely human but rare personal quality, which can be learned and measured, and increases with age through advanced cognitive and emotional development that is experience driven' (p 677).

Wisdom, in the ways described above, points to a very distinct capacity that is viewed as uniquely human and related to older age. However, it begs the questions: Are all old people wise? Can 'wisdom' be a benevolent yet damaging label in later life? Kathleen Woodward (2003) suggests that the label of 'wise' gets placed on older people indiscriminately, not based on any theoretical notion or defined concept, but just because of chronological age or physical appearance. When wisdom is used in this way, Woodward argues, the label implies passivity in some respect. The wise person contemplates, rather than acts, is peaceful, not angry. She cautions that using the label of 'wise' can rob older people of their right to be angry and react to issues affecting them. By rejecting 'wisdom', they are then at risk of being ignored or viewed as 'deviant' in some way. Wisdom should therefore be used with great thought and not applied to all people.

Creativity, the arts and later life

This final section looks at the growing interest in creativity in the arts in later life for diverse groups of older people. In many respects, the arts challenge 'science'. Their effects are not easily measured. The response can differ from person to person and range from having created a profoundly meaningful change for one person to causing no reaction in another. It is not a 'one size fits all'. What the arts can do, however, is change the way we think about health and wellbeing.

The cultural arts are defined as 'the practice of creating perceptible forms expressive of human feeling' (Langer, 1966, p 6). Helga Noice Tony Noice and Arthur Kramer (2014), for example, conducted a systematic review of participatory arts (that is, arts in which the person is actively involved in the creation of some artistic product rather than an observer) interventions for older adults. Artistic forms studied included dance, expressive/autobiographical writing, music, theatre and the visual arts. They found positive quality-of-life outcomes in 31 of the studies reviewed but did not find strong evidence for other outcomes. Part of the challenge in this type of research, they note, is inconsistent use of standardized measures, varying research designs and lack of clear outcomes. However, their findings did point to the importance of creative outlets in overall life satisfaction. Another important work on arts and aging was produced by the Mental Health Foundation (2011). Like Noice, Noice, and Kramer, the Foundation reported findings from studies involving the participatory arts. Again, although empirical evidence was often lacking, participants' subjective views of engagement, enjoyment and attitudes about quality of life support the importance of the arts.

Arts and dementia

An interesting intersection in the topics of narrative, creativity and aging is that of creativity and the arts in dementia care. Findings from several cultural arts programs have pointed to their potential to be a high-impact and low-cost alternative to other dementia therapies. For example, in one small study, Lee and Tabourne (2009), evaluated the effectiveness of the Dancing Heart™ program to improve function (for example, flexibility, energy, balance) and reduce falls in eight community-dwelling residents. The Dancing Heart™ program involved improvisational dance and personal storytelling led by professional dancers. The program met once a week for 90 minutes. Qualitative data revealed that participants felt increased socialization and less fear of falling. The small sample size, lack of standardized measurement and lack of an appropriate control group limit the interpretation of findings. In another small study, a grounded-theory approach was used to understand the psychological and social effects for eight caregivers and their loved one with dementia (Roberts, Camic, & Springham, 2011) when viewing art in a museum. Caregivers reported feeling emotionally engaged and supported through the activity.

In addition to these, other individual studies involving the cultural arts and arts interventions in dementia care point to promising avenues for future research (increased pleasure, improved quality of life) (Teri, McCurry, Logsdon, & Gibbons, 2005). However, like the studies cited earlier, systematic reviews have dampened enthusiasm by citing poor study design (for example, lack of randomization, lack of adequate control groups), small sample sizes and other methodological weaknesses.

There are several challenges to understanding the cultural arts in the context of the complex systems of dementia care. Arts programs are developed with the overall goal of 'meaning making'. The arts provide the opportunity to create meaningful experiences through which people can connect with themselves and their larger environments (physical and social). The goal of the cultural arts is sometimes in contrast with an implicit goal of clinical interventions, which are created to effect a particular outcome (for example, reduce anxiety). Consequently, these practices have focused on clinical measures of success rather than considering alternative interpretations and approaches to learning about how the arts operate in positive ways that may differ from traditional therapies and treatments.

Summary

Counter to many of the negative ways that aging has been framed, narratives and studies of creativity and wisdom provide new ways to focus on the 'growth' part of growing old. Specifically, narrative work can shed light into what it really means to grow old, not only from the perspective of those who have reached old age, but also through the imaginative perspectives of novelists and other artists. Creativity in aging is also an important area because it emphasizes new potential. Cohen's and others' work has challenged previously held views that the brain faces inevitable decline. Creativity, according to many, is certainly possible in later life. In addition, growing interest in the cultural arts and opportunities for meaningful engagement in later life show great promise from an experiential standpoint, even if measurement of their effects cannot be obtained.

Further reading

Cohen, G. D. (2006). *The mature mind: The positive power of the aging brain*. New York: Basic Books.

de Medeiros, K. (2013). *Narrative gerontology in research and practice*. New York: Springer Publishing Company.

Edmondson, R. (2015). *Ageing, insight and wisdom: Meaning and practice across the life course.* Bristol: Policy Press.

Kenyon, G., Bohlmeijer, E., & Randall, W. L. (2010). *Storying later life: Issues, investigations, and interventions in narrative gerontology.* Oxford: Oxford University Press.

References

Ardelt, M. (2003). Empirical assessment of a three-dimensional wisdom scale. *Research on Aging, 25*(3), 275–324.

Baltes, M. M. (1988). The etiology and maintenance of dependency in the elderly: three phases of operant research. *Behavior Therapy, 19*(3), 301–319.

Baltes, P. B. (1997). On the incomplete architecture of human ontogeny: selection, optimization, and compensation as foundation of developmental theory. *American Psychologist, 52*(4), 366.

Becker, G. (1997). *Disrupted lives: How people create meaning in a chaotic world*. Berkely and Los Angeles, CA: University of California Press.

Birren, J. E., & Cochran, K. N. (2001). *Telling the stories of life through guided autobiography groups*. Philadelphia: Taylor & Francis.

Black, H. K., & Rubinstein, R. L. (2004). Themes of suffering in later life. *The Journals of Gerontology Series B: Psychological Sciences and Social Sciences, 59*(1), S17–S24.

Bohlmeijer, E., & Westerhof, G. (2011). Reminiscence interventions: bringing narrative gerontology into practice. In: G. Kenyon, E. Bohlmeijer & W. L. Randall (Eds.), *Storying later life: Issues, investigations, and interventions in narrative gerontology*. New York: Oxford University Press, pp 273–289.

Bowen, L. M. (2014). The literacy narrative of Chadwick's *The First Grader. Age, Culture, Humanities: An Interdisicplinary Journal*, 1, http://ageculturehumanities.org/WP/the-literacy-narrative-of-chadwicks-the-first-grader/.

Bruner, J. (1991). The narrative construction of reality. *Critical Inquiry, 18*(1), 1–21.

Burnside, I. (1996). Life review and reminiscence in nursing practice. In: J.E. Birren, G. M Kenyon, J. Ruth, J.J.F. Schroots, & T. Svensson (Eds.), *Aging and biography: Explorations in adult development*. New York: Springer Publishing, pp 248–264.

Butler, R. N. (1963). The life review: an interpretation of reminiscence in the aged. *Psychiatry, 26*(1), 65–76.

Butler, R. N. (1974). Successful aging and the role of the life review. *Journal of the American Geriatrics Society, 22*(12), 529–535.

Butler, R. N. (2002). The life review. *Journal of Geriatric Psychiatry*, 35(1), 7–10.

Chase, S. E. (2003). Taking narrative seriously: consequences for method and theory in interview studies. In: Y.S. Lincoln & N.K. Denzin (Eds.), *Turning points in qualitative research: Tying knots in a handkerchief*. Lanham, MD: Rowman & Littlefield, pp 273–296.

Cohen, G. D. (2001). Creativity with aging: four phases of potential in the second half of life. *Geriatrics, 56*(4), 51.

Cohen, G. D. (2006). *The mature mind: The positive power of the aging brain*. New York: Basic Books.

Cohen, G. D. (2009). Historical lessons to watch your assumptions about aging: relevance to the role of International Psychogeriatrics. *International Psychogeriatrics, 21*(03), 425–429.

Cohler, B. J., & Cole, T. R. (1996). Studying older lives: reciprocal acts of telling and listening. In: J.E. Birren, G. M Kenyon, J. Ruth, J.J.F. Schroots, & T. Svensson (Eds.), *Aging and biography: Explorations in adult development*. New York: Springer Publishing, pp 61–76.

Cole, T. R., Ray, R. E., & Kastenbaum, R. (2010). *A guide to humanistic studies in aging: What does it mean to grow old?* Baltimore, MD: Johns Hopkins University Press.

de Beauvoir, S. (1972). *La vieillesse.* New York: Putnam.

de Medeiros, K. (2005). The complementary self: multiple perspectives on the aging person. *Journal of Aging Studies, 19*(1), 1–13. doi: 10.1016/j. jaging.2004.02.001.

de Medeiros, K. (2007). Beyond the memoir: telling life stories using multiple literary forms. *Journal of Aging, Humanities, and the Arts, 1*(3–4), 159–167. doi: 10.1080/19325610701638052.

de Medeiros, K. (2011a). Self stories in older age: crafting identities using small moments from the past. *Amerikastudien/American Studies, 53*(1), 103–122.

de Medeiros, K. (2011b). Telling stories: how do expressions of self differ in a writing group versus a reminiscence group? In: G. Kenyon, E. Bohlmeijer, & W. L. Randall (Eds.), *Storying later life: Issues, investigations, and interventions in narrative gerontology*. New York: Oxford University Press, pp 159–176.

de Medeiros, K. (2013). *Narrative gerontology in research and practice*. New York: Springer Publishing Company.

de Medeiros, K., Kennedy, Q., Cole, T., Lindley, R., & O'Hara, R. (2007). The impact of autobiographic writing on memory performance in older adults: a preliminary investigation. *American Journal of Geriatric Psychiatry, 15*(3), 257–261.

De Vries, B., Birren, J. E., & Deutchman, D. E. (1990). Adult development through guided autobiography: the family context. *Family Relations*, 39(1): 3–7.

DeFalco, A. (2010). *Uncanny subjects: Aging in contemporary narrative*. Columbus, OH: The Ohio State University Press.

Edmondson, R. (2005). Wisdom in later life: ethnographic approaches. *Ageing and Society, 25*(06), 339–356.

Edmondson, R. (2009). Wisdom: a humanist approach to valuing older people. *Valuing older people: A humanist approach to ageing*. Bristol: Policy Press, pp 201–216.

Freud, S. (1905). On psychotherapy. J. Strachey (translator). *Standard edition of the complete psychological works of Sigmund Freud*. London: Hogarth Press, pp 257–268.

Gubrium, J. F., & Holstein, J. A. (1998). Narrative practice and the coherence of personal stories. *The Sociological Quarterly, 39*(1), 163–187.

Gubrium, J. F., & Holstein, J. A. (2012). Narrative practice and the transformation of interview subjectivity. In: J.F. Gubrium, J.A. Holstein, A. B. Marvasti, & K.D. McKinney (Eds.), *The SAGE handbook of interview research. The complexity of the craft* (2nd edn). Thousand Oaks, CA: SAGE Publications, pp 27–44.

Gullette, M. M. (2004). *Aged by culture*. Chicago, IL: University of Chicago Press.

Haight, B. K., & Haight, B. S. (2007). *The handbook of structured life review*. Baltimore: Health Professions Press.

Haight, B. K., & Webster, J. D. (1995). *The art and science of reminiscing: Theory, research, methods, and applications*. Washington, DC: Taylor & Francis.

Jeste, D. V., Ardelt, M., Blazer, D., Kraemer, H. C., Vaillant, G., & Meeks, T. W. (2010). Expert consensus on characteristics of wisdom: a Delphi method study. *The Gerontologist, 50*(5), 668–680. doi: 10.1093/geront/gnq022.

Kaminsky, M. (1984). *The uses of reminiscence: New ways of working with older adults*. New York: Haworth Press.

Kaufman, S. R. (1986). *The ageless self: Sources of meaning in late life*. Madison, WI: University of Wisconsin Press.

Kemper, S., Greiner, L. H., Marquis, J. G., Prenovost, K., & Mitzner, T. L. (2001). Language decline across the life span: findings from the Nun Study. *Psychology and Aging, 16*(2), 227–239.

Kempermann, G., Wiskott, L., & Gage, F. H. (2004). Functional significance of adult neurogenesis. *Current Opinion in Neurobiology, 14*(2), 186–191.

Kenyon, G., Bohlmeijer, E., & Randall, W. L. (2010). *Storying later life: Issues, investigations, and interventions in narrative gerontology*. Oxford: Oxford University Press.

Kenyon, G.M., Clark, P., & de Vries, B. (2001). Narrative gerontology: an overview. In: G. Kenyon, P. Clark, & B. de Vries (Eds.), *Narrative gerontology: Theory, research and practice*. New York: Springer Publishing, pp vii–ix.

Kenyon, G. M., Ruth, J. E., & Mader, W. (1999). Elements of a narrative gerontology. In: G. M. Kenyon, J. E. Ruth, W. Mader, V. L. Bengtson, & K. W. Schaie (Eds.), *Handbook of theories of aging* (1st edn). New York: Springer, pp 40–58.

Langer, S. K. (1966). The cultural importance of the arts. *The Journal of Aesthetic Education, 1*(1), 5–12.

Lee, Y., & Tabourne, C. (2009). Effects of Dancing Heart Program (DHP) as therapeutic recreation intervention on risk of falling among elderly. *Annual in Therapeutic Recreation, 18*, 157–163.

Lindauer, M. (2003). *Aging, creativity and art: A positive perspective on late-life development*. New York: Springer Science & Business Media.

Lindauer, M. S., Orwoll, L., & Kelly, M. C. (1997). Aging artists on the creativity of their old age. *Creativity Research Journal, 10*(2–3), 133–152.

Linde, C. (1993). *Life stories: The creation of coherence*. Oxford: Oxford University Press.

Maines, D. R. (1999). Information pools and racialized narrative structures. *Sociological Quarterly, 40*(2), 317–326. doi: 10.1111/j.1533-8525.1999.tb00550.x.

Mental Health Foundation (2011). An evidence review of the impact of participatory arts on older people. Retrieved 9 August 2012, from http://www.baringfoundation.org.uk/EvidenceReview.pdf.

Mishler, E. G. (1986). *Research interviewing: Context and narrative.* Cambridge, MA: Harvard University Press.

Myerhoff, B. (1980). *Number our days.* New York: Touchstone.

Myerhoff, B. G., & Kaminsky, M. (1992). *Remembered lives: The work of ritual, storytelling, and growing older.* Ann Arbor, MI: University of Michigan Press.

Noice, T., Noice, H., & Kramer, A. F. (2014). Participatory arts for older adults: a review of benefits and challenges. *The Gerontologist, 54*(5), 741–753.

Pennebaker, J. W., & Seagal, J. D. (1999). Forming a story: the health benefits of narrative. *Journal of Clinical Psychology, 55*(10), 1243–1254.

Polkinghorne, D. (1988). *Narrative knowing and the human sciences.* Albany, NY: State University of New York Press.

Polkinghorne, D. E., & Birren, J. E. (1996). Narrative knowing and the study of lives. In: J.E. Birren, G. M Kenyon, J. Ruth, J.J.F. Schroots, & T. Svensson (Eds.), *Aging and biography: Explorations in adult development.* New York: Springer Publishing, pp 77–99.

Powell, J. L. (2009). Social theory, aging, and health and welfare professionals: a Foucauldian 'toolkit'. *Journal of Applied Gerontology, 28*(6), 669–682.

Ray, R. E. (2000). *Beyond nostalgia: Aging and life-story writing.* Charlottsville, VA: University Press of Virginia.

Riessman, C. K. (1993). *Narrative analysis* (Vol. 30). Thousand Oaks, CA: SAGE Publications, Incorporated.

Riessman, C. K. (2007). *Narrative methods for the human sciences.* Thousand Oaks, CA: SAGE Publications, Incorporated.

Roberts, S., Camic, P. M., & Springham, N. (2011). New roles for art galleries: art-viewing as a community intervention for family carers of people with mental health problems. *Arts & Health, 3*(2), 146–159. doi: 10.1080/17533015.2011.561360.

Rubinstein, R. L. (1987a). Childless elderly: theoretical perspectives and practical concerns. *Journal of Cross-Cultural Gerontology, 2*(1), 1–14.

Rubinstein, R. L. (1987b). The significance of personal objects to older people. *Journal of Aging Studies,* 1(3), 225–238.

Rubinstein, R. L. (2001). The qualitative interview with older informants. In: G.D. Rowles & N.E. Schoenberg (Eds.), *Qualitative gerontology: A contemporary perspective*. New York: Springer Publishing Company, p. 137–153.

Rubinstein, R. L., & de Medeiros, K. (2005). Home, self, and identity. In: G.D. Rowles & H. Chaudhury (Eds.), *Home and identity in late life international perspectives*. New York: Springer Publishing, pp 47–62.

Rubinstein, R. L., & Kilbride, J. C. (1992). *Elders living alone: Fraility and the perception of choice*. New Brunswick, NJ: Transaction Publishers.

Savishinsky, J. (2001). The passions of maturity: morality and creativity in later life. *Journal of Cross-cultural Gerontology, 16*(1), 41–55.

Simonton, D. K. (1990). Creativity and wisdom in aging. In: J.E. Birren (Ed.), *Handbook of the psychology of aging* (3rd edn), San Diego: Academic Press, pp 320–329.

Sohm, P. L. (2007). *The artist grows old: The aging of art and artists in Italy, 1500–1800*. New Haven, CT: Yale University Press.

Swinnen, A., & Stotesbury, J. A. (2012). *Aging, performance, and stardom: Doing age on the stage of consumerist culture* (Vol. 2). Münster: LIT Verlag.

Teri, L., McCurry, S. M., Logsdon, R., & Gibbons, L. E. (2005). Training community consultants to help family members improve dementia care: a randomized controlled trial. *Gerontologist, 45*(6), 802–811. doi: 45/6/802.

van Langenhove, L., & Harré, R. O. M. (1994). Cultural stereotypes and positioning theory. *Journal for the Theory of Social Behaviour, 24*(4), 359–372. doi: 10.1111/j.1468–5914.1994.tb00260.x.

Webster, J. D., & Haight, B. K. (2002). *Critical advances in reminiscence work: From theory to application*. New York: Springer Publishing Company.

Woodward, K. (2003). Against wisdom: the social politics of anger and aging. *Journal of Aging Studies, 17*(1), 55–67.

Wyatt-Brown, A. (2000). The future of literary gerontology. In: T.R. Cole, R.E. Ray, & R. Kastenbaum (Eds.), *Handbook of the humanities and aging* (2nd edn). New York: Springer Publishing, pp 41–61.

Yetter, L. S. (2010). The experience of older men living alone. *Geriatric Nursing, 31*(6), 412–418. doi: http://dx.doi.org/10.1016/j.gerinurse.2010.07.001.

Zeilig, H., Jamieson, A., Harper, S., & Victor, C. (1997). The uses of literature in the study of older people. In: A. Jamieson, S. Harper & C. Victor (Eds.), *Critical approaches to ageing and later life.* Buckingham, PA: Open University Press, pp 39–48.

Glossary

Active aging
Defined by the World Health Organization as the process of optimizing opportunities for health, participation and security to enhance quality of life as people age.

Activities of daily living
Basic activities one needs to be able to perform in order to live independently, such as bathing, using the bathroom, dressing, eating, transferring (walking) and continence.

Activity theory
Posits that people desire to maintain the activities and attitudes of midlife throughout older age.

Acute disease
Disease that is relatively short in course, with a quick onset and often with severe consequences such as death.

Ageism
The systematic discrimination of a person based on his or her age, including assumptions about abilities and functions based on perceived age.

Age norms
Expectations regarding 'appropriate' behavior or performance level based on chronological age.

Age-segregated housing
Housing for which one must meet a certain age criterion to live there. This includes private developments marketed to a particular age group (for example, 55 and over) or government-sponsored housing.

Aging
See Biological age, Chronological age, and Functional age.

Alzheimer's disease
A type of dementia characterized by the presence of neurofibrillary tangles and beta amyloid plaques.

Assisted living
A type of housing in which a person lives independently within a defined, structured community and generally age-segregated retirement community (as opposed to remaining at home in the larger community) but receives assistance with personal services such as meals, housekeeping, transportation and activities of daily living. In the United States, this type of housing is regulated at the state level and is generally paid for out-of-pocket.

Bereavement
Refers to the person who has experienced loss. This differs from grief, which is the response to loss.

Biological age
The product of time and a series of events – some random and some purposeful – that ultimately end in an organism's death. Biological aging begins at the point when an organism reaches sexual maturity.

Chronic disease
Disease that last three months or longer and cannot be prevented or cured.

Chronological age
The number of years an organism as lived.

Cohort
A group of people banded together because of some shared similarities such as year of entry into an educational program, birth year, shared historical event or others.

Communicable diseases
Diseases that are contagious and are passed from one person to another.

Compression of morbidity
A hypothesis that suggests that the same interventions that have led to increases in average life expectancy may shift the onset of illness and disability to later in the life span, closer to death.

Congruence model of person–environment interaction
Proposes interrelationship of seven dimensions of congruence between personal life space and environmental influences: segregate, congregate, institutional control, structure, stimulation/engagement, affect and impulse control.

Continuity theory
Perspective that assumes that people apply familiar strategies to maintain internal (for example, personal preference) and external structures (for example, interacting with familiar physical or social environments).

Convergence theory
An early gerontological perspective that suggested that through industrialization, nuclear families would strengthen and ties to extended family would weaken.

Counterpart theory
Proposes that there are latent structures of behavior such as emotions, cognition and motivation that are carried forward from earlier experiences.

Cumulative advantage/disadvantage
Proposes that people who begin their lives with advantages (for example, wealthy) or disadvantages (for example, poor) will accumulate more benefits (for example, education, leading to high-paying job) or disadvantages (for example, lack of education, leading to low-paying jobs) over time. These will ultimately affect later life.

Cumulative inequality
Describes how personal trajectories are shaped by the accumulation of risk, available resources, perceived trajectories and human agency.

Death anxiety
Fear associated with anticipating a nonexistent self. Three components include past regret, future regret and the perceived meaninglessness of death or whether the person can make sense of death.

Death salience
Awareness and acceptance that death is inevitable.

Defined benefit plans
Provide a monthly benefit based on age, job tenure and earnings.

Defined contribution pensions
Specify the contributions paid by employers and employees.

Dementia
A general term describing progressive cognitive and/or behavioral symptoms that affect ability to function due to memory loss, cause difficulty in acquiring new information, poor judgment or reasoning, language impairment and/or changes in personality or behavior.

Demographic dividend
Describes the positive impact and benefits that a country might experience while transitioning from a 'young' population to an older one.

Demographic transition
The interrelated changes in fertility, mortality and migration that result in the rapid growth and aging of a population.

Dependency ratio
The number of working-age adults (aged 16–65) relative to the number of people assumed to be non-working (aged 15 and under and 65 and over).

Development
From a biological perspective, changes that prepare an organism for sexual maturity and the ability to reproduce.

Disability
Defined by the World Health Organization (WHO, 2015a) as 'an umbrella term for impairments, activity limitations and participation restrictions. Disability is the interaction between individuals with a health condition and personal and environmental factors.'

Disability Adjusted Life Years (DALY)
A measure of the burden of premature death, injury and disease. It is calculated by adding years of life lost due to premature mortality to years of life lost due to disability.

Disease
Defined by Merriam-Webster (2015) as 'an impairment of the normal state of the living animal or plant body'.

Disengagement theory
An early gerontological theory that describes a mutual yet adaptive social and psychological withdrawal of an individual from society

and society from the individual as a person ages. Originally, 'disengagement' was believed to start at around age 50.

Ecological model of aging
Explores the relationship between the individual and the environment based on levels of the individual's adaption in relation to the environmental forces (that is, press) that are placed on the individual and his/her personal competence.

Eldercide
The purposeful killing of older people.

Expansion of morbidity
A hypothesis that suggests that the same interventions that have led to increases in average life expectancy will lead to higher levels of chronic disease in later life.

Extended family
A group of people who are related in some way (for example, legally, socially, biologically), regardless of living arrangements.

Family
A set of relationships that may be determined biologically (for example, child), legally (for example, spouse), or socially (for example, partner) and that exist even in the absence of contact or involvement.

Filial obligations
The obligation of adult children to show respect toward and care for their parents.

Flourishing
The promotion and maintenance of mental health, as opposed to just the absence of a condition such as depression. Three dimensions of flourishing are: emotions, psychological functioning and social functioning.

Fourth age
Period of later life characterized by decline and dependence.

Frailty
Decreased reserve and resistance to stressors that leads to cumulative decline and vulnerability to adverse outcomes.

Functional age
Physical and cognitive performance abilities, as compared to those of an average adult.

Generativity
The idea that people expend energy to guide the next generation or contribute to society in a way that will benefit future generations.

Geriatrics
A medical specialty focused on old age.

Gerontology
The study of old age and later life. It is derived from the Greek words 'geron' (old man) and 'logia' (study of).

Gerontological perspective
The broad idea that the object of interest in research, inquiry or practice is older age, later life and/or older individuals themselves.

Green old age
Describes a time of fitness and activity with some failing powers.

Grief
Grief is the response to loss. This differs from bereavement, which refers to the *person* who has experienced loss. Grief includes the emotional, cognitive and somatic aspects of a person's response to loss.

Hardiness

A combination of commitment, control and challenge within an individual that allows him or her to counter the effects of stressful events without ill effects.

Health

Defined by the World Health Organization (2015) as 'a state of complete physical, mental and social wellbeing and not merely the absence of disease or infirmity'.

Healthy Life Expectancy (HALE)

The average number of years a person can expect to live in complete health, calculated by subtracting the years lived with disease or injury.

Hostels

Residences with limited assistance for individuals with deficits in the activities of daily living.

Independent housing

Describes housing not specifically designed for an older person. This includes multi-generational homes, apartments, houses. The majority of older adults in the world live in a form of independent housing.

Kinship

Networks of people related by blood, as well as friends and other non-blood relatives who are recognized by others as being family.

Learned dependency

A passive behavior that is learned so as to gain a desired outcome (for example, attention). Because of assumptions that older people are prone to dependency due to incompetence, over-protective environments are created whereby older people are 'rewarded' for adhering to dependency scripts.

Lewy body dementia

A type of dementia that is the result of the presence of the protein alpha-synuclein in the brain's nerve cells.

Lifecourse perspective
Describes the real and anticipated age-related role transitions (for example, age of full-time employment) that occur over one's lifetime.

Life cycle hypothesis of savings
Suggests that people keep their consumption levels relatively the same over various periods of earning and retirement.

Life expectancy at age 65
The average number of additional years that a person at age 65 could be expected to live if age-specific mortality rates remain unchanged.

Life expectancy at birth
The number of years a newborn infant would live if prevailing patterns of mortality at the time of its birth were to stay the same throughout its life.

Life review
Describes the process by which a person evaluates his or her life, especially as one comes closer to death.

Life span
The theoretical biological maximum length of life that could be achieved under ideal conditions. The human life span is theorized to be 120 years.

Life stories
Stories people tell about themselves.

Living apart together (LAT)
A partnered relationship where two individuals do not share the same household yet still consider themselves to be a couple and participate socially as a couple.

Living arrangements
Describes the people with whom one lives. Living arrangements may be culturally dictated, the result of economic status, or individually selected and managed.

Loneliness
Describes the deficit between a person's desired versus actual quality and quantity of social engagement, or distress due to the perceived absence of social interactions.

Median age
The age that divides a population numerically into two equal groups whereby half are younger and half are older.

Mild cognitive impairment
Cognitive decline that is greater than expected for an individual's age and education level but not so severe as to interfere with the activities of daily living.

Modernization theory
An early theory proposing that changes in status of older individuals are due to changes from agriculture-based societies (high status) to industrial ones (low status).

Mourning
A social expression of grief or how grief is made known.

Multi-generational family
A living arrangement of three or more generations or people with family ties who live together.

Narrative
The telling of some aspect of self through ordered symbols. Narratives can be told using language, gestures or other representations (for example, music, art).

Normal aging
The biological process of ageing that may involve functional decline but is not identified as a disease.

Nursing home
Institutions the serve frail elders by providing 24-hour care (see also Skilled Nursing Facility).

Old age dependency ratio
The number of people aged 65 and over who are assumed to be non-working, relative to the number of people assumed to be in the workforce (those aged 16–64.)

Organisation for Economic Cooperation and Development (OECD)
An international organization, established in 1961, whose mission is to 'promote policies that will improve the economic and social wellbeing of people around the world' (OECD, 2016). There are currently 34 member countries.

Pathological aging
Functional loss that is due to disease and not the process of aging itself.

Pensionable age
The age required for eligibility to draw retirement benefits.

Personal adjustment
Change in behavior in order to successfully adapt to changes in a situation.

Political economy of aging
Perspective that examines ways in which social and economic forces, generated from a production mentality, are damaging to older individuals.

Productive aging
Refers to the economic benefits of older individuals as consumers, investors and volunteers.

Residential home for the aged
A housing institution that serves elders needing some level of medical and/or personal care that can be provided by a visiting nurse.

Resilience
Conveys the idea that plasticity or compensatory mechanisms in some individuals enable them to avoid negative outcomes despite negative conditions or exposures.

Salutogenic model
A guiding theory of health promotion that views health on a continuum rather than focusing on health and disease as two dichotomous conditions.

Sandwich generation
Describes family members who are caring for younger children and aging family members.

Sarcopenia
A geriatric syndrome characterized by age-related decline in muscle mass and strength.

Selective optimization with compensation
Describes three elements involved to response to changes: (1) selection, which requires directing resources to some domains while ignoring others; (2) optimization, which describes maximizing a behavior for a desired outcome; and (3) compensation, which means implementing new resources to achieve a goal.

Sex ratio
The proportion of men to women in a given society.

Skilled nursing facility
This is similar to the definition of nursing home. However, in the United States and other countries, skilled nursing facilities can be used for short-term stays primarily for rehabilitation for conditions such as

hip replacement. Once rehabilitation has occurred (generally in less than 6 months), the person returns to his/her primary residence.

Skip-generation households
Households composed of grandparents and grandchildren, where the middle generation (that is, the parents) are absent.

Social assistance programs
Non-contributory programs generally targeted to poor or otherwise vulnerable members of a society.

Social convoy model
Describes the social network (for example, family, friends) that surrounds individuals over their life span and assists with changes and challenges over the lifecourse. Although convoys may change in some ways, they remain relatively stable.

Social exchange theory
Shifts in power dynamics that individuals must make when providing or receiving services such as informal care.

Social insurance programs
Contributory programs in which people receive some type of benefit or service in return for their contribution.

Socio-emotional selectivity theory
Suggests that as people get closer to death, either with age or disease, they will increasingly choose to invest their time in meaningful relationships, as opposed to acquiring new knowledge or less-meaningful relationships.

Subjective wellbeing
Positive evaluations that people make about their lives.

Successful aging
There are several definitions of successful ageing. (1) The conditions whereby the individual gets a maximum of satisfaction and happiness;

(2) an adaptive process that enables the individual to reach his or her goals in aging; (3) a state in which the aging individual maintains a low risk of disease, high mental and physical function and active engagement with life.

Thanatology
The study of death and dying.

Third age
Period of later life characterized by high function and independence.

Vascular dementia
A type of dementia caused by impaired blood flow to the brain.

Wisdom
Describes a person's ability to understand a deeper meaning of life, to be reflective and self aware and to have a diminished sense of self-centeredness.

Index